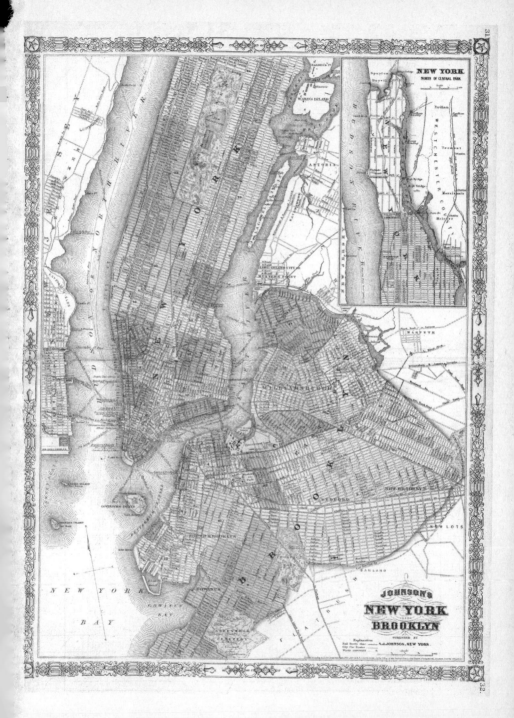

NEW YORK
NORTH OF CENTRAL PARK

JOHNSON'S
NEW YORK
AND
BROOKLYN
PUBLISHED BY
A. J. JOHNSON, NEW YORK.

THE EDGE

BECOMES THE CENTER

*An Oral History of Gentrification
in the Twenty-First Century*

DW Gibson

The Overlook Press
New York • NY

This edition first published in hardcover in the United States in 2015 by
The Overlook Press, Peter Mayer Publishers, Inc.

141 Wooster Street
New York, NY 10012
www.overlookpress.com

For bulk and special sales, please contact sales@overlookny.com, or write
us at the address above.

Cataloging-in-Publication Data is available from the Library of Congress

Book design and type formatting by Bernard Schleifer
Manufactured in the United States of America
ISBN: 978-1-4683-0861-7

FIRST EDITION
1 3 5 7 9 10 8 6 4 2

For all citizens of New York City—
especially Gigi.

THE EDGE BECOMES THE CENTER

1.

"Opportunity in New York springs from strong neighborhoods. When we demand that big developers build affordable housing, and fight to keep our hospitals from becoming luxury condos, it's not to punish the real estate industry. We do these things so the everyday, hardworking people who anchor our neighborhoods can live and work and be healthy in the communities they love. That's how we all rise together."

*I*t is November 5, 2013, and Bill de Blasio stands on a stage surrounded by an exalting audience. The crowd sways to Lorde's anticapitalist anthem "Royals": That kind of luxe just ain't for us. We crave a different kind of buzz. *Victorious on this election night, de Blasio will soon be a mayor in charge of a budget with more than three billion dollars in surplus. The money started flowing into the city several decades ago, the spigot dripping steadily by the early 1990s when Rudy Giuliani and William Bratton built a police force muscular enough to frisk its way to a city free of broken windows and tagged stoops; a city with a lower rate of violent crimes, capable of seducing developers to buy up abandoned buildings. The capital surged under a twelve-year Michael Bloomberg administration, despite the fact that he took office three months after the city's two tallest buildings, its welcome beacon to global capitalism, collapsed.*

Now here we are: Bill de Blasio, recently arrested while protesting the closure of a hospital, becomes the 109th mayor of New York City just as a leading real estate agent says that 80 percent of his clients are hedge funds; not individuals concerned with the quality of vegetables at the corner bodega but corporate entities who see potential in the bodega's square footage.

I set out to understand how gentrification affects lives and not far into my trip I realized the word gentrification is useless—rendered so by overuse, too broad to adequately capture a huge range of disparate experiences, contexts, and, ultimately, meanings. But no matter how idiosyncratically one defines gentrification, it is an idea that never strays far from money—investment, capital moving into the neighborhood.

"I've spoken often about a Tale of Two Cities. That inequality —that feeling of a few doing very well, while so many slip further behind—that is the defining challenge of our time. Because inequality in New York is not something that only threatens those who are struggling. The stakes are so high for every New Yorker."

The stage where de Blasio stands is not a curtained number in a midtown Manhattan hotel ballroom; it is a temporary platform constructed in the center of a stone and brick building that was originally an armory for the 14th Regiment of the National Guard on Eighth Avenue in Brooklyn. The building has had several incarnations, a YMCA at present. This is Park Slope, de Blasio's neighborhood, and thus a meaningful place to party, but more to the point: one hundred and eight mayors preceded this man and not one chose Brooklyn for his election night celebration—a fact not to be underestimated. This outer borough feels front and center.

Outside the YMCA the streets are relatively calm. The flames of the de Blasio fire only carry so far. Voter turnout for this revolutionary election was 24 percent. This is not an easy city to rile, politically speaking, particularly when the violence of gentrification that fuels the de Blasio battle cry is so subtle, less like a bullet or a blade and more like the slow encroachment of carbon monoxide, filling one building after another. The mayor's neighborhood of Park Slope—reminiscent of The Cosby Show *and the affluent middle class—is already subsumed and the vapors are advancing on the crumbling brick facades farther into Brooklyn.*

I follow the vapors.

By the time I reach Lincoln Road in Prospect-Lefferts Gardens, there is no trace of the din from the de Blasio uprising. I find a forty-five-year-old man on the front porch of a towering Victorian home. It is late, deep into the night but still his snug, gray suit remains unwrinkled. His polka-dotted pocket square hasn't budged. The pinpointed fashion shaves ten years off the bachelor's age; his demeanor has a confident bounce to match. Prospect Park—formed by glacial debris some seventeen thousand years ago, sculpted by Frederick Law Olmsted and Calvert Vaux in 1867—is two blocks away.

My name's mTkalla. I always get questions. mTkalla?—how do you say that? And I tell the story: My full name when I was born was Martin Kennedy Keaton. My mom named me after both Martin Luther King and Robert Kennedy. I was born in 1968. I used to win awards as a kid doing Martin Luther King speeches. I remember once when I was nine I did the "I Have a Dream Speech" and a woman in the front row—an older black woman—was balling with tears and she told my mother, "I can't believe that a little boy did this speech." I performed like I was in front of Martin Luther King.

Then in '88 or '89 there was so much violence against black American men in Brooklyn. People getting beat up. People getting shot by the cops. I was doing some research regarding the whole middle passage and people getting brought here, European names being forced on them. I read Assata Shakur's autobiography and *The Autobiography of Malcolm X*. Here's a man whose only true god was the truth as he understood it. He could go on for years and years saying one thing, but once he understood the truth to be different, he admitted that the truth is different now. He lived that. And he continues to be an inspiration for me.

So recently I decided to change my name officially. I decided to put the silent *m* in front of the name Tkalla. The *m* is homage to MLK.

The result sounds like Ta-KAH-la. There is an unkempt yard in front of the porch where we sit. Up against the sidewalk, an overgrown hedge hides us from the street. A busted car (broken windows and flat tires) lists in the driveway alongside mTkalla's Porsche SUV (tinted windows and polished tires). The house looks mostly empty through the windows; a few walls have been partially removed and drywall dust covers the floors and banister and built-in shelving of the decrepit mansion.

This place is part of my story actually. I'm moving from Park Slope—my mom's still there. You familiar with Park Slope? My father bought a couple of houses there a long time ago. Had to take out a big mortgage to pay off the family to keep the properties. A lot of debt. He passed about fourteen years ago. So I decided to sell everything and have a house free and clear. I had an opportunity to move somewhere else, some suburb, some palatial something. But why would I move away from Brooklyn? I consider it the planet. So I bought this house—*he points back over his shoulder at the looming structure*—which is a little bit of a big deal because my mom always wanted to live in a place like this. But there's a lot of effing work, man, there's a lot of work.

When I tell people that I'm moving out of Park Slope back to Lefferts Gardens people are like, "You're crazy. You're bugging out. How could you move? You're one of the only black dudes that owns in Park Slope," da da da da.

And I'm like, "First of all, you don't even know what I'm moving to. If you saw where I was moving, you'd get it."

"No, you're bugging out."

And then they come here and they're like, "Oh, I get it."

I'm so excited about this house.

The lot is a hundred feet wide and a hundred feet deep and you can fit like eight cars in the driveway—there's a two-car garage.

mTkalla escorts me over to his driveway, which extends the length of the property. In a city where drivers circle for hours searching for a spot and spend $747 million on parking tickets in one year, the long driveway looks even longer, feeling more like a landing strip for small planes.

To have a driveway—*mTkalla smiles like a conquering teenager*—I just like saying it: driveway—I could just repeat driveway, driveway, driveway . . .

The smile runs on with the incantation of the word until mTkalla turns and walks toward the garage. He stops suddenly—I'm no Hugh Hefner or anything like that but—*and continues walking.*

Someone shot a short film here not too long ago. If I'm talking too fast or moving too fast just let me know. I'm trying to say three sentences at the same time.

We walk around to the backyard. The jungle that I saw in the front yard is deeper here, richer. And there are certain additions: various piles of garbage and demolition—splintered wood, bent siding. But for all of that, it is still a backyard in the center of New York City—the center of Brooklyn, to be precise, which, for mTkalla, is the center of everything—he requires Manhattan for nothing. Manhattan is a museum dutifully toured when friends from out of town visit. mTkalla has not been there in a month.

Circling back around to the front of the house, we enter through the main door and stand in the parlor. mTkalla envisions the following tweaks:

We're going to paint a little bit darker to give it more of that richer look. I want to leave as much undisturbed as possible.

We'll keep that—*pointing at the fireplace before ascending the dark wood staircase to the second floor.*

Originally, I wanted to move from Park Slope to Bed-Stuy 'cause a lot of my business is in Bed-Stuy. But those homes are, at the most, twenty feet wide and for someone who doesn't really do stairs—my mom can't use the stairs—that doesn't really work. She's seventy years old. And I'm not going to move any place that my mom doesn't approve of, 'cause she sacrificed so much for me and I need her last few years to be good. So I came here, and I stood right in this place—*pointing at the recently sanded flooring beneath his feet*—and I started getting chills all over my body. I went home, I said, "Hey Mom, I found the house."

She said, "Really?!? You found the house?"

"I found the house."

We walk down a hallway here, a hallway there, and wind up in a mostly empty room with an unmade bed in the middle of the floor.

I've kind of co-opted this room until everything else is done downstairs. You can control the construction better when you're on-site. Eventually, this will be my master bedroom.

He points to one massive window between two other massive windows:

We're going to do a deck off there. This is away from the street, this is southwest exposure, I mean, you know . . .

He rolls his eyes, displaying a bit of ecstasy, and continues:

We'll rip out the kitchen. We're going to do a nice, all-white kitchen, Carrara marble, blah, blah, blah.

This is going to be my living room.

That room will be the family thing.

That's a classic baby room. I have no babies so I have no idea what's going to happen with that.

This is actually the only house on the block that has a legal commercial space. This room is an addition—they used to run a little school out of here. So I'm using it as my office, consultancy, whatever—where there's film, editing, music production, design. I plan on blowing that wall out there, keeping the ceilings kind of raw and doing a nice industrial type of kitchen in the corner. A three-quarter bathroom. And this will be the reception area for the mTkalla Group, the Casa Brooklyn, the whatever the hell—

we want to take over the world. Or take over Brooklyn. Because it's not about taking over the world. If you take over Brooklyn, it's partly like taking over the world.

He laughs and heads back out to the last traces of sunlight on the front porch. Across the street is an apartment building with three or four or five men standing near the entrance, laughing and talking, coming and going. The rest of the block is lined with spacious, free-standing homes like mTkalla's, making the street seem misplaced in a city where most people live in boxes stacked much closer and higher.

I can't wait for this to be somewhat done so we can just relax and have people over. Raise a family or create a vibe, man.

It's funny because I remember growing up in Bushwick, six blocks from here. I was a nerd, and people would say, "Where you from?"

I had to drop it in a certain way: "Yo, I grew up in Bushwick." People would be all, "Really?"

Now people say, "Ah, Bushwick, what does that mean? Hipsterville?"

Even if I could have afforded to live in Park Slope I would not have chosen it. There's no vibe. I think Park Slope is definitely one of the more Manhattanized parts of Brooklyn. When you walk the streets it doesn't feel like Brooklyn. There's something cold about that neighborhood. A lot of people who live there, who own there, who rent there—they'll say the same thing.

For all the time mTkalla spends distinguishing between different neighborhoods—and there are distinctions to be made—these neighborhoods don't correspond to borders observed on a map—not always, anyway. Urban historian Suleiman Osman writes that before the 1970s "Brooklyn had no real neighborhoods. Those who did use enclave names could rarely distinguish where the area began and ended. Early attempts to locate Brooklyn's authentic neighborhoods were not by local residents but by two groups of outsiders with very different motives: community organizers and real estate agents." The labeling— and, ultimately, branding—of Bushwick and Fort Greene and Clinton

Hill and Sunset Park and Stuyvesant Heights and Park Slope et al. is
recent and evolving. And regardless of the monikers, a neighborhood
is where daily life plays out, and daily life does not involve lines on a
map; it is a spectrum of places: a home, a school, a playground, a diner.
And the people who fill those spaces:

When I talk about a neighborhood, I think 70 percent of it is
the people and how they relate to each other. And a lot of people
who are in Crown Heights or Bed-Stuy—particularly African
American folk—come from the South. Both sides of my family
come from the South, from Virginia. My pops came from Bloom-
ingburg. I remember driving down this road there and everybody
that passed, my dad waved to them. Every single bloody person.
I'm ten years old and I'm like, "Hey Pops, do you know all these
people?"

And he's like, "No."

"So why are you waving at them?"

"That's what you do! When you come down here you wave
at everybody."

And I'm like, "Are you serious? It seems tiring to me!"

He laughs.

And we'd go into a store and people were taking their time,
and I was like—*he snaps three times in rapid succession*—and he
said, "You need to calm down man, you're on Brooklyn energy.
You need to turn it down."

My father came up here with his brother in the '50s and they
bought property when New York was going through a recession
and no one wanted to live in Brooklyn. The two homes he bought
in Park Slope, they were either seventeen or twenty-seven thousand dollars.

I don't ask mTkalla the current sticker price for the Park Slope
properties though it's safe to say the going rate on those homes is up-
ward of three million dollars. But you could fit two Park Slope brown-
stones inside his palatial spread on Lincoln Road and there'd still be
plenty of driveway, driveway, driveway.

I used to be a deputy tax sheriff, when I was nineteen, twenty years old. Public Enemy and X Clan were real big at the time. So I used to go collecting taxes in all black with a beret on. I was looking like little Shaft—it was too funny. And because I was a young African American, people would assume that I was a delivery dude. Then I'd flip out my badge and be like, "I'm Martin Keaton, department of Taxation and Finance." And once I flipped that badge everything changed.

But I couldn't really do the nine-to-five thing. I have a butterfly brain. It definitely doesn't work that way. So I went to college. I studied black and Puerto Rican studies. Was exposed to poetry. That lit up my heart. I started writing my own stuff and it was one of the most amazing experiences ever. When I would perform my energy would be kind of a cross between James Brown and Busta Rhymes. It was really lit up. High energy. We'd go and perform in prisons and do workshops.

I started out with very political poetry, very antiestablishment poetry and then I was confronted by a guy on the corner in Brooklyn: "Yo, I go to these poetry readings and everyone's talking about how their girlfriend did them wrong or their boyfriend did them wrong or how they hate the government. Every community has beauty—how come we're not hearing that on the poetry scene?"

And I heard that.

This dude, his name is Ginger Brown, he made me reflect on who I am. In my heart I'm a romantic dude. I said to myself, you need to have your stuff reflect that. So my poetry's all about love and sensuality.

In 2005, I owned my dad's houses, I had tons of debt, I was still poeting. I was popular, I guess, in my little underground scene but I was broke as crap. I needed to make some money. I'm an egghead—I'm not a hustler from the street or anything—so I thought, my parents come from real estate, I've been around real estate, I've been a landlord, and I love people, I love Brooklyn, so maybe I can just bring those gifts and see how it develops.

The first couple years it was pretty hard. I had to be some-body's assistant who was younger than me but definitely more knowledgeable. This dude was from the Bay Area, and he said, "I saw San Francisco turn around quickly. Light speed. So in order for you to be an effective marketer of real estate here, you can't be focused on what this place was. You have to be focused on what it is and what it can become."

I finally caught up to that. And I have vision as well so that helps.

Now I'm a real estate agent over here; I'm a poet, filmmaker, music dude over there. And as time's gone on, real estate has given me the capital to build my studio and create a center where I can have artists come together where we can share ideas. I need to ex-ecute my ideas. For me, work is kind of about the crossing of boundaries and some type of understanding and some type of sub-mission. And I think that the real estate game is also about people coming together and being understanding and being courageous and breaking through the space where they were and making something new in the universe for themselves.

You know, people always talk, "Yeah, if I'd bought in Park Slope in the '70s or the '80s or the '90s I would have made all this money." And then I say to them, "Well, in the '80s, Park Slope wasn't the Park Slope you know."

All these places that have value, there's a challenge. And peo-ple don't want to deal with a challenge. They want to sit back and say, "I don't know if I want to buy in Ridgewood or Crown Heights." And then when these places blow up they say, "Oh, I should have bought there." But they don't want to do the heavy lifting. They don't want to be a part of the community to help build it up. Which is where part of some of the animosity comes from with the whole labyrinth that is the gentrification conversa-tion. Some renters feel like, hey, I had vision for this place twenty years ago and I made this my home and I helped build it up and some of the new people don't see some of the old people as the folk that helped stabilize the neighborhood. They see the old people as old people and they are holding their breath, waiting until they move on.

In New York City you have rent stabilization. So you can have these four million dollar places but the building across the street can be rent stabilized. People who live in these buildings can't get kicked out. So when their lease is up the landlord is obligated by law to renew their lease until their rent hits a certain amount. It's going to be a decade or fifteen years or more before that person can be moved out. If you go to other cities or counties, the landlords can do whatever they want. The thing that's amazing about New York City is you have people who are billionaires rubbing elbows with people who are panhandlers because everyone's always kind of on top of each other. Which, if you're a landlord, can be a real pain in the ass.

But I believe as a principle that we don't need to dominate other people, we can just share. Because there's enough for everybody. Maybe I'm naive, but I don't think that it has to be this person's Brooklyn or that person's Brooklyn. There's a lot of space here and the variety of it all is what makes it hot. When you're greedy you starve. Or when you're greedy you're always hungry—even if you're full!—which is like starving.

Working in real estate for the last eight years, when I look at Brooklyn I see four sections.

First, there are people who are renting, just five years ago they could have found a full-floor apartment for $1,000, and now that single apartment has appreciated 100 percent but their salary hasn't appreciated 100 percent. So they're like, "Where the hell do I go?" Now they think about moving deeper into Brooklyn. Some of these folk have this fear that things are changing around me and I don't know how I'm going to survive. And that's real. In the more frustrated sections of the community, that fear turns to animosity for what they perceive to be the new people. Sometimes they think the new folks are being arrogant, they're not talking to us. So they move around the new people in a way that can sometimes be intimidating. Because they're like, "Fuck you."

The second section, the people who own, they're not mad because it's either I own and I'm good, or I'm about to sell and I'm about to make a grip. You know, Brooklyn Heights is $5 million right now, Fort Greene is $3 to $4 million right now. There's a certain type of person who can afford to do that. Economic fences get erected when more capital moves in. The people that are buying these properties now are coming with all cash or with 50 percent down and I'm like, "Come on dude!" Really, who are these people?

We had a joke the other day: the most affordable part of Brooklyn right now is Queens. Who would have even thought that would be a sentence ten years ago?

So when people talk about new people moving the old people out, I'm saying, "But they're paying the old folk a grip of money!" This isn't eminent domain. Nobody's being forced to sell at gunpoint. And some of the old folk may just buy an apartment around the corner and an estate down South somewhere. In terms of their trajectory and how they see their lives, that may be an improvement.

Then you've got a section of people who come to Brooklyn, and they dig Brooklyn. And they could be considered the gentrifiers but they dig it here. They're not holding their breath. They say, "I want to participate in how this becomes." It's good for new people to come into a place and regenerate it. Because if you're in a place for so long you view it as "it's been." And you've already created possibilities for yourself ten years ago. But a new person steps in on the scene it's like, "Oh, anything is possible—let's do it!"

And you're like, "I don't know if you can do it."

And they're like, "I just did it."

And you're like, "Oh shit, maybe I can do it!"

Then you've got a whole other core, the last section. You've got new people that are moving in just because the price is cheaper and they couldn't give an eff about Brooklyn. They don't care about these neighborhoods and they're holding their breath until the old folk go. You can almost see it on their faces, like they're holding their breath because something stinks. They're like, "I'm just going to keep it straight ahead." That's not a good plan. 'Cause you're creating a box, a fence around yourself and people don't dig "the other."

I don't like to deal with those people at all. When I sense those people, I'm not your dude. Seventy-five percent of the folk in Brooklyn are my people. And the other people who are holding their breath, I hope they don't like the smell and they leave. I have no time for them. You know we get to choose who we spend our time with. And I'm not spending it with any of them.

One time, I was showing this apartment and I had a woman ask me, "Well what do you think about the neighborhood?"

I said, "I think it's great."

She said, "Well, what do you think about the safety?"

I said, "You could be comfortable here."

"Are you sure?"

"What do you mean?"

And she said, "Well, I'm just afraid."

I said, "What are you afraid of?"

She said, "I'm afraid I'm going to be the only white woman walking down the street. Am I going to be the only white woman walking down the street?"

I said, "What do you mean? I don't understand your question. What are you really saying?"

And she had to just float in her own ignorance.

I said to myself, I'm not going to come at her in a certain way, angry, but I'm not going to feed it either. That blew my mind! You can't ask me that question and get an answer. Obviously—hopefully—I very much identify as black. I almost had to go home and look in the mirror. Is there something I'm giving off that would make people feel comfortable saying that to me?

As a real estate agent you don't want to say certain things, but I'm a human being: if you look at the history of violence in New York City, most of it was not African American vs. European. Most of it is otherwise. So it always bugs me out when people from certain neighborhoods come and say, "Am I going to be safe?" I mean, we don't protest against other people moving into our neighborhoods. We don't resist it on that level. For the most part the energy's kind of open. Whereas if I were to want to move to a certain neighborhood, cats might be like, "No, this house is not for sale."

I'd be like, "But I called this morning and you said this was for sale."

They're like, "Yeah, we got an accepted offer."

Wow.

When I was growing up, I know that when people moved into our neighborhood we didn't have that level of resistance. Not to say that people don't get mugged, but, for instance, lets say somebody gets mugged. I don't condone that but usually there's an economic motivation. A lot of time when we've been in other areas, people were not robbing us, people were just saying, "Get the fuck out." That's crazy! And you're dealing with that in the '80s and the '90s. There was a dude named Yusef Hawkins, who went to Bensonhurst in 1989, and he was shot to death because they thought he was coming to visit some European lady and they were like, "Naw man, that's just not happening."

You'd be hard-pressed to find those examples in African American neighborhoods. I'm not saying there aren't examples, there might be examples, one or two, but not thirty examples.

He pauses, leaning forward to shake his head at the reality of what he has said. Then he sighs and falls back into his chair.

I was born in Brooklyn. I'm making my way economically here and I love this place. So going from Park Slope to here is me planting a deeper flag in Brooklyn: I'm here to stay. Even if I get other properties around the world, this is my base. I'm gonna ride and die for Brooklyn. And I'm going to have influence because I choose to have influence in this city. And I'm not going to be afraid.

I think vulnerability and a willingness to be open is a true springboard to freedom. I want to see the world. I want to be with people and check the vibe.

About a month or so ago, the brothers who were hanging out across the street they approached me and were like, "Oh, I see you're moving in. Don't worry, you'll be safe. You know it's cool," blah, blah, blah.

I was like, "Dude, I grew up around here."

"Really?"

"Yeah, seven blocks from here!"

He laughs.

And one of the guys was like, "We're happy that you have the place." Which really means: the trend here is that the new people who buy may not look how I look. It's almost a given that if there's going to be a turnover, the turnover isn't going to be to someone who looks like someone from the community. And they were kind of surprised that the person who was getting this house looks like me. But then, I don't know if it's the way I walk or talk but I'm still approached as though I'm a gentrifier. Because, again, gentrification isn't about color, it's about perceived class.

There has to be some way that I'm able to contribute, or help build a platform where different people in this city have the opportunity to meet each other and mingle. Not in a political forum, not in a seminar. Just somebody's having a barbecue, different people come. Once people have different experiences they say, "Oh, this is not what I thought." And sometimes it's that simple, because you can't legislate to change somebody's heart.

The thing my business partner says is really attractive about Brooklyn is that things are still evolving, there are more possibilities here. Because there's some places you can go in Brooklyn where there are empty storefronts, or affordable storefronts, so regular people can participate in starting something here. And when I'm saying regular people I mean people that don't have a net worth of $10 or $20 million. And that's not to say those aren't regular people, they're people, they're human beings—I get that—but they're operating on a different strata. Even a person with a six-figure salary can struggle in New York City. People like that can have an original idea, rent out a storefront, and test the idea on real people. Whereas in Manhattan, how much would it cost for you to get a storefront? Man! That's a whole level of backing, it's many millions of dollars and that's too much, that's too pro-hibitive for a lot of folks.

Listening to my mom, she talks about fifty years ago, about the Fox, the Paramount—you used to have all these cultural cen-ters in Brooklyn, and people who lived in Brooklyn didn't need to go to Manhattan to entertain themselves. And she feels like some-thing happened in the '60s or the '70s where certain powers that be said, "We need to drive more traffic to Manhattan so these things are going to stop." I grew up thinking that you had to go to the city to entertain yourself 'cause there was nothing here in Brooklyn. But now Brooklyn has how many restaurant rows? And there's the Barclays Center. The thing that trips me out: it was a hole in the ground for decades. Nobody wanted it. All of a sudden a developer comes round, he's got multimillion-dollar plans to de-velop it, says, "I'm going to create a stadium, I'm going to create thousands of high-rises."

And people are like, "Oh no! This is crazy!"

Really? How many people got displaced by that? And it wasn't displacement. These people got paid for that—that's the truth. And the people that held out the longest got paid the most. And now people from Brooklyn, instead of going to Madison Square Garden to root for the Knicks, they can wear Brooklyn on their chest. Do you know how many people from Europe wear Brooklyn on their chests? People come to Brooklyn from all around the world. There are people at Brooklyn Nets games who don't even care about basketball; they just want to be in Brooklyn.

They just want to do that. There's no chant in Madison Square Garden like, "Go New York, Go New York, Go—" gimme a break! And I'm a Knicks fan! I'm a die-hard Knicks fan! But now I say the Knicks are my mistress because I give my money to the Nets. Whoever you give thousands of dollars, that's where the commitment is at, right?

He laughs.

I don't know what it is about Brooklyn. I think there's something to be said about word power. For the first eighteen years of my life I was Martin Keaton. And when I changed my name to mTkalla, people just reacted differently to me. And the feeling of saying the word Brooklyn, I don't know if it's the double *o*'s or the way it drops, but when I was touring Europe, people would say, "Are you American?"

I'd say, "No I'm from Brooklyn."

And they would always say, "I get it. We feel you on that."

Now when I've been talking to people about Brooklyn becoming the primary city, or the primary attraction of New York City, people aren't looking at me like I'm crazy. Queens doesn't have that gravity. Manhattan doesn't have the same energy. Manhattan is concrete. And you have to have a certain amount of power to puncture that. Brooklyn has real people, they're down people that care about each other. There are people who have been here for decades and they came and spotted that southern influence that allows the seeds to get into the ground and germinate and really become something different. 'Cause there's soil here.

2.

*T**he story of mTkalla's name has not been told in its entirety:
several days later he emerges from a weekly sales meeting;
breezing by his desk, rarely if ever visited, he passes his as-
sociate, Adam Sikorski, who greets him as "TK." The nickname further
complicates the man.*

*The brief conversation between mTkalla and Adam is obscured by
arcane real-estate speak, indecipherable to the rest of the world. Adam,
forty-two, is just three years mTkalla's junior but mTkalla has been in
the business longer and brought Adam to the bosses to get made over
a year ago. mTkalla has added a fedora to his gray suit; Adam wears
a hand-loomed, herringbone scarf artfully wrapped around his neck,
somehow not incongruous with his burly, thick beard. His chest is thick,
too, and in his wool hat, he brings to mind Yukon Cornelius from the
1964 claymation television movie* Rudolph the Red-Nosed Reindeer.
*Adam offers to let me tag along with him out to Bedford-Stuyvesant—
Bed-Stuy—the Brooklyn neighborhood where the mTkalla Group is currently selling several homes, or, as they would put it, moving a lot of
inventory.*

*Adam barely touches the door leading out of the building but it
seems to fly out of his way as he bursts onto the sun-splashed sidewalk.*

What a fucking gorgeous day.

He hustles toward the nearest intersection, talking the whole way.

I'm Jewish. I don't know if you knew that. My great-grand-father immigrated to this country from Russia at the turn of the century, but I was raised in California. I'm not super religious in the least. I wasn't bar mitzvahed—I guess a lot of people would say I wasn't a Jew. But that is in my bloodline, and there's some-thing about it that made me gravitate toward entertainment and real estate—as pigeonholed as that is. I don't know why. It's strange.

He laughs, scanning Carroll Street for his car.

See I entered this strictly as a buyer. That's how I met TK. I was coming out to Bed-Stuy all the time, 'cause I did a lot of home-work to get myself up to speed. I was looking for the bargain, and really, the bargain was out in Bed-Stuy up until about a year and a half ago. Now the bargains are over. Now it's on fire.

Ride with me.

As soon as Adam climbs into his car, he docks his smartphone in a case attached to the dashboard, and in an instant, the interior of his Volvo is wired—calls automatically come through the speaker system, a bright screen provides navigation, and a computerized voice reads his text messages aloud if he is not on the phone. But mostly he is on the phone. Updates from contractors, updates from other brokers, up-dates from clients and lawyers, updates from Ernesto, Nacho, and Jimmy—the trio Adam connects with buyers and sellers looking for strong and wildly efficient movers available on short notice for twenty-five dollars an hour. At one point Adam speaks with a contractor about whether they will meet at two or two thirty; they split the difference with two fifteen.

With him, everything is a negotiation. You're never going to get it at the first try, you have to just know that off the bat.

Despite the endless calls, fragmented by bad connections and yet more incoming calls—each usually regarding one deadline or an-other—and despite the clogged streets and their punishing traffic, Adam shows no trace of agitation or impatience. His voice stays soft and calm; and he keeps gesticulation to a minimum, as if offering his tranquility to the swarm of drivers, pedestrians, and bicyclists who share Myrtle Avenue with us. Most impressively: he always—always— yields to the car trying to take the lane in front of him.

When I met TK we discovered a lot of parallels. I'd been working in the entertainment business for about fifteen years, mostly on the music side, and TK came from a performance background, so we paralleled each other even if we didn't know each other. When we connected on the real estate thing, there was a deeper level there, where we discovered we're both inspired by film and creativity and music, art, architecture, fashion, food.

We like being a part of this. This is where it's all happening, at least for me. And the essence of what I do now is kind of the essence of what I did in the music business. I connect people. I facilitate deals. I'm a dealmaker. I like finding the undiscovered thing and making it something that it wasn't before. I enjoy when people discover something that they didn't see at first. I like being around when the lightbulb goes off. I like to be in the know. I'm the guy who walks through the kitchen to get to the club. I'm not the guy who waits on line out front for two hours.

Nearing his destination, Adam parks at the end of the street and walks halfway down the block to a four-story brownstone with various layers of paint peeling from every corner of the facade. Three men stand together at the curb in front of the house, speculating about the sale of the building; a kid rests on his bike next to the trio, listening in; Henry, the agent showing the place, stands at the garden-level entrance, next to a for sale sign with his name on it. Adam shakes Henry's hand and tries to get his client Izzy on the phone while we all loiter in front of the house. Henry, the three men at the curb, and the kid on the bike are all dark-complected; Adam and I are not. We are the duo that stands out because we are clearly the only ones here who do not live on this street—until Izzy arrives, floating across the street in bright blue pants, sunglasses, and a crisp, collared shirt unbuttoned halfway down his chest. A recent transplant from Tel Aviv, he works to manage the weight of the giant Nikon camera in his hand.

Henry gives a tour of the house, currently registered with the city as single room occupancy, or SRO. He opens a door on the second floor to reveal the layout of one of the rented rooms, which has the feel of a disorganized closet with a bed lodged in the middle; the shared bathroom on each floor sends the smell of an unflushed toilet up and down the hall. Izzy isn't feeling the place—he doesn't even take the lens off his camera—so the tour is brief.

Adam and Izzy walk to the end of the block and Izzy says the place needs "too much work for eight hundred thousand dollars." Adam reminds him that the "six hundred thousand dollar days are gone." He is firm when conveying the realities of the Bed-Stuy market but comforting when he tells Izzy to take a few hours to consider it, maybe "talk about it with some of your guys." Izzy agrees to report back by the end of the day, as other buyers will offer by then. They shake hands, and Adam hustles back to his car, on to the next appointment.

Controlled presentation is the name of the game. There are lots of different kinds of pressure points where a deal can fall apart. So my job is to alleviate the pressure points to the best of my ability, to actually get it to the end result, which is a transfer of title. Somebody pays for something, somebody gets something, and everybody walks away happy. Ultimately, that's the driving force of this: connecting the dots, putting together a deal.

Nine times out of ten, the buyer and seller never meet each other until the day you're actually walking in to sign the papers. It's all behind somebody who's behind somebody else. And while you're representing an interest on one side of the table, you can also be representing the interest on the other side of the table. It's kind of the veiled reality in the business. You never want to put a buyer and a seller in the same room at the same time, especially before they've executed the transaction. Control is really the name of this game because all kinds of crazy shit can jump up.

His phone rings again and he takes the call, which then necessitates that he make two more.

When it rains it pours. And they all want answers yesterday.

My effectiveness is being ahead of the curve. If I'm not super on top of it, fifteen other people are going to get what I'm looking for and walk away with it. My boots are on the ground right now, and if I don't show up to an appointment when I need to, or if I don't get that text and return it now, they're on to the next one.

There's never a dull moment. I'm anxious all the time, dude. But if I don't get panicky, I think it affords me more leeway—if I can chill people out, too. I think at the end of the day, people just want what they want when they want it, so you have to manage expectations, and when you manage those expectations, try to do it with a cool demeanor; otherwise, you'll go crazy in this kind of job. It can be very demanding, and all at inopportune times. When this business is ready to go, it wants to go. There's no relaxing. I can barely keep up with this thing.

He flicks his smartphone with his finger.

Technology has definitely changed the business of real estate considerably. Access to information. Receiving and sending, being able to communicate with so many people so quick. That's how business gets done. That's the new efficiency of it all.

Social interactions are more specific and directed than they used to be. You used to crash into people. It wasn't as direct and focused. Your happy accidents—I feel like happy accidents have been marginalized by technology. Like back when I was hanging out at D&D Studios between sessions. The community that grew out of those recording studios, those chance meetings, you know, when people hung out on the downtime, that's when it was really interesting and amazing and inspiring. That's gone but the momentum that was in the music business in the '90s, where it was just so the place to be—that's what's going on in Brooklyn in the real estate market right now. It's the same exact kind of exuberance and interest and discovery and change. I like that. There is an energy that I can swim around in all the time: you can touch it, you can feel it, you can taste it. And that's what's going on. You either get down with it, or you gotta get out. Some of it's dirty and some of it's fantastic, but you're in it, and it's happening in real time, and it's live, and it's exciting. That gets me off. I like that a lot.

I had a friend of mine from Los Angeles, took a trip to Paris and he called me saying, "Oh my god. Dude. The hottest restaurants in Paris right now are Brooklyn-inspired restaurants, and everywhere I go in Paris, people are talking about Brooklyn!"

I think it's the underdog story. Brooklyn has always been the underdog. Big, shiny Manhattan kind of throws its weight around and turns its back on little Brooklyn. But Brooklyn has kind of been like, that's cool; we're cool with that. Let's go do our own thing.

I also think there's kind of been this migration of cool. Follow the cool people away. So the cool people don't live in Manhattan anymore. Cool people live in Brooklyn. And it's probably purely an economic force that's driven that, but now it's been branded. There's been a stamp that's said the migration of cool has come here, and if you want to be a part of that, don't even waste your time over there in Manhattan anymore. It's not dangerous anymore. Brooklyn is dangerous. Or at least it's perceived to be dangerous. And danger loves to hug cool. Cool and danger hang together. They are homies.

Stopped at a light on Myrtle Avenue, formerly known as "Murder Avenue," we are shadowed by train tracks that run over the center of the road, and Adam points at an unmarked door hiding a speakeasy coffee shop serving lattes to a room full of laptops. His take on danger hugging cool echoes urbanist Neil Smith. Decades before "cool people live[d] in Brooklyn," Smith wrote about the false sense of frontierism experienced by those moving capital into neighborhoods: "Where the militance or persistence of working-class communities or the extent of disinvestment and dilapidation would seem to render genteel reconstruction a Sisyphean task, the classes can be juxtaposed by other means. Squalor, poverty, and the violence of eviction are constituted as exquisite ambience."

As it happens, most of the guys who are in this game are Jewish. It's just a fact. And what's really interesting is when you start
to see the different strata and how they go about their business.
Like some guys drive, you know, the 600SL with all the bells and
whistles. And some guys don't even drive. It's interesting to see
how they express themselves, and to see which American ideal of
success they relate to.

The Persian Jews tend to be the slickest. They're the ones that
are so heavily impacted by a perceived expression of wealth, and
they want to be seen as, wow, you guys are the high rollers. They'll
spend the money on the cars, and they'll spend the money on the
clothes. They wanna be like, we made it, and this is what success
in America is. And a lot of them have incredibly bad taste when it
comes to picking finishes.

He laughs.

You know, they want to make it like the Venetian at Las
Vegas, and you're just like, wow, the market doesn't want that.
So that's been interesting, to give them notes and rein them in a
little bit towards the norm, because the way they express their
taste—well, it behooves them not to.

You've also got the Hasids, the ultra-Orthodox. There's kind
of two factions. There was a central figure in the ultra-Orthodox
community; he passed away and the two sons have kind of been
fighting for control. And it's been a big to-do within the Hasidic
community. But they're the first comers. They like to be landlords. They're not into flipping or selling. They're into buying
and holding. They tend to have a deeper connection to the place.
The Hasids are growing the community on the Williamsburg/
Bed-Stuy border—that little pocket over there. They're reinvesting money, they're reinvesting in Brooklyn. They're invested in
what this place is and they're not looking for an exit. If Hasids
keep something, they tend to want to keep it forever. Their
endgame is to generate a portfolio. Also, as I've been reading, it's
kind of inherent to the ultra-Orthodox Talmud, based in religious

scripture, the idea that you have to devote a certain percentage of the money you make to real estate. So it's almost like a religious proclivity to be involved in real estate. The religious component informs you about what someone's endgame is. That's been interesting for me to uncover.

The Hasids are very different from the mentality of a new immigrant to the country, like an Israeli immigrant. Because these guys are all about go, go, go, fast, fast, fast, fast, buy it, flip it, sell it, keep it moving, go, go, go. It kind of feels like, with the new guys, it's just a job, and they're wham-bam, thank you ma'am. A lot of the newcomers don't live in Brooklyn. They live in Long Island. And they come in and do their thing, and then they go back—they leave. That's definitely something that, if you threw a lens on it, I think you'd make a lot of people really upset.

Adam arrives at a two-unit home where he's arranged a meeting between his cabinet guy and a client, David; the two of them are already standing in front of the stoop, looking at samples. David is almost done renovating the place, which is immaculate: exposed wood beams and clean white walls frame open rooms drenched in sunlight pouring through windows—and skylights in the unit on the second floor. Adam is investigating the latest work in the first floor apartment bathroom when a woman suddenly appears. She is African American, looks to be in her mid-forties, and walks through the front door of the place with confidence and curiosity. Adam doesn't flinch at the sight of an unexpected person standing in the room with him. His calmness is always something to be shared.

Adam: Hello. How are you?

Neighbor: I'm fine, thank you. I'm just looking around because I live next door and this house was a mess.

Adam: Oh, I know. We hooked it up!

Neighbor (*smiling*): I knew the lady that lived here. She had about fourteen kids. Fifteen kids! And more people hanging out, having parties. It was a mess, let me tell you.

Adam: Wow.

Neighbor *(moving farther into the apartment, peering into the backyard):* That's going to be a deck, huh? Oh that'll be real nice.

Adam: I know I'm about ready to go hang out there right now.

Neighbor: Me too!

Adam: C'mon let's go grab a beer!

Neighbor *(laughing):* I don't drink beers. Only Sunkist soda.

Adam: Alright.

They laugh together. She goes upstairs to take a look at the second unit and Adam wanders out to the front of the building to squeeze more samples out of the cabinet man. Adam isn't happy with any of the faux wood choices, and neither is David. As the three men discuss possible alternatives, a second neighbor approaches. She is also African American, early fifties, and she's pointing at David's renovation, waving her finger with a question on her lips:

Neighbor: Can I ask one question, please: Around how much does that siding cost?

Adam *(hesitating):* You know, I don't know how much this costs.

Neighbor: Because I can get the aluminum for a thousand.

Adam: Okay. I think this might be a little more like three.

Neighbor: I still have the original siding and it's time, you know, it's time . . .

Adam: Little upgrades?

Neighbor: Yeah. There's a lot of money in that house and we try to keep it a certain way but it's not easy. *(Point at the new siding.)* I love this but I can't afford this. But I want this!"

She laughs.

Neighbor: I want this. I love it.

Adam: We're trying to make the neighborhood pretty.

Neighbor: Sure, sure. Lord knows we need all the help we can get!

She makes Adam laugh. She lingers while the cabinet guy, a Hasidic man with a barrel chest to rival Adam's, returns to the matter of natural finish options, promising to send samples by the end of the week. Adam walks with the neighbor down the block; I follow close behind as they talk siding, their broad smiles and earnest tones seem somewhat squeamish about moving past the established topic. At the corner they wave good-bye to each other and Adam looks over his shoulder to confirm I'm keeping up.

There's a lot of interesting moments that happen in a day. The people who are not planned, but drift in and out. I get that all day long. And nine times out of ten, it's positive. She wanted to put her two cents in, and at first I thought, "Oh boy. Here it comes. She's gonna lay into us." But then she was smiling and had a cool vibe and it was kind of like, "I like what you're doing. Thank you. And I'd like to do it myself." So that's cool. I like happy, unexpected interactions that just happen. Nobody had to really over-analyze it. It was just like, "I live on the block, and I want to see what you guys are doing. Wow, this place is great."

But there is that slice of interactions where we'll get a face like, you low-down, dirty—look at what you're doing. Who are these dudes to come into the community and turn it into something that could be worse—or could be better—but why are you here doing something? Who gave you permission to come in and do something? You enacted something that we didn't do, and we're not sure if we like that.

You know, these guys from Long Island, they come in, they buy the place, they renovate it and they sell it—and they're going to make a profit. It would be easy to judge them and demonize them and be, like, fuck those dudes—man, those dudes came over here, and they bought that place from somebody that we used to know, and they were some local down on their luck, and they took advantage of them, and now they're just gonna go ahead and sell it and keep it moving. But what you didn't see in a knee-jerk reaction is what that development meant to the immediate community.

That woman came inside the house back there because she knew what it had looked like before and she wanted to see what it looks like now. She knew who lived there. And what was her reaction? Oh, by the way, the people who lived here, they wrecked this place. They jacked it up. And they had parties. And they didn't respect the block. And we're happy that they're gone—happy that you came in and fixed it up and made it pretty and made it beautiful. That's when the story turns on its head. But that's not a good storyline. That's not a good angle. Because then you don't have a bad guy in the story. There's no one to hang out to dry.

He laughs.

On a couple of different listings, I'll work with guys that have negotiated some sort of distressed purchase of a property. Maybe the sellers were underwater, they couldn't make their mortgage payments, they lost their job, shit was bad, they weren't able to pull out of whatever tailspin they were in, and they needed to sell. They needed to sell now. And they didn't want to market it, and it needed to be cash. My clients who buy those places, they'll say, "Listen, Adam, put it back on at market." So I put the property on at market after it closed a month ago at half-price, and they haven't done anything to it—but it's fair market. They found the property that had more than 150 percent of equity that was left. And that's that. But then people walk into an open house with a bone to pick. 'Cause people are so diligent—there's a lot of different ways you can find out, well, when did this sell last? There's new technology that's in place for full disclosure. And they come in looking—*he widens his eyes*—saying, "What the fuck? Dude, this guy bought this for three hundred grand a month ago, and you're selling it for seven hundred and fifty thousand? Fuck you!" That's usually the lead. At first it's anger. They weren't even really interested in the place. They just came in to the open house to kick up some shit and vent and be like, "Fuck you, asshole. Because I wanted the three hundred thousand dollar deal."

And I just have to say, "Hey listen, guys, if you want the deal, you're going to have to pay for it. I'll go find you the deal. But you're going to have to pay me to be your bird dog." You know, these guys who get these deals, it's not just luck of the draw, they happen to find a great thing, and woo-hoo. They have full staffs. This is their job. This is what they do professionally. They've got people in the neighborhood that work with them and hang out at the barbershop, that go to church, that talk to the communities. "What's going on with old Joe's mom's house? Are they okay? It looks like shit's falling to hell in a handbasket over there. Listen, I know somebody, he can help you. He's all cash. He'll pay you what you want, and then you can be free. You can move on." And these guys have to pay on the side to have access to that information. So what closes on paper and what they've actually spent often times are not the same.

And then all of a sudden they're saying, "You mean I have to pay to get the deal? You mean the diamonds aren't just laying around on the beach? And I can't just walk down to the beach and trip over one and put it in my pocket?"

But people still look at that margin, and they say, "I want that margin—and fuck you!" A lot of people are frustrated because the market is moving so fast, and they feel like they're marginalized, and they're not in the loop, and they can't get what they perceive as the deal. So managing that is interesting, too. You've gotta just roll with it. If you're thin-skinned, this isn't the gig for you.

The majority of my experiences have been respectful. I think, for the most part, people let you do your thing. It hasn't been some really heavy, bad trip. I know sometimes you can feel a turned eyebrow at your back, like those dudes when we rolled up to that house with Izzy—but I've never experienced something where somebody just came right up to my face and called me out, or gave me some kind of bad trip. It's always basically been very, "This is what you do, dude, and you're doing it, and you're nice to me. I'll be nice to you and we'll keep it moving." And that's it.

I think it's easy to frame the story and say gentrification is such a dirty, bad, awful word to the people that want to make it that, to make it this gross, awful, horrendous, hindering, handicapping kind of thing. But when you really see it, people are also reaping the benefits. And everybody has to share! If you don't want to share, if you don't want to live in the city, you cash out. You cash out, keep it moving, and go somewhere where you don't have to share, where you don't have to be affected by all these different people moving in and out and back and forth and up and down and all around you. If you're not down with it, that's cool— good-bye. But if you can manage it, then you say, "Hey, listen. It is what it is: things are changing." You either get on board with it and you take advantage of the positives and you manage your negatives, or you pack up and you bounce. Period. The end.

I don't see powerlessness; I don't feel that. I feel like there are choices, there are options. Everyone has the power to participate in this in a positive way. And I think a lot of people choose to. They say, "I can deal with it or I can't but either way it's bigger than I am and this is what's happening." To be on the fence here, it's not a good place to be. You've gotta commit to it or you've gotta leave.

3.

Shortly after dropping his two-year-old daughter off at Brooklyn Friends School, Adam gets a call from MJ Mai. MJ is the contractor handling the gut renovation of a two-story Brooklyn home Adam and his wife bought one year ago. It is a wood-frame house in Clinton Hill and one of the first on the block to be reimagined with an influx of cash. The Sikorskis have been long-term, temporary residents of a one-bedroom apartment while MJ and his crew work. Moving in will mean more space and a backyard for the family. And income property, of course—a duplex apartment. In this city the American Dream often comes with a tenant or two.

Work on the house is so close to completion that Adam can smell it: fresh paint, sanded wood, the plastic of new appliances. But on this morning, MJ's tone of voice is spiked, shooting out of Adam's car's sound system. As Adam listens to his contractor, his expression grows uncharacteristically anxious and for good reason: his new washer and dryer, delivered just the day before, are gone. MJ says they were lifted in the night along with a couple thousand dollars worth of tools. Adam tells MJ to call 911 and does a U-turn, heading for the house.

By the time he arrives, a dozen cops have descended on the scene. The junior officers, made to do the busywork of writing out the report, are more interested in Adam's modern, bright white spread than his missing property.

Cop: Amazing! From the street you'd never know this place
was here.

*Adam tries to get the cop to refocus on the stolen property, and the
cop reluctantly starts taking down the information, doing so with the
lethargic posture and slack jaw of someone convinced there will be no
meaningful outcome, other than perhaps an insurance claim, resulting
from his task.*

*MJ decides to cut his losses and leaves for his office. And half an
hour later the general contractor has already brushed off the theft. He
must. He's already back at his desk working the phone. He pauses to
take off his glasses and rub his eyes. He looks at his watch and shakes
his head. Glasses back on.*

I was born year of horse. Not a good year.

He laughs.

Horse, working hard. That means I'm working hard.

*He wakes up at six thirty to begin his workday. Each morning in-
cludes a glass of fresh soymilk, consumed hot, even in the swampy late
August haze. He is a short but stout fifty-nine-year-old man. His thinning hair, bushy eyebrows, and trimmed moustache are all dyed black—
not one gray root left exposed.*

*He lives in the Elmhurst neighborhood of Queens but he keeps his
office for Great Will Construction in Manhattan, just off of Canal
Street, along the blurry border between Chinatown and the Lower East
Side. A shrine to Buddha is built into the corner opposite MJ's desk.
There's also another figure on a shelf above Buddha.*

That's Guan Gong. It's a god to protect our business.

*Guan Gong and Buddha are both encircled by jars of incense,
bowls of oranges, and bottles of wine.*

Wine for me.

*He smiles but still does not recline in his chair. Various phones
continue to ring every five minutes: sometimes it is his mobile, sometimes it is the direct line to his desk, and sometimes it is the phone at
the front of the office so the receptionist yells down the hall in Chinese
to convey the caller. Occasionally she yells down the hall while MJ is*

*already on the phone, and he delivers a quick response for her without
interrupting the call. Most conversations are in Chinese but a few are
in English. Though it is his second language, MJ communicates well
in English: despite the odd disordered word and unpredictable verb
tense, his sentences are efficient and clear. Sometimes he extends a single word while gathering a thought and his voice jumps from one pitch
to another, like a sudden burst of song.*

In China nobody trust the government. Communism. Actually
my father died by that. You know the Cultural Revolution? My
father was teacher in Shun De, our village near Canton. Nineteen
sixty-six—the Cultural Revolution just starting—and my father
died. I was twelve. When he died, I move out. I can't live there no
more. My sister go to my auntie's home. And my other sister go
to my father's teacher's home. The worst is the Red Guard, at the
time, they go down to my father's teacher's house when my sister
was there. So bad . . .

His eyes water so he squeezes them shut.

So bad, that story. I don't mention it.

Some years later my father's teacher used my family story to
write a book. My mom moved to New York, and we found out
she became a citizen. They told my mom, oh, all your not-married
kids can come with you. That's why I come down here in 1982.

When I first came to New York, I don't like here. Everything
is a stranger, you know. I only speak Chinese, right, no English.
And I feel bad, so upset, really upset. I don't have any dream. I
just come down to start my new life, looking for work, that's all.

In '83, after I live in New York for some time, I went back to
China to see my girlfriend and we married. Then she come down
to New York. We have two kids. The first one is a girl and the
second one is a boy. That's perfect—I tell you why.

*He grabs a scrap of paper and draws two Chinese characters. He
points at the first:*

That means *daughter*.

He points at the second character:

This means *son*.

He points at both characters:

These two combined together means one word: *good*. That's what I have. That's perfect.

I just told my kids, you know, I'm not really requiring you to become lawyer, or become doctor, something like that. I said I am only requiring you to not become the garbage. In Chinese, we say, "Don't become the garbage." That means you can support yourself. They could live by themselves. Not just depend on somebody. You can be useful. That's what I require them. That's all.

When my children were in the elementary school a lot of gang people walk around the street and we were scared. We always worry every day about gang people attacking them. It's better now. A lot's changed—security most of all. More security, more security—here, in Chinatown and the Lower East Side, more security.

My first job was the Chinese restaurants. Bad job.

He laughs.

Then I worked in the supermarket. After I found that job then I like New York slowly. After a couple years I feel I could get everything if I want it. You know, it's simple: you're working hard, you can get better—whatever you want. You pay more effort, you get more. That's what I trust.

At that time, I can speak both Mandarin and Cantonese but I don't know English at all. And I know that English is very important. So I go to the evening school for learning English and the first school I go to is in a church, because it's free. Free is important for me.

He laughs.

Later, another worker in the same supermarket told me that Confucius Plaza, they have an adult education program. So I register and took almost four years, just learning English. Every week we have two classes until 10:00 p.m. I'm working in the market from 9:00 a.m. I come back home almost midnight for four years.

And after four years we go to Florida for a personal reason: my brother disappeared. Nobody knows where he goes. So I go down to help his wife. Even though they divorced I still look at her as my sister. I spend three years there and help her to be independent. Then my friend called me and he says he formed a general contracting company in New York and he wanted me to come as a partner. He gave me a good offer, and that's why I'm coming back.

But after coming up, he changed his mind. No more offer.

What can I do? I cannot do anything. He changed his mind.

MJ shrugs and flips his hand in the air. It seems to take no less than the atrocities of the Cultural Revolution to even slightly rattle this man. All other misfortunes, including moving across several states for a job that, in the end, doesn't materialize, are met with an upright posture that will not collapse, a blasé tone that refuses to bark back at circumstances that cannot be firmly gripped. MJ drops his hand back down onto his desk where it forms as a fist.

I had to find work. I know New York area so I started my own contracting company. Great Will Construction is the name I give. I got the license and started my own work.

After just about half a year, another friend, he have a big job. The problem, he don't know English so he wanted me to get involved, to help him, and then I joined his project. It take almost one year. After the project finish, the general contractor, the owner—it's a big company—gave me a call and he gave me a very good offer. So I join him. I was vice president over there and took care of all the construction work. I stayed at the company six years until about 1994.

But then I quit the job because of personal reason.

It's bad for me. Really bad for me.

You know I have my brother, right? Well, when I'm working for the company, my brother call me. He's in Hong Kong and he's coming back to New York. I was shocked. Really, really shocked. He said he wanted me to help him to start a restaurant in New

York. A Japanese restaurant. I told him I don't like to do anything in restaurants. He said, "I don't need anything," he said, "just be my credit to get a loan from the bank."

So I do it. I help him to get the loan from the bank: $140,000. I'm not nervous, I trust him.

When we open the restaurant: loss. Total loss. Every month is a minus.

And the most harm: my brother disappeared again. Less than six months after the restaurant open he left.

After this happened we never talk. Not one time.

It killed me at the time—the loan, the lease, the money. The landowner, every month he sends somebody down to collect the rent. Six thousand five hundred per month. So I look for somebody to take over the restaurant. Nobody. Finally one guy, he come down, take a look and he said, "Okay. I only could take over the lease. Forget paying for all the restaurant equipment."

So I say, "Okay."

I gave everything to him. Total loss. I lost almost $200,000.

That's why I go back to my own construction business—just the regular contractor, starting over from there, looking for clients, looking for work.

In 2001, I have a friend and he get the project for the 434 Lafayette Street. It's an old building. A two-story house on top of the theater. It was a big project, about five thousand square feet. One point one million dollars. That's too big for my friend. Also he don't know how to go through the architect drawing. So he bring the drawing to me and I go through them and I said I could do it. Then he say, "Why not we do it together?" So we started. And I supervise the project from beginning to finish, the whole project.

The whole interior design is not the regular design. Something special. The walls are not the regular Sheetrock, it's called resin wall. The texture, it looks like the fiberglass. It looks different, not like you see before, very special space. They sent the resin walls from Ohio and use a crane to lift them to the back of building. Crazy.

From that project I started working with that architect—MESH Architects—doing more jobs. We work on the Atrium House in Brooklyn, in Williamsburg. Nineteen Powers Street, near Union Avenue. This one.

He points to the 2012 Building Brooklyn Award that hangs on the wall behind him.

Actually the Atrium House was posted in *New York* magazine. It is originally a one-story garage. Nobody using it, nobody in building. Then the architects they see it and decided to change the garage to a live-in unit. They have an extension to become a two-story and we build the house around a courtyard. It's beautiful. It looks so different. The sunlight comes in and there's grass and the grill for the barbecue. Not like you see so much in New York. Something new.

Now I'm doing building projects in New York for about twenty years. I'm still here.

He smiles.

I have ten people working for me. So far, even though I try to find somebody to help me lead, I can't find anybody. You know, many people they know how to do the work but no English. Or I got the people could speak English but they don't know how to do the work.

Most of the construction workers that come from China now are older, same age as me. They know how to work but no chance to get English. No chance. They pay certain money, $60,000 at least, and then somebody help them get into USA. They set up the payment schedule. They have to work for five or six years at least to pay back the money. You know, some are making something like $1,000 a month, right, because they don't have any skills. They only work for construction, or maybe restaurants. The maximum they get is $1,000, something like that. Assume they give two hundred dollars to pay back the cost to come to US, they have only eight hundred for the rest of living.

One job we did on Madison Street, the government wanted someone to help take over the building, to clean up all the violation. I went there to take a look. The room like this, same size.

He motions to the walls of the well-ordered 12 x 15 office where we sit.

Even smaller than this room. And guess how many people live there? Twenty-two. I cannot imagine. Three layer of the bed. And then the shoes all around the floor. Twenty-two people. I saw the paper on the door of the fridge. The name and how much money they pay for the rent. Twenty dollars a month. Just for a bed. The whole building was like that.

And a lot of people are still coming down from China. In New York still get better pay than in China. Now most of people come from Fujian, right, Fujian province. In Fujian area, if the family have nobody living in USA, they have no face. That means—I don't know how to explain—if they don't have any relative in the US, they will have no honor and people look down to them. So, many people, they want to come.

I want to keep my office in this neighborhood but this space is no good for me. I need to move. The reason is Chinese tradition, the feng shui. The entrance is narrow and also the most worst thing is the bathroom right here.

He points over his shoulder toward the back of the building.

No good. In Chinese tradition it's no good. All the money go through the bathroom! Supposed to put the bathroom on the side and not face the entrance. That's common sense. That's normal common sense.

My friend hired a fortune-teller and when I met her I ask her, "Hey, what you think about my office? It's good or bad?" I told her address.

"Get out," she said. "I know the space. The bathrooms are bad, right? The front is narrow."

I said, "Yeah."

She said the former tenant in this space is also contractor. He just rent it for six months and give up. "I told him same thing: get out."

It's really scaring me, you know. Since I moved here, the business still keep busy but not make any money. No money, no money. Some clients still have the balance they not pay me. A couple years already and I'm still waiting. So I started looking for new space. Just need the space that fits my use. Still in Manhattan. Manhattan is a link to all the different boroughs. I can manage anybody, from my client, to my architect, to my worker. Even though in Brooklyn the rent, it's cheaper, right, but it's not the good location. You know my old fortune-teller, he die already, but he told me Manhattan—in the whole New York—Manhattan is the best location. Best land. For everything, for everything, for everything: Manhattan. I don't know why. Only God know that.

He laughs.

I want to find the right space for my job because I still like my job. When I finish a new project I feel good.

A smile brightens his face.

You know, I don't know how to say this feeling: when I start a job, the building, the interior it's always bad condition or worst design, something like that, right? After I finish the job it's a beautiful living area, it's a new space. A new part of New York, you know? Then I have a special feeling.

4.

I stand in front of 434 Lafayette, ringing the buzzer to see if the owner will let me up to take a look at the resin walls from Ohio that MJ put in place. There is no answer and the silence sounds like it is telling me: private property, come back never. I turn around and look across the street at the mid-nineteenth century stone building where the Public Theater has operated since 1967. It is a towering red-and-brown-colored Neo-Romanesque structure that the Landmark Preservation Commission saved from demolition at its first hearing in 1965. It was the first order of business. Shortly thereafter, the theater company's founder, Joseph Papp, persuaded the city to let him use the building for the theater. More recently, the Public spent $40 million on renovations. I head to the offices of the architecture firm working with the theater, seeking the person in charge of the historic undertaking:

Have you seen the new building? That's mine. I've worked with that building for over ten years. If you look closely, it's actually three identical buildings. It looks like it was all done at once. In fact, it was done over the course of fifty years. Those walls are a meter thick, solid brick. Anything that's done now is a veneer of brick, behind it is something else. Nobody lays ten layers of brick anymore. Nobody can afford it. It'll cost billions and billions.

Stephen Chu bites into a grilled chicken sandwich. He is wedged into a hobbit-sized booth at Corner Bistro on West Fourth Street and with every bite, he magically succeeds at keeping the sauce off of his sculpted goatee. He was originally accepted at Berkeley as pre-med but switched to architecture, seeking a middle ground between his artistic tendencies and his father's demands for a practical degree—his father was an engineer and first generation immigrant from China.

I did their green room and their dressing rooms. I did their offices. I repaired their roof. This last job was actually the first job that someone could see. I restored the facade. The original scope of the work was to improve the face, the outside, for the public—lowercase *p*. The lobby turned out to be the most efficient thing to accomplish that.

The design that we ended up doing was extremely complex from the city agency perspective. We wanted to put a stoop on the building. I had to get the people at Landmarks to say okay before I could do anything. We spent months preparing a presentation, which I gave five years ago. To make the case, I based the entire scope of new work on history. So I started from day one, the beginning of that building. I said first of all the use has changed. It was the first New York City Public Library. And then the Hebrew Immigrant Aide Society gut the building and it became a dormitory with a big kitchen, like a halfway house to help immigrants before they moved on to permanent housing. In the '60s, a developer wanted to tear it down and build something else. And Joe Papp came along. He and Giorgio Cavaglieri, who was a well-known architect of the time, completely gut it again and made it into what it is today, which is six theater venues and a library. So, many uses over many years.

And during the '20s when they built the subway, they widened Lafayette and they tore the centerpiece stoop off. They shoved the stairs into the lobby. You went up the stairs and into the lobby, which wasn't even a lobby anymore because you had these damn stairs in it! So we said we're going back to the historical condition, putting a stoop back.

There's a lot of cultures in New York City that have a whole history of hanging out on the stoops. Here's an institution that's already based in bringing theater and the arts to everybody. It makes perfect sense that that stoop should be there, a community amenity. If you go on a sunny day, you'll see everyone's there having lunch. Nowhere to do that before. And there was nowhere for people to line up when standing in line to get free tickets for Shakespeare in the Park. I made the case that the stoop would improve the bond with the community.

So Landmarks, in fact, commended me. The commissioner said this is an excellent presentation. We got our approval. The only thing they asked was that we make the handrails bronze.

He laughs.

Bronze handrails? No problem.

They spent millions of dollars restoring the facade. The canopy is glass, okay, so it's modern but it's what's called revocable consent. The city can take it all off if they decide. They have that right. They can take the stoop off; they can take the canopy off. So I designed the whole thing carefully: the canopy is supported by two points and if you cut them off the whole thing is gone. And it hangs off the facade so you don't do anything crazy to the building. Now, once you're inside we modernized it, but it's been gutted so many times. The arrangement we came up with was bringing back the original purpose of the building: prosody, opening the archways up, the balcony. All of these things would increase visibility and sense of space.

It's interesting because civic or public works pop up more in gentrified areas. I think there's actually lobbying, pushing political dollars. Not that there may not have been a need for it before. I think you can't help but look at the pros and cons of gentrification and whom it's for.

I've done work for NYU. I did the genomics building. I've worked on the biology building—that process was interesting. NYU's in a tough situation. A university that's really done well for themselves in recent years, they've gone up in desirability and the ratings. They have little room to grow. Any time they do work near Washington Square it becomes a huge community upheaval. The neighbors get very upset. And ultimately it causes a lot of reducing of scope of most of NYU's efforts to expand.

I had to do several presentations to the community board. Sometimes they help us understand the neighborhood and what happens around it and the dynamics of the neighborhood during different times of day. We're hired by an institution that, with or without us, will do something. It's not that without us they just won't do it. So if we have the opportunity to make it better, we will. That's one of our main concerns, really.

I like to think that the architecture works with the environment. We don't want to just plop something down that's designed in a bubble and just dropped on the site. Noise, future plans, zoning changes are all extremely important factors. Because we're talking about buildings that could last for fifty years. There's a long lifespan in this environment. To be responsible you have to care about all those factors.

You know, it's never good publicity for a university to be seen as somebody coming in and taking away old folks or people that have been living there their whole lives and moving them out and causing disruption. That's never good publicity for anyone. So I think they would be thrilled if we could produce designs that the neighbors could appreciate and think add value to the infrastructure of their neighborhood.

I follow Stephen over to his office in the Meatpacking District. His firm occupies several floors of a modern building, all of them connected by a glass staircase at the center of the room. The open work areas are slick and modern, verging on futuristic—not unlike the countenance of Stephen and his colleagues. I feel like an antique visitor who has stepped out of a time machine. I am on the deck of a spaceship that is sailing through galaxies in search of tomorrow's landscapes. Clustered desks, each with a pristine widescreen monitor, are covered with un-

furled plans and unstained coffee cups. Stephen is only mid-career but his resume must be written in ten-point font—it's crowded with civic and cultural projects from around the world. He beams with satisfaction as he shows me an image of Stanford University's Bing Concert Hall, a project for which he served as lead designer.

For my own projects I enjoy sketching the possibilities much more than working on the one that I'm actually going to do. The dreamy side of it is always fun and there's a lot of that in architecture.

A lot more clients are steering towards adaptive reuse instead of new construction. It's more sustainable. So I've done a lot of work that's adaptive reuse.

We did a little work on a restoration piece at Carnegie Hall. We restored Stern Auditorium and then we were hired to build a new theater below it so there's Zankel Hall, and it has a very modern character. It's interesting to see that within one block you restore this and down below you create a new thing, which in some ways has a relationship with what's above. I think those are the projects that I like the most: there's the existing and there's the new and the new is not trying to copy the old, it has its own language. But there's a dialogue with the existing and not just crashing the new on top of it, or drawing a line. The two want to work together. And I think the history of time plays itself out in architecture. Visually you can understand that's what's happening.

My own house is by no means historic and by no means has a significant facade. It's on a worker's housing block, built in the 1930s, intended for lower-income residents. It wasn't the brownstone, it wasn't the stately townhouse. It's a three-story brick box.

He laughs.

With fake shutters attached to the brick, which I tore off immediately.

We're in Ridgewood, Queens. I've been in the house for ten years now and my block has changed. There's more of a sense of community. My neighbors own their own houses. They take care of them. There's pride in that. I know all the neighbors on my block. Some of that is because I spent a year off work. And spent four months at the house every day, renovating. You tend to get to know your neighbors; a lot of them are around all day. So they'd want to come by, see, and we'd have a chat. It's kind of nice. There's a lot of kids on my block. Now I've got two kids. There's a pretty nice feeling there where you know your neighbors, say hi every day, people watch out for you. If they see something weird going on they'll let you know. I like that. In my neighborhood some of my neighbors are out on stoops twenty-four seven.

I rent out the top unit in my house. I just put two signs up and I got calls like crazy, people showing up and wanting to give me cash on the spot. I think the first person that came by is the person I ended up renting to. I had a good feeling, and they've been there for four years. They're friends now. And I haven't touched their rent because I'd rather have people I like and trust than get more money and deal with somebody who's a pain in the butt. My doors are open to them so when I leave and go away they access my house. They take care of my cat. I take care of their cat. That kind of stuff makes a difference. It's that kind of stuff that's hard to find when your life is in the city.

I didn't buy the house because it was a little Queens brick house. I bought it because it straddled residential and commercial warehouses. Ten years ago I was already thinking if anything's going to change it will be the warehouses. I didn't want to be in the middle of pure residential. I felt that was too static for me. I wanted to see the change, I wanted to see development out there. Because I'm an architect and building is what I do.

There are certain areas that are up for being rezoned and I got an email for a petition to block it. When I hear people say, "Oh, it's changing the character," I ask, "Is that a bad thing?" It's an evolving process, it's living, right? It's like language. Language changes and so does use of language. So does land.

5.

*P*aula Segal moved into an apartment across from a vacant lot and couldn't help but wonder about its evolution:
I talked to the old dudes on my block and asked what was up with the lot, and asked everybody else what was up with the lot. Eventually a lot of people had a lot of shards of a story of all these broken promises and a press conference that had happened ten years before. So I called a community meeting at the local school. Passed out flyers, worked with local organizations. A lot of people came, a hundred or so. It was pretty amazing. There was still a lot of pent up anger about a half-a-million-dollar project that never happened. There were a lot of people that had a lot of feelings about that big hole in their neighborhood.

And now it's a big beautiful community garden and park called Myrtle Village Green. We've been open about a year. It's a garden and there's a dog run. People just had a wedding. There's a little production farm that's a CSA.[1] Movies get shown on a wall. There's a bunch of communal space, communal garden beds, individual beds, the kids from the elementary school have little

---

[1] "Community-shared agriculture" or "Community-supported agriculture," a system for farmers to sell city-dwellers a subscription to the crops, delivering them weekly to a designated spot in the city.

beds that they grow—it's just a shared space in a neighborhood that doesn't otherwise have that.

And I got priced out of that neighborhood just before we got access. I don't live there anymore.

Paula was born in the former Soviet Union in present-day Ukraine. Her family immigrated to Boston when she was eight years old. Her first memories of the United States were of supermarkets.

Really cheesy but it's the truth.

She walks into the kitchen of her shared workspace in a loft around the corner from Wall Street. There are two men in an office next to Paula's and one emerges to ask her if she knows anything about the broken dishwasher. It is four in the afternoon; Paula arrived only minutes ago and she is wondering aloud why two men waited for a woman to arrive so they could ask her to deal with the broken dishwasher. She lays into the man who slinks back toward his office, gently shutting his door on the way to his desk. I feel guilty by association, men, and offer to help wash the dirty dishes; Paula takes up the task herself and offers to make me coffee.

It's late in the day, a last burst of heat hits the windows, and we sit in her office while the grounds settle in the French press on her desk. As we talk, Paula rests her hand on the touchpad of her laptop, ready to click at a nanosecond's notice. Her eyes are mostly turned toward the screen, even while she is the one speaking.

She graduated from the CUNY School of Law, and emphasizes that her program of study, the social justice initiatives, was not originally structured as a law school but as a public interest school. "Law in the Service of Human Needs," reads the mission statement of her alma mater.

Conversations with Paula seem to work better when there is sparring involved, not so much because she's a lawyer but more so because she's too smart to tolerate anyone who passively absorbs what she says. She wants questions, demands for elaboration—her brain is too sharp and too fast to go more than a moment or two without a challenge.

When she moved to New York twelve years ago, she picked her apartment, the one she was eventually priced out of, because of the twenty-four-hour hardware store in the neighborhood.

The lights were on at eleven at night and I thought, something about this feels safe. There's always someone around. This must be a community. This makes sense.

When I ask her what gentrification means, her dark eyes, a bit perplexed, shrink under her brow. I try to figure out if the expression has to do with my question, or with something she's just seen on her screen. She confirms it's me:

I don't use this word, *gentrification*, it doesn't mean anything. It doesn't describe anything in the world. It's a noun, right? So you should be able to point to something in the world. It's a nebulous word that has to do with the movement of capital and increased land worth. But as far as dealing with the work on the ground, day to day, the issues are about displacement and about people's quality of life and about the places they live.

I try not to use the word *community* either because—what does it mean? Does it mean the people that are there? Does it mean the people that are going to be there after you've elevated the land values? Or does it actually refer to the space?

In the process of getting access to Myrtle Village Green, we started working on other ways to get information about vacant public land. When we started, you had to buy the database for $300 a borough, updated every six months by the Department of City Planning. We really hammered the department because charging for this was illegal. We got tons and tons of people to send in freedom of information requests. Now it's free.

We had to do a lot with the data to make it useful. The city thinks of its land in terms of uses and taxes, broadly speaking. But uses are defined in a very market-driven way. So "vacant" encompasses many things. There is no separate layer for city owned land. It's just "not tax collecting." So we had to do a couple of things. We had to manually remove all of the existing community gardens based on a community garden survey. We had to pull out all the nonprofit organizations that are getting tax abatements and have vacant land. The original map missed the MTA and other public-private entities, so we added them in as we learned about them. We also had to take out all the gutter spaces—all these spaces that are maybe two inches that run the length of the whole block, and places that don't have street frontage. We actually looked at each parcel on Google Street View and on Oasis. We had to do a lot of manual cleanup on that first set of data before it made sense. And that got us closer to a better picture of what was going on, on the ground.

We figured out this map of all the vacant city land that's not tax collecting. Our cutoff for the size of the space that we include is if you can't stand in it, it's not a space. If you can stand in it you might be able to do something. If you can stand in it and put your arms out—*she does*—it's a space. You could grow something there.

I was invited to do something for the Ideas City Festival so I made a couple hundred of the maps with a friend of mine, Julius Samuels, and we handed them out at the festival. A bunch of people signed up for the mailing list and I was kind of like, "Whoa, people really want this." So we started pasting the maps onto foam board and put out about ten on particular lots that we'd identified.

Then somebody named Eric Brelsford got in touch with me. He said, "I'm a computer programmer. Do you actually have this data that's making up this picture? Because if you do, we could put it online."

And I said, "Sure."

And now Eric and I are the two employees of 596 Acres.

She smiles and sips on her coffee.

We turn data into information that people can use. So we are really focused on connecting people with resources and control of land use decisions. We put out a lot of print materials. We do workshops. If there's a place that's out of energy and isn't working, we'll go and have a meeting there. Getting angry in person is actually much more fulfilling.

She laughs.

The meetings bring in new people and we work out whatever fights have been happening on the block. When I host a meeting suddenly everybody's getting along, everyone is recentered.

We started with Brooklyn and at this point we've mapped all five boroughs of New York City. Staten Island's information is up but it's password protected. People in Staten Island who we work with have it. But I feel like putting information on the internet first is creepy and I want to make sure that we can support people in neighborhoods and that we're getting information to people in neighborhoods first.

A lot of people don't have access to the internet. I know it seems like we live on the internet but, you know, that's you and me.

The other way to look at our work is that we're trying to sort of heal the scars of urban renewal.

In her current project, "Urban Reviewer," Paula is studying 150 master plans, often called "urban renewal plans," that were adopted by the city beginning in 1949. Most of the plans were carried out under the leadership of Robert Moses, who amassed colossal political power without ever holding elected office. Famously dubbed "The Power Broker" in Robert Caro's 1974 biography, Moses served as the head of various public authorities from the 1920s to the 1960s, always taking the power with him by retaining control of development funds. Handling the money for public projects—parks, roads, bridges—allowed Moses to circumvent much of the legislative process. To say that he designed twentieth-century New York is not an overstatement—it's hard to find a corner of the city free of his influence. Moses did not renovate old buildings—he demolished them. He prioritized private cars over public transportation and pedestrians. And his fingerprints are all over the urban renewal plans Paula is studying. The plans reveal Moses's brutal, systematic approach: identify "blighted" or "obsolete" neighborhoods, clear them of existing buildings, and bring in new development, public and private. The people who lived in the "blighted" and "obsolete" neighborhoods never made the decision to identify their communities as such; instead, the city's Committee on Slum Clearance made the designation.

In many cases, the urban renewal plans were begun but never completed, more specifically, the city often never made it past the slum clearance stage. So Paula is documenting the shocking overlap between the slum clearance sites—the bulldozed businesses and apartments and schools—and the 596 acres she identified in her exhaustive survey of vacant land. It turns out that much of the land that was cleared decades ago—land that was never developed or modernized, as promised—is still lying vacant. Or as Paula puts it:

Capitalism just didn't do what it was supposed to do next.

It's all about what people can actually do, right? And giving people the ability to build their own neighborhood. This is a very nerdy and direct way to take people's rights to the city seriously and enforce them as rights. In a truly legal sense. People have the right to create their city. Especially in these spaces that are public spaces.

I really believe that people's ability to make decisions about the spaces that they're in is a kind of security that lets you take the next step in your life. The anxiety of having other forces making decisions for you is untenable.

So the spaces we work with are rather important because they're for people that are in a neighborhood at a particular moment whether they've been there for thirty years or three months. They can acknowledge that they're all there together and make decisions even if it's about this bounded space. And it builds a political force with the people in the neighborhood across class, across race, all kinds of religious lines. It really is a way of taking control and reducing some of that anxiety and some of that anger that people feel.

At one site, someone had offered to set up a composting toilet, solar panels, electricity, and Wi-Fi, and they went back and forth and back and forth and back and forth, and ultimately they nixed the toilet because they were like, "We don't want people pooping here." They liked the solar panels and they liked the electricity. They want to show movies and they want to play music. But they nixed the Wi-Fi because they were like, "This is not that kind of space. We talk to each other here."

All of the spaces where we've worked are constantly being created. They're always public and that means that the process is always beginning again, every single time people are encountering themselves in that space. If that's not the way it works the space stagnates.

6.

*S*hatia Strother does not stagnate in her Bedford-Stuyvesant *apartment—the woman and her home are abuzz:*

So I was going to visit my great-grandmother—saying hi, keeping tabs on her. And as I was leaving, I passed the lot next to her house—it was a vacant lot with no real purpose. And something made me do a double take because something was out of place. And I realized that there was a sign. So I looked and it was a map that had been posted by 596 Acres.

Shatia is unpacking bags filled with vestiges from her long day: laptop, mail, groceries, spillover from her son's backpack. Sean is eight and they came home together not ten minutes ago; as they were walking down the block, the boy's voice echoed with questions to ask, anecdotes to relay, facts to share (mostly about bugs), and dinner requests to make. Shatia managed to get her son, her dry cleaning, her bike, and her bags up the stoop of the brownstone where they live on the second floor. Shoni—stepfather to Sean, husband to Shatia—will not be home from work for several hours.

I remember when I was a kid, maybe ten, and one summer the lot was opened and a lady started an arts program under this pavilion that she had built for the kids on the block. I don't know if it was lack of funding or lack of interest but she was only able to do it maybe two or three weekends over the course of one sum-

mer and then it was shut down. When I saw the 596 Acres poster
that memory came back and I thought someone was trying to redo
the workshops, or revamp the lot, or do something else. But when
I really looked at the poster, I realized it was an organization trying
to get other people to do things. So I was like alright, that's cool,
and I contacted Paula, said, "Hey, I saw the sign. I've lived in this
neighborhood almost my entire life. I want to do something."

Paula put me in contact with another girl, Kristin, who was a
transplant to Brooklyn, and she said, "You guys are both interested. You should link up."

And that's sort of the beginning of the garden story.

*Shatia interrupts herself to check on Sean who is in the bathroom,
supposedly getting ready for a bath. His high-pitched voice, yet to stop,
is made indistinct by the running water, which has now been going for
several minutes. Shatia gets up and opens the bathroom door to discover that her son forgot to put the stopper in the tub—all that water
gone—and he's fiddling with a notebook instead of getting undressed.
He is resisting the familiar sequence of events. She enforces this sequence with a totalitarian glare, which carries authority beyond her
twenty-eight years, and holds it for several seconds.*

You're pushing me.

*As soon as Shatia steps out of the bathroom, the door closes behind
her. It squeaks meekly, echoing her son's retreat.*

*Shatia finds a bottle of wine, already open, and fills two large
glasses. She gives one to me, and motions toward the couch; she takes
a chair on the other side of the coffee table. The apartment is cluttered
with stacks of paper and textbooks and laundry and life. Sean finally
stops the bathwater and his mom shakes her head. She has big, bouncy
hair that matches the brightness of her smile and her energy in conversation, even after a long day. She talks of her past, pinpointing
events that changed her life:*

I'd been working in the fashion industry for about seven years.
It was what I wanted to do. I wanted to be a designer and I wanted
to be famous and I was going to make these beautiful clothes and

everyone was going to know my name and it was going to be awesome. As I got older I realized I wasn't that shallow. I actually woke up one day and realized: holy shit, you thought you were this shallow and you're not. But I still did it because I made really good money. And at a certain point I realized it wasn't enough because my job consumed so much of my time. It was becoming a thing that didn't leave room for the things that I loved. It didn't leave room for me to be instrumental in bettering my neighborhood.

As time went on I got more jaded. I was working for this company and I remember being in this meeting where my boss was trying to decide whether or not she should report the results of lead testing on these belts from a Chinese factory. She looked at the cost to do the recall and it was too much so she decided to sell them and let the chips fall where they may. And if anyone got sick, she would settle potential lawsuits. So we're just going to cross our fingers and hope no one gets sick. Hope that nobody's kid chews on their belt. And I remember sitting in this meeting thinking fuck that! This is crazy! What kind of world am I living in? I cannot possibly work in a place like this and contribute to this type of carelessness when on the side I'm talking about being all for my people and justice for all and fight the good fight. You can't do that. It's not okay. That's one of the biggest contradictions you could possibly commit. That was the turning point. So I decided to leave.

I had talked about wanting to go back to school and applied to NYU for their masters in sociology program. Unfortunately none of my fashion design credits transferred.

She laughs.

They accepted me with a partial scholarship. So that's where I'm at right now. This is my first year. I'm loving it. It's hard work. It's exhausting. I have a fifteen-page paper that's due tomorrow morning and I still have six more pages to go. Once he goes to bed—*motioning over her shoulder, rolling her eyes*—I'll be doing that all night. And I love it. Because I'm doing something that has a purpose now.

Shatia thinks about social work as a field capable of bringing gardening skills and food policy awareness to targeted neighborhoods. A few months ago she took a job with the Northeast Brooklyn Housing Development Corporation. Included in the organization's purview is a range of programs to create more access to healthy food in Brooklyn: renovating a food pantry, adding a demonstration kitchen, hosting free cooking lessons.

It's the first time I've had a dream job. I get to work in my neighborhood. And my work is directly involved in improving my neighborhood. The biggest thing that attracted me to the position is that I would be at the forefront to new programs. I would be instrumental in developing new ideas and solutions in my neighborhood.

My family has been here for five generations. My great-grandmother was born in North Carolina and moved to Brooklyn in her early twenties. She had a few jobs. She was a line cook for a restaurant at one point. Eventually she was able to buy a brownstone here in Bed-Stuy. She ran an underground club in her basement. And her brother, my great uncle, ran the band. It was like a little speakeasy.

Her daughter, my grandmother, grew up in that house and still lives there. She'll be eighty-nine this year. My dad and his brother grew up in that house, too. And then me and my siblings grew up in that house. My son is the first generation that hasn't grown up there. But he still has a connection to it because we live three blocks away.

She motions out the window and takes a drink from her glass.

Hopefully it will continue if my son decides to stay here when he's an adult. So that's one, two, three, four, five generations of us in Bed-Stuy.

My great-grandmother bought it, I think, for $80,000 in the '50s. Right now I think the value is $665,000. I mean it's in complete disrepair. It's falling apart and shit. But we still own it, it's still in the family.

And now there's a garden next to it because I saw the 596 Acres poster.

That's a lot that was vacant since the '70s. When I was a kid I remember that lot being empty and us running around in it. My dad played there—when he was cutting and smoking weed with his friends that was the lot they went to. And now it's been turned into a community asset so my son doesn't have that same relationship to it.

She laughs.

First we had to find out who owned the lot. Turns out HPD owned it—the Housing Preservation Department of New York City. We had to secure a license agreement with them, saying that they would allow us to use the space during whatever interim before a developer came in. We had to sign all these agreements and prove that there were interested people in the project and that we had outreach in the community. And at that point it was just a waiting game for the keys, which took a while. So I decided to rent some bolt cutters and cut the lock and just start working in there while we were waiting. They'd already told us we had the space, and it was taking them a while to send us the finished paperwork. So I was like, "Fuck this, let's just cut the lock open, we already know we have it. What are they going to do? Relock it?" So that's pretty much how it happened. I wanted to get started. This is something I'm really excited about.

We decided we wanted to create a gardening space to be open to the community. We didn't want to turn it into this garden club that was always locked. That was a huge, sensitive topic to me: the amount of entitlement that goes into people starting projects, saying this is for us, and the community at large is not always welcomed. That coupled with the fact that we have a lot of newcomers in the neighborhood who aren't necessarily engaging with the culture of the neighborhood. So I really wanted to make sure that we were open and transparent and a community asset, and not this elitist group of gardeners who wanted to hang out in this space and not include everybody.

One of the biggest ways to do that was nonverbal: we open the garden when the sun comes up and we lock it when the sun goes down and whoever walks by or is interested in being in the garden can be in the garden. There's rules about no smoking or no kids unattended or no illegal activity. But anything else and this is your space.

We gathered a whole bunch of donated seeds from events and workshops. So aside from a few private beds anything that grows in the garden you're able to harvest without permission, without oversight, without guidance. Here, we have extra garlic—take it. We have extra tomatoes—take them. And then we started conducting workshops, and incorporating education into the space. Now we partner with a couple of schools. Our way of showing people that we are an open community asset is by making everyone feel like they're getting something out of it.

I'm not getting paid whatsoever. Sometimes when you're in the heat of frustration and you have garden members who aren't pulling their weight or you're frustrated with a specific project, I'm always like, "I should get paid for this shit!"

She laughs.

But then I realized that I don't want that. It really comes out when I'm angry or frustrated about something that I'm passionate about. Other than that, I do it for the love of it. And I do it because, honestly, I want to see more people of color having leadership roles in our neighborhood and the wider community. I feel like it's something that is lacking. Because I'm involved in the food justice community and every workshop I go to, everything I'm involved in, it's always majority white women. That is consistently the majority. I went to a cooking workshop last week and it was right at the projects at Fulton and Malcolm X. I went in with an open mind, potentially to pull in some partners with the work that I do.

This workshop was run by three white girls in their twenties, teaching old black women in their sixties how to cook.

Shatia holds her breath for a moment, letting the image settle: three young white women instructing a group of aging black women on the elusive art of cooking. Then she explodes with laughter.

The idea they put out there was we're not going to teach you how to cook, because we already assume you can do that, but we're going to teach you how to incorporate healthier items into your ingredient repertoire. That's what they said they were doing. But then it's these three white girls, and they say, "Oh, can we get anyone to volunteer to help with the cutting of the onions?"

I think they were making jambalaya.

So this woman gets up and she says, "Sure I'll help you with the onions."

She's this older woman—like fifties, sixties, can't tell which but she's up there—and she starts cutting the onion and the girl's like, "No no, no—that's not how you cut an onion."

And the older woman goes, "Woman, I've been cutting onions for thirty years. I've been cutting onions since before you were even born. I know how to cut an onion!"

That was the most condescending thing I've ever heard. I would never think to tell a woman, one of my elders, how to cut an onion. I'd be looking to her to teach me things. Even if I assume she doesn't eat healthily, at least she knows how to cook. That's a big source of pride.

I think there have been long-standing stereotypes and ideas about seeing a white face as the authority—and the only authority. There needs to be some measures for correcting that, for saying, "There are people like you who know things. There are experts who look like you." It's that same idea of telling a little black boy that he could be president because: look, there's somebody that looks like you. I think that should start on a local level. And I'm not going to say that these girls didn't know what they're talking about, that they aren't suited to the task, but I think it's important for everyone to know that people who look like them have important roles and they're doing things and they're making changes and they're leaders in certain ways. Because a lot of people don't feel like the black population gives a shit. A lot of people feel like the black population is lacking leaders, lacking people who are involved. I think that workshop might have been more appropriately led by a group of women of color, or a group of men of color, or a group of men and women of color.

It isn't something that you should manufacture. You shouldn't have affirmative action with this formula where you say, "Well, you know, all of our workshops are sixty percent this." I think it's something you tailor to your audiences. Today we have A, B, C people coming. Let's think about what that means. Let's think about how we can make this the best it can be for them. That should be something that's constantly in the forefront of your mind when you educate a group of people. What would be best for them? What do they need to see? Or even ask them! I think it's another condescending thing to say, "I'm going to go in and teach them." Find out what they want to be taught. I don't feel that happens very often.

When I got involved in activism, I just assumed white people do everything. "There's not going to be many people like me, not very many black people. They don't do this." And I knew better! As someone who prides myself on being open-minded and educated, it's surprising how easy it is to fall into stereotypes. I know of many, many, many amazing black leaders throughout history and even currently but still I catch myself with those thoughts sometimes. Does that make any sense? I can't really explain the contradictions. I knew there were people of color that existed in my community and in the larger community of New York and also America but I walked in saying to myself that I was going to be the only one. It's just a thing you have in the back of your head. It's ridiculous but you still feel it.

I think that where the disconnect comes in is that black leaders are not widely publicized, they're kind of behind the scenes and no one is connecting the dots. So you'll have one person in East New York doing one great work, and then you'll have a person in Bed-Stuy doing another great work, and there's not much cross-referencing of these resources and ideas.

One of my ambitions is figuring out a way to create a coalition of these leaders that is very public and very present. How's that going to happen? No idea! But it's going to happen. I shouldn't have to scour the earth looking to find my people.

In a rapidly changing landscape, the search for "my people"—a community united by a shared sensibility or a common aesthetic or a vision for what a neighborhood can become—often feels especially urgent. In the 1970s, many new Brooklyn residents began to identify themselves with the moniker "urban Thoreaus" (rather than "gentrifiers"). Regardless of each person's longevity in a neighborhood—a month or five generations—there is often the desire to feed off the electricity of others, or, in the case of Shatia, to harness disparate currents, new and old, running throughout the borough.

When I was growing up here, we always lived in the part of Brooklyn people called Stuyvesant Heights. That's where all the really beautiful original brownstones are and a lot of gorgeous architecture. And that's where a lot of the wealthier residents lived. So I grew up in this little pocket on my mother's side. They are significantly wealthier than my dad's side. My great-aunt on my mom's side of the family, she owned a brownstone before she passed away. Estimated value maybe like $1.8 million. She was packed with money. My dad's side of the family is lower working class. My experience in Bed-Stuy has always been kind of weird because when I was with my mom's family I stayed very insulated from the world at large. And then being with my dad's side on the weekends, I realized: oh shit, there are poor people and Bed-Stuy's a lot bigger than these fifteen blocks that my mom's side of the family tries to keep me contained in. So I've always had this weird sense of wealthy vs. poor and being a part of both worlds. Once the influx of wealthy started coming into Bed-Stuy, that didn't really faze me because I already knew there were pockets that existed. They'd already been here. Just not in such large numbers and not in this take-over mentality. Plus all the wealthy people I knew when I was a kid were black.

She laughs and refills her glass with wine, a more modest pour— not long now before she starts with her homework. Her son is draining the bathwater, inching toward bed.

I really started to notice when I would walk to the train and there were more white faces than black faces. That's when it became real to me. But that's also when I became aware that I had a very skewed view of gentrification because I never thought of black wealthy people as gentrifiers. It always had this racial connotation to it. And I woke up and realized that gentrification is a class issue, it's not a race issue, and it took all the white faces to move in for it to occur to me that gentrification has been occurring for a very long time, it's just now it has a white face.

Right now my world is in chaos, I have to tell you, because I have so many competing ideas of what this all means. If I was on one side of the fence it would be so much easier to deal with this. If I was just a wealthy white girl, or a wealthy black girl, moving to a neighborhood, I could take a stance. If I was just a poor resident I could take a stance. But I come from a unique position of knowing both sides—knowing a bunch of sides.

It is refreshing to hear Shatia shift from the idea of "both sides" to a more complicated story—that of multiple perspectives. Gentrification is often saddled with an us vs. them framework, with "us" and "them" redefined ad infinitum—no two people ever talking about the exact same thing when it comes down to what "we" want and what "they" are doing wrong. Most of the time this idiosyncratic bifurcation is, as Shatia puts it, about class: wealthy vs. poor with everyone on either side of a centerline. But Shatia's own experiences, the contradictory spaces she lives in, obliterate that clear line. As Neil Smith puts it in The New Urban Frontier, *"Many people occupy 'contradictory*

class' positions; the source of contradiction . . . might involve anything
from the occupation of an individual, to the level of class struggle in a
given period. Classes are always in the process of constitution."

Shoni and I, our wealth has fluctuated. When I was in fashion
we were what Obama calls the middle class, the $200,000 or
more, we were there. Then I decided to be a crazy person who
leaves all that and works with my hands in the dirt and, well,
we're still middle class but our household income is less than what
it was.

And when me and Sean's dad were together, when we were
first starting out, I was fiercely stubborn in the idea that I didn't
want family help. So we lived in a shelter. I know what it's like to
live in a shelter for three months. I know so many perspectives
and you would think that would be something that helped but it
just confuses me. 'Cause I actually don't know how to feel about
it all.

Even outside of myself I have friends all over the spectrum. A
lot of my friends are people that moved into the neighborhood recently and they're considered the problem. But I love them. And
they're all really invested in their community and you can't really
hold them to blame for being successful. One thing I hear is all
this "rich this," or "wealthy that" or "you make more so you
think you're better." I would hate for someone to begrudge me
for being economically successful! Why wouldn't you just be
happy that I made it?

Then I started to realize that maybe that isn't the issue. Maybe
the negative impact of gentrification has more to do with the dis-
engagement of the people who are moving in. So I started to hone
in on what I saw as the target of my anger. I found out it's not so
much the neighborhood changing and displacing people, which is
a legitimate problem that I'm angry about, but I think my biggest
problem is people who move here just because the rent is cheap
and they see this as a pit stop to wherever their path is in life. They
decide to come here but they decide to not be fully invested in their

community. So they come here like we have a little more money, we're driving rents up, we're not going to be involved, we're going to walk down the street with our headphones. We're just here to find the cool bars and restaurants, and we're not really engaged in the larger community. Those are the people I'm angry at.

I refuse to wear headphones.

I've started going on this campaign where if I'm walking and I notice that you have your headphones on, I'll step in front of you and say, "Look up!"

She laughs.

And I'll say, "Hi, how are you? How's your day going?"

And the reactions have been hilarious. Some people jump. Because sometimes I'll jump when I approach them and go—*she stands to demonstrate, springing forward with both feet*—"LOOK UP!"

I told my husband about it. I said, "So I've started yelling at people on the street."

And he was like, "What're you talking about?" I told him what I was doing. And he said, "No. There is no way. I know you've done some ridiculous shit but this is just—you're going above and beyond."

And I said, "I feel really passionate about this and I'm going to continue to yell at people on the street. If you don't look up, I'm going to yell at you to look up." I think he only halfway believed me.

So we were on the way to this friend's house, maybe last week or the week before, and I did it to somebody. And he said, "How has no one punched you in the face yet?"

She laughs.

But I haven't gotten any negative reactions.

She laughs again.

For me it's principle. When you're walking down the street, no one wants to be invisible. Look people in the eye. Just look and nod. Smile. I don't know—frown. I don't give a shit. Look at me and acknowledge that I'm existing and that I'm walking past you. Something to acknowledge that we are here. We are existing in the space together. That's a phenomenal thing. Just the idea that two people are sharing a space at any given time deserves acknowledgement.

7.

I have taken note that our shared spaces tend to have one thing in common: they offer refreshment. It can be beer, or coffee, or water, but the general principle holds firm across class, geography, religion, and history. Whether it's a South Texas icehouse in the first half of the twentieth century or the break room water cooler in the second half of the same century, or a British coffeehouse three hundred years earlier, the experience of occupying these spaces with a refreshment is restorative and comforting—maybe even enlightening. We like to gather wherever beverages are involved. Even in the present, when our definition of "community" has less to do with sharing physical space and more to do with sharing virtual space, we still shuffle into darkened rooms and huddle around espresso machines and beer taps, if only to commune with whatever device ferries us to the internet.

Tarek Ismail, however, just put his phone away in the pocket of his pants. And his bright blue headphones are wrapped in their cord and placed at the corner of the table where we sit. He has just swooped into his seat at Patisserie Des Ambassades, a French-African bakery in Harlem on a stretch of Frederick Douglass Boulevard peppered with new restaurants and bars and coffee shops that border spots that have held steady for ten or twenty or a hundred years.

I arrived early, and I'm already halfway through my coffee, but Tarek has yet to get the staff's attention. The service is shoddy but no-

*body cares because everyone is in a good mood. Tarek has lived in the
neighborhood for three years and he picked the place. He did not pick
the Starbucks a few blocks down, nor did he pick the place directly
across the street from the Starbucks called Double Dutch, which offers
Wi-Fi, shots pulled at 204 degrees (we are, after all, at sea level), and
natural sweeteners.*

If you go into Double Dutch, it's kind of out of touch with
the history of the neighborhood. But it's packed every single day.
What's interesting is that it's owned by these two guys that own
two other coffee shops uptown. Both of them are real estate agents
and they opened these coffee shops to drum up business in the
neighborhood. So it all sort of feeds on itself in this way that's un-
comfortable.

*Originally from Toledo, Ohio, Tarek is twenty-nine. His mother
was born in the United States to Palestinians; his father was born in a
Palestinian refugee camp in Lebanon. His extended family, uprooted,
has been cast throughout the Middle East.*

*Columbia Law School brought Tarek to New York. Three months
ago he took a job with a public defense organization; he works with
parents whose children are taken by the city because of neglect or
abuse.*

They're really difficult cases. Very emotionally fraught, as you
can imagine. The facts of the cases, sometimes they're not the pret-
tiest facts. It's kind of this seedy underbelly of society that we
don't really interact with much when we're sitting in Double
Dutch. But it's important for me. And as a lawyer it's important
to cut my teeth doing this kind of work.

*Tarek still hasn't had the chance to order coffee. He sits patiently
with his tie knot poking out from the top of his green sweater, which ri-
vals his blue headphones in brightness. He carries a backpack instead
of a briefcase. At Double Dutch the beards grow unkempt; Tarek keeps
his cut close. He looks over his shoulder once more then gives up on
the coffee.*

My sister's working at the Starbucks right here. She just

moved in with me three or four months ago. She gets really good benefits. And the benefits move outward to all of us. I have a pound of coffee for my office every week.

He laughs.

What's interesting to me is that this Starbucks serves everyone. In the mornings, cab drivers come in and get a cup of coffee and a croissant. They don't do that at Double Dutch, I can tell you that for sure. And in a strange way these giant corporations seem like home to a lot of people: at my job I'm working with these families who are dealing with Children's Services Administration and whenever you ask them where they take their kids they're going to say McDonald's. Because that's the sort of thing where they've learned to feed their kids and feel comfortable. And I think that's what happens with Starbucks. This Double Dutch thing feels foreign. It's the ambiance and who's sitting there and who's behind the counter.

There's actually a funny story about this Starbucks that one of my friends told me. He said—and I'm going to curse but you're going to understand why—he said when Starbucks first moved in ten or fifteen years ago they hired people from the neighborhood. It hadn't been gentrified at all and it was still Harlem as people knew it. And they weren't really complying with the way things went in a Starbucks. So someone walks in and they order a Caramel Macchiato. They call back the Caramel Macchiato and this guy's like, "My nigga, Caramel Macchiato!"

He laughs.

That doesn't happen any more.

Whole Foods just broke ground up at 125th. I don't know how it's going to go but there are four or five Whole Foods around the country that are community Whole Foods, where they reduce the prices and make it affordable to people in that community. And I think what they decide to do with the Whole Foods will say a lot about the future of this community. And whether or not they are willing to preserve the identity of the community that exists here today. I don't know what direction we're going to head in.

The farther east you go in Harlem, it's kind of virginal in a way. You can see that there are new properties just waiting to become new businesses.

Tarek knows the terrain because he is looking for a place to lease. He wants to find an empty spot in the neighborhood and fill it—that much he knows. Other than that, he hasn't settled on many specifics. Beverages will likely be involved, possibly food. This flirtation with entrepreneurialism has roots in his experience as a student:

Law school ends up, at least in my experience, being something like violence on the mind. It forces your brain into a certain way of thinking so that you're not thinking creatively; you're not sharing ideas with people. You're not able to sit down and talk about interesting questions you've got going on in your life because you start to critique people's thoughts in a way that is not entertaining and feels aggressive and no one wants to do it anymore. So basically, to maintain my sanity, I started having people over for brunch once a month on Sundays.

And college makes you think that, for life, you'll just be able to hop over to your friend's house whenever you feel like it and dig something out of their fridge. But you lose that after college. In this city there's so many people but often you feel so lonely, anonymity becomes the hallmark. Groups of friends become less tight. It's a lot of people who, present company included, have to schedule in advance who they're going to meet with and when.

He's right: here we are in the middle of March and I first asked him to meet for coffee at the beginning of February. Previous to this we met only once, at a dinner hosted by a mutual friend. Perhaps if we had a thicker history this might have happened sooner but I don't think so: the brevity and rarity of Tarek's emails led me to believe that control of his inbox is perpetually slipping from his grip.

I'm bad at keeping a schedule. It's not how I grew up and it's not my style. I'd rather just hang out with people—as simple as that may sound, and maybe irresponsible as that may sound. I don't like arranging my meet ups with friends to be responsibilities, I prefer that the friendships themselves are the responsibilities.

The brunches are something I continue to do today. And now my sister's involved and we both really enjoy creating that space and feeling responsible for a space like that. That's the impetus for opening a business.

Me, my sister, and a friend of ours, we've been toying with the idea for a while and we've been looking at different spaces, trying to figure out what would work because it's kind of a foreign concept to all of us. But it's not foreign enough to deter us. I think it's very doable while being cognizant of what's going on in Harlem and the ways we would play into it or not play into it.

We're thinking about how to feed back into this community—which I'm really starting to call my own. We're considering what's the best way to frame a space in this neighborhood that relates to all members of the neighborhood, whether it's a coffee shop, or a communal space that doesn't really exist right now.

The idea of community as where you go and hang out is important. Having other people around you doing stuff is something that has existed since the beginning of time. Interaction has also been a critical part of that equation and more and more that part of the equation has been falling by the wayside.

I saw someone post something today to the effect of "I'm creating a new social network, you know what it's called? Outside!"

He laughs.

And it's true, right? This idea of space, of communal space, warm communal space—it's foreign in this city. It's just so strange because so much here is communal. The transportation is forcibly communal here but in a way I think there's not much communing that happens. And I miss it. That's what I come from. That's what I knew growing up in Ohio. And there's no reason to not have it. It's so easy to facilitate. It's just a matter of figuring out how to do it while feeding ourselves and keeping the place open.

He laughs.

Someone once told me that if you really love cooking, instead of opening a restaurant, you should invite a bunch of people to your house, use the finest ingredients, and take a big stack of money and light it on fire and you'll have had more fun than opening a restaurant.

He laughs.

That's the message I've gotten. So that's why we're excessively cautious and thinking about what it is we want to do and what we want to create.

When we first were talking about this, we went downtown to all the different coffee shop owners, asking what they thought of opening a coffee shop in Harlem. People literally told us, "I don't know if black people drink as much coffee."

And we were like, "Excuse me?"

He laughs, still in disbelief.

"Thanks for the advice buddy."

One product we're considering building into whatever community space we hope to make is called manakish, which is basically a very thin pie that you put in the oven. It's Middle Eastern. In essence it's peasant food, really casual. It's not meant to be more than a few bucks. What's weird about this neighborhood is that if you look around there's not a lot of grab-food-and-go places. It's all fancier sit-down places that close kind of early. You do feel a separation of society when you go into any of these restaurants that maybe you don't feel when you go into the grocery store for example. So that's one thing we've been thinking about.

We've also been thinking a lot about the ways in which our identities and what we're doing mix with the identity of the community in which we live and want to be a part of—whether or not we want to impose our identity onto the community or feed into a broader identity. We're spending a long time thinking about whether or not we want to be another ethnic restaurant gentrifying the community or, instead, if we want to be somewhat thoughtful about our role here.

I think that to some degree you have a new neighborhood and you have an old neighborhood. So those are two communities. But at the same time you have all these immigrants that have been here longer than the new neighborhood but not as long as the old neighborhood. There's a huge West African community that has been here and they bring their culture with them in the way that I do and the way that you do. There's a sort of communal reality to that.

But people feel offended by newer communities that don't appreciate the history and don't appreciate the difficulties that were in the community before we got here. To some people it's offensive, I think, and for good reason.

I'm projecting myself onto a history that I haven't experienced but: I feel like it's as if I were to go back to whatever village in Palestine where my grandparents are from and see what's being done with it now, I would probably feel the same hostility. I would feel expelled. In that case there was an actual expulsion but in Harlem there's a de facto expulsion in a lot of ways—whatever it is: price, access, comfort, community. So I imagine that's the feeling I would have, and it's not a good feeling. It's an angry feeling. So I relate to it and I sympathize with it in a real way. And it makes me wonder if I should stay here. And so that's another reason I feel like I've got to feed back into this community in a way that does more than just take.

8.

*R*aul is bouncing his knee, and his body with it, but somehow his voice remains steady as his eyes scan the sidewalk:

I try not to be judgmental. Puerto Ricans, they criticize everything. I try not to be like that.

But new people, they come from wherever they're from and they try to make New York like where they're from. So why don't you just stay where you're from? You know what I mean? In Brooklyn, ask a kid how to get to Prospect Park. They can't tell you. But they can tell you how to get to somewhere in Iowa. People are very book smart and scholarly, savant, but they don't know common things to get around. They're very clumsy that way. I hate these kids that come from other places that are here for two or three or four years that are like, "Oh, I feel like I'm so New York."

You have nothing to do with this place!

People get here and they think they represent New York. No, you don't represent New York at all, dude. You're misinformed. Get a good decade underneath your belt. You start getting attached to the city.

Raul is six feet tall, his chest is broad and thick, and he hesitates at nothing. His eyes are dark, almost black. Only his resonant voice fits his age, forty-six. Everything else about him seems younger—with his gym shorts, colorful Nikes, and a hooded sweatshirt with front pockets where he can hide his hands, Raul generally looks like he's going to or coming from a pickup game. When winter descends, he covers the uniform with a puffy jacket from The North Face.

He's just back from watching that movie—the title escapes him but it had LA gangs and cops and blood.

I took my grandmother to see that shit.

He cackles. Raul's always cackling, and when he does it is equal parts sinister and vulnerable. There is a hint of something underhanded or plotting in his cackle but you also hear a need—a longing for some discernable response. Show me, Raul seems to say—show me that we are connecting. And if that doesn't happen quickly, he'll pull out his phone to check for messages, browse status updates, temporarily exit.

He leans on a wobbly sidewalk table at a taco shop just north of Houston Street, not far from his apartment. He takes a moment to gauge the girl sitting alone at the table next to us; she is the only person within earshot but she's wearing earphones, swaying away in her own universe, and so he continues:

That's the second movie my grandmother's seen in her whole life. She's from Puerto Rico. It's a dead town. There's a theater a couple of blocks up the road but according to my mother, she didn't go. I was like, "Ma, she's never been to a fucking theater?"

She just moved here because she's old and she got sick. Her husband died. He was a bootlegger, womanizer. He had businesses, grocery stores, wives, a lot of wives, a lot of kids. He was bugged out. He was no walk in the park. I didn't miss anything.

My mother's originally from Bedford-Stuyvesant, Brooklyn. I guess she kept annoying the doctors because she's good at annoying people, so they're like, "Yo, go to another hospital!" So she went to Coney Island. That's where I was born.

She bounced on my father when I was three. Then she was hanging out here in the East Village with her girlfriends. There's two kinds of people: live in Brooklyn, stay in Brooklyn, or some people are curious to see what the fuck is over the bridge. My mother crossed the bridge. Eleventh Street and Second Avenue, she still lives there to this day. Rent control, papi![2]

He cackles.

Me and my friends used to walk around. My mother said, "Don't go past Third Avenue." We went all the way to the Hudson River. Forty-Second Street, we used to cut school, we'd jet up there. You go to Forty-Second Street and see kids from all over the city and meet them—the Bronx, Staten Island. Everybody's gonna be at the arcade buggin' the fuck out.

It was real up there on Forty-Second Street. The hookers and shit. The pimps, all dressed up. It was bugged out. Crazy realities up there. I remember I had a friend, a Chinese kid named Jimmy, he worked in a shoe store on Forty-Second and Eighth. He would get me some things, you know, wholesale or whatever. One time these dudes were fighting and they came into the store. It was crazy, knives and stabbing each other. It used to get ill. Mid-'90s, they started taking everything down, started building it back up. Toys "R" Us, Dave & Buster's—all that big, clean shit. Funny enough, I enjoy it as an adult. It's nice up there. People think it's corny. I ride my bike and when I come back from Central Park I always go through Times Square. I like it. I've changed and that place has changed.

I ride my bicycle for exercise—and to keep up with New York City. Do you go to FDR Drive, look at the water? They fixed it up real nice. Better late than never. You can sit underneath the Williamsburg Bridge sometimes. I like to ride my bike down by Water Street. Cherry Street. It's like the neighborhood that time forgot over there. It's real peaceful. It's not that gentrified.

---

[2]   New York apartments under rent control are extremely rare. If rent-stabilized apartments—whose rent increases are regulated by the city—are an endangered species, apartments with rent control, where rent hikes have a fixed ceiling, are nearly extinct. They make up less than 2 percent of the housing stock.

Growing up in the city, you get a double education. We hung out with older cats. They were thieves and criminals but, you know, you listen to them all night. Education, man. You learn a lot by watching.

My mother and my stepdad, they were in love. Beginning of everything they were bugging out.

"You want to go to Puerto Rico?"

"Alright, let's pack a bag and jump on the first plane."

Get drunk or get happy on the drop of a dime. They tried to break up a few times but he reeled her back in. I was a little kid. Twice, we came back. He was cool. He was a—he had businesses—a fur business and businesses and stores and stuff, okay: he was a banker. Before there was the Lotto, he played numbers and shit. He had a candy store that was the front. And in the back was numbers and you could bet on anything you wanted. He was in charge of the south side. The Jewish mafia was over there. He was Puerto Rican but he was good with numbers so they hired him and he took over the whole neighborhood. Being a banker is very important. He was in charge of everybody, the whole neighborhood. Zip code. It's a lot of responsibility. That's how he met my mother. He saw her and that was it.

It was a good neighborhood, the East Village. It was bugged out, rich people, poor people. Everybody's on top of each other. I was like eight, seven and I had this friend, his name was Richard, black kid—we were like brothers so we would walk around intrigued by the city itself. We didn't know what the hell was going on, we was just buggin' out. We'd go all the way to the West Side Highway, when the West Side Highway was still up high and we used to climb up there. I used to look at the graffiti on the walls. I noticed it. I wondered why somebody would do that. I was curious.

I loved to play basketball. It wasn't going to be my ticket but I still loved the game as much as anybody else. I was the first dude ever to rock green suede high-top Nikes in 1979, I was fourteen.

Everybody was like, "What the fuck are those, dude?" I saw Magic Johnson wearing them—I was already reading *Sports Illustrated* when I was a little kid and dudes in my neighborhood weren't reading *Sports Illustrated*.

I went to a lot of high schools. I played on the team and I would never go to school. I wasn't really a student athlete. I was an athlete student.

There's the cackle again.

Tenth grade I went to La Salle Academy but I wasn't going to play varsity because the dudes were mad good. I went to Seward Park when Seward Park was ill. I was shitting on myself when I went there. It was ill kids from Avenue D. But I played on the basketball team and I knew all the black dudes so I was good money. We used to smoke weed over in that park on Essex.

I played at West Fourth court but it wasn't because I was all that. One of the coaches put me on a team just because he knew my mom. I played once in a blue moon. The greatest thing that happened was being on the court at the same time with Joe "the Destroyer" Hammond. He was the greatest player that never made the NBA. The Lakers drafted him but he was also a big dealer. They offered him money to play and he was like, "I make half a million on the streets." I was killing motherfuckers for this old man. You should have seen the picks I was setting. It was better for me than meeting fucking Obama.

It's interesting because nobody that hangs out at that park is from that neighborhood because the A, the B, the C, the D, the F—all the trains leave you right there. So you have all these kids come from bumfuck whatever to this park. Once you step inside you're no longer at Sixth Avenue and Fourth Street. You're in another world. It's hustlers in there. They're playing dice, they're playing cards, they're smoking weed and selling stolen goods, you could put bets down, it's fucking crazy. They have dudes that been hanging out there for thirty years, forty years. It's generational in there.

Last five, six years the level of competition went down the drain. Now it's just dudes want to play at West Fourth to say that they played at West Fourth because the fuckin' court is so fuckin' famous. It sucks now. If you want to relive your youth with your fuckin' high school friends and you give a check, you'll get on the team. No background checks.

Raul has some pictures from his playing days that he wants to show me. So we pay the bill and move to his apartment, which is a loft crowded with stacks of clothes and magazines and—well, all kinds of things: autographed baseballs encased in plastic pedestals are lined up on a rectangular table; coffee table books share a corner with promotional VIP swag. Raul is nothing if not a collector. His apartment feels like a small warehouse with an unmade bed shoved in the corner. There are a few sections of wall that aren't buried behind inventory, and most of them display something remarkable: a Jean-Michel Basquiat drawing, a framed Babe Ruth baseball card.

Opposite the bed, a dozen pairs of Nikes rest on individual acrylic glass display shelving just as they would in a department store. Raul walks to the far end of the loft, where the sun streams through big windows overlooking the street, and shuts off his television, which is somewhere in the clutter—you can tell it's there because the local news is on loop. He moves behind a giant forest of shoeboxes, stacked in a dozen or so inexact columns reaching near the ceiling. Despite the chaos, Raul knows where everything is. He emerges from behind the boxes with a stack of old Polaroids and the ingredients for a frightfully large blunt.

He goes back and forth between singling out pictures and assembling the blunt. One image reveals a teenaged, mustachioed Raul on a subway car. He has a friend on either side of him and each boy holds his own jar of ink—the same ink that's brazenly wiped across their shirts and jeans. Raul points at his younger self:

That's a fuckin' punk right there. That's a punk! He thinks he's a man. He knows everything. You can't tell him nothing. If I knew then what I know now—*he shakes his head.*

He was alright, he's a good kid.

I used to write—graffiti, whatever. It's just like a thing amongst them, the gods, they don't mention that word *graffiti*. It's *writing*. I fuck up and call it graffiti all the time.

He points at the picture:

That's my friend on Ninth Street. I used to keep him near me because he had mad ink and supplies in his house. And he knew how to get into spots. It was kind of like my first little crew. You notice the train car is mad clean. Used to catch them clean. You put your shit on the trains, the kids in the Bronx are going to see you and you're gonna be a celebrity up there, everybody's gonna know you because the trains connect the whole city. So you're gonna pick a line by your house, or a line that you can get to, and a yard that you have access to and you're gonna try to dominate it. Whoever dominates is the king of that line. That's a big deal.

Writing on trains is the ultimate. You can't stay there all day. You gotta be in and out. Time is not your friend. Don't strain your brain, paint the train. I wasn't great by any means, but I went to New Lots, I went to the J Yard, I went to the Ghost Yard, I went to prestigious yards where we would just stop and look around—where the fuck am I? I've been to mad, grand, crazy yards.

When I was sixteen, Patti Astor and Bill Stelling, they opened up the Fun Gallery, thank god. They made graffiti expensive. Fab 5 Freddy is the reason. He did Andy Warhol soup cans on the trains, so these niggers go, "Oh, these kids aren't stupid and they know about art. They know their place. They have taste." Fab 5 Freddy brought it all together on my block. It was good. I'm lucky. Things happened to me, random, Random Raul.

Another cackle.

I went across the street and introduced myself. My friends, they were scared, they wouldn't go. I didn't give a shit—they were on my block! That's my block! I grew up there. If it was on another block, I would never in a million years have introduced myself to them. I was just like fuck it. Jean-Michel, Keith Haring, those dudes, they were on my block. I didn't give a fuck about school anymore.

I didn't graduate. I was two credits short. Algebra or trig or some weird shit. It didn't affect me. I was hanging out with rock stars, gods.

Rene Ricard, he's an art critic. He was one of the stars in the Andy Warhol movies. Went to Harvard. Rene Ricard's not his real name. I know his real name but I can't tell you. So he wrote an article on Jean-Michel in *Artforum*. Jean-Michel started making mad whop. He wrote an article on Keith Haring and that's it. Every time this guy wrote an article on you, you were set. Who the fuck is this guy? This guy's got the Midas touch. So I had my little graffiti crew, the TSC, The Style Counselors, and I said, "Listen to me, find this fucking guy, Rene Ricard, and bring him to my house. When you find him, call me."

Couple of days later this kid in my crew: "Yo, I got this guy Rene here, what do you want me to do with him?"

"Yo, bring him to my house—I'm eating, bring him over."

So he brings him over. This guy is the fucking genius art savant. We used to hang out. He was like a big mentor, big, in my life. He's the kind of guy, you go to Europe, he'll write you a letter of introduction. You show it to the people at the hotel, they treat you like a god. He used to like me. He had the hots for me, but I wasn't gay. I'm pretty sure, maybe, he said he slept with me to people, but I didn't give a fuck, it was an honor hanging out with this fucking guy. He had the hots for me and I had the hots for his knowledge, for his brains, like who the fuck are you? What do you know? And that motherfucker, he introduced me to Clemente, Julian Schnabel, Brice Marden. I had never met people like that before. They took me in. I was like the little kid in the group. It's almost like I'm spoiled from that time, like nothing really impressed me after that. Good time to be alive and shit, that's what I'm most proud of: I'm nobody but I was around during good times. I'm going to fuckin' Warhol parties, eating seaweed. What the fuck is this? I would just eat it because everybody else was eating it, I didn't want to be a fuckin' idiot.

And this is how I think—this is how a sixteen year old thinks: So Futura was doing a mural for Citibank on Seventeenth Street, which is now the W Hotel. This is how a sixteen year old thinks: I'm gonna steal that shit and I'm gonna tell him that I found it, I'm gonna give it back to him. Me and my crew, we took all this down. And everybody was like, "Oh my god, somebody stole it!"

And I was like, "Yo, I know where to get it—you want to get that back?"

He's like, "Yeah."

And I gave it back to him, and we became friends ever since then.

Jean-Michel, he didn't stand a chance with these people. The big, big dealers. They kind of study you as a human being and shit. It's not even about your artwork. They just want to see what kind of person you are, and project an image to sell your work. It's psychological shit. All this fucking money. It changes your relationships, obviously. You're giving your friends drawings, they're selling them and shit.

He points at another photo:

The top three graffiti artists are Lee, DONDI, and S-E-E-N. The funniest thing about graffiti is when you see a European kid doing it—I don't know. When a New York kid does it, it's like he's from New York, he's got the style, he's got this attitude, he's from New York. When a European dude does it, they're imitating it. I can't explain it. New York is different from energy anywhere else.

On the trains, before they used to give you a fine and nothing happened to you. Now you get caught on a car, you going down. Last painted car was—what?—1989? Yeah, 1989. The death of subway graffiti. This kid Mike said something really interesting. He said, "We lost the trains but we gained the world. Because after we got off the trains it spread through the whole city." It was really a beautiful way of putting it. These motherfuckers, they can't write on trains no more so they got to do the next best thing: really hard to do shit, like turn the shit into a James Bond movie.

I can't go out with cans now, I'll get caught, my age. Forty-six years old. Graffiti used to be like, oh, this poor kid, but now all these new art kids are like, check out what I can do. So the niggers are doing wild stuff on the streets.

Raul lights his blunt and stands in front of his graffiti-covered refrigerator, pointing out each signature:

This is one of the first superstars in graffiti history. This nigger, Stay High, he just died. Stay High 149. He fucked everybody's head up. You know, it looks corny to you right now but he did that shit 1970, 1969—that was a big fucking deal. When you see tags like this when you're a kid, you're like, "What the fuck is going on right now?"

He points to another name:

Yo, Phase 2. Greatest graffiti writer of all time, this nigger basically invented graffiti right here. That's why this refrigerator ain't going nowhere. He invented drips, arrows, numbers, everything. All this shit, putting a 2 by your name. We wouldn't be having this conversation if it wasn't for him. His name is Lonny, he's totally nuts and amazing.

He points at other signatures on the side of the Kenmore:

That's Zephyr.

That's Futura.

Futura took me to his house out in Brooklyn. I was fucking freaking out and shit. Smoking weed. I didn't really like coke. I just did it like seventeen, eighteen, nineteen because everybody else was doing it but it's not really me. That white powder takes you to weird places. Going up is the way to go, but coming down, it's like the worst fucking feeling ever, fuck me! Slippery, slippery slope. It's weird, people love that shit. They have an insatiable appetite. I'm a weed guy. I'm a pothead. I used to be buying this cheap weed and they were smoking green buds already. C— was the first one to bring buds from California to New York and we were like, "What the fuck is this shit, nigga?" Cali, nigger! He brought that shit from Cali. That was jumping, the weed scene, it just turned green—'80, '81, '82.

That's when New York was New York. Mud Club, Max's. A good time to grow up. Andy Warhol used to always be in Keith Haring's studio. I was scared to death of him. Sometimes on Sundays he would have these little picnics at Central Park. Used to go. Bugged the fuck out. Fucking Andy, he was alright. I used to have a baseball team and he'd always come watch us. *Interview* magazine had a baseball team, and we used to beat the shit out of them all the time. My team was Futura; Fab 5; Zephyr; Ricky Pow, used to be a famous photographer; the Beastie Boys; two or three kids from my neighborhood who were really good at baseball; and me—and we would kill it.

I was working getting weed for people and shit. I was working on my own with that, and then this big deal, this lady named A—, she got robbed and shit, and someone said to her, "Yo, you should have Raul do it for you." And she did.

So I had the weed thing and I used to steal linen canvases from Utrecht and sell them to all the big painters. My dream was to be—I used to want to work in Duggal, to have these big machines that print the big color photos. They're these beautiful, awesome machines. I sold weed to this girl that worked there. She used to let me come in, we used to smoke and she'd print and let me see it. It was like, "This is what I want to do with my life."

But the interviews didn't go too good. They didn't hire me. I was dressed nice. Whatever. That's when I really got into the weed thing. What do they say in the movies, in the books? "The rest is history."

I had a rent-controlled apartment, a little studio. I was in love with this girl and shit. It was time to move on. And we moved to Mercer Street. All of a sudden I went from paying $400 to two grand. That was a big fucking jump. I was in love with this girl, and I had to provide and man the fuck up. I remember I was walking the streets thinking, where am I gonna get the money for this fucking apartment? I ran into this guy I knew—hadn't seen him in five years, so I was bugging out. He was a booker for a model agency. He asked, "You know where I can get some?"—*Raul mimes sucking back on a joint even though there's still half a glowing blunt in his other hand*—I was like, "Do I?"

He took me under his wing, introduced me to everybody. It was a big deal, the model industry. I went from having, like, a nickel in my pocket to—I had two hundred grand on me in one year. That's unbelievable. I had never had that kind of money. It was overwhelming at twenty-seven.

People were kind to me and took me under their wing, and I always remember that. Roberto Clemente said if you can help somebody and you don't, you're wasting your time here on earth. I enjoy everybody. I enjoy bums in the fucking street. As long as you have a good heart, I don't care if you're rich or poor, I'll be your friend. I don't judge nobody. I don't care if you're a freak. I'm a freak, everybody's a freak. But if you have a good heart, you're a good person, I'll try to help you out. If you're evil with bad intentions, get the fuck out of here!

I stopped smoking when I was thirty for ten years because I had to concentrate on that shit. I was a one-man company. Five g's, six g's a week, ten years. The older I got, the better I was at it because when I was younger I was more temperamental and angry, and you gotta have temperance with people. You gotta be patient with people because they're probably stupid. You can't get mad at every little weird thing that happens. You can't be arguing or fighting with people. It takes one person to flip on you and rat you out.

I'm a good evaluator of character—I have to be. If I'm sticking my neck out, I have to see if I feel you. I get a good vibe. I'm always pretty much dead on. I can always tell who I'm going to see again, who I'm not going to see again. It's a whole art. Gaining

people's trust, you know, go to their house and shit. It's discipline.
Etiquette, too. Not any idiot could do it. You could do it on the
low end and be on the street, but if you're gonna deal with really
rich people, celebrity, it takes a little bit of—you know.

Je ne sais quoi.

*Raul has expanded his product line over time, adjusting inventory
according to demand. Recently someone asked him if he had any acid
and he responded: "Get the fuck out of here. What do you think this is,
1970?" The oversized pockets of his hoodies and puffy jackets are filled
with what will move: cocaine, a grab bag of prescription pills, maybe
a little ecstasy for lingering aficionados, and, of course, weed, which
is masked by generously applied cologne.*

*Raul is proud of his clientele, always managing to rattle off the
names of high-profile patrons. I have seen Raul in action with the kinds
of people who are never far from the cameras on Oscar night, or
Grammy night, or Emmy night. And many of his stories invoke the exotic—the New Yorkers who carve out niches so strange, so unexpected,
that they could only thrive in this city. The city cannot resist these people: Raul opens an old issue of a prominent magazine and points to a
giant color photo of a man and a turtle.*

That's my friend E—, he lives in the building. That turtle is
worth a million dollars. He's into conservation. Nigger goes to
these crazy places and buys mad turtles. He keeps them on the
roof. There ain't none there right now. He'll have them here and
then he sends them out to Cali. He's got a compound. They try to
do anything possible to keep these motherfuckers going, breeding
them and shit. They're like gold, man. Half a million dollars to a
million, a million and a half, they're mad extinct.

When I first started it was a lot of people doing what I was
doing and I had to separate myself. You have to prove to people
that you're a righteous dude. It's just relationships. That's what
business is. Relationships. You gotta be cool when you meet them
and be consistent of course, punctual and all that shit. Sweat the
small stuff. A lot of people, they look to me, not because of what

I have, it's how fast I get it to them—they're into that. When they call, they know it's happening. It's not "maybe"—oh no, it's gonna happen. They're into efficiency. They're hooked on that more than anything.

I saw people back in the days, in the late '90s and shit. They be like, "Yo, I'll fly you out to Paris right now." Shit like that. I used to go out to the Hamptons a lot. I used to be going there twice a day. Hamptons in the summertime. Helicopter. I'd bring my girlfriend. Go there, have lunch, go to the beach for a second. Get on a helicopter, come back. Go back that night.

When I was still really young, twenty-six, twenty-seven, I had the concierge of the Carlyle on my payroll—you'd be surprised what goes on in that hotel. I remember going to see my guy, standing behind Nancy Reagan. "Just say no"—that was really funny. I'm right behind her. Secret service dudes. And it was just me and her.

Some dudes, they do this job and they take advantage of girls. Like ugly girls or strung-out girls. I take advantage of socialites.

He cackles.

Royal people. Royalty I've been with! Billionaire heiresses. Fucking billionaires up in my crib and the husband's in the Mercedes-Benz outside right here waiting to go to dinner—at the restaurant that I suggested they go to! It's crazy realities.

I'm like a therapist or something. People tell me their fuckin' crazy secrets and shit that nobody should know, they just feel comfortable, they open up. Here's the thing about me I've been the most proud of: you can take me anywhere. You go anywhere, to the 'hood, or to some elegant dinner, I'm your Huckleberry. I can fit in, talk to anybody. You gotta have lots of sides in New York. A lot of realities, you know? People have dark sides and they want to be wild and shit. Some people don't know how to get it out. People project an image of what they want you to see them as, but they're not like that at all once you get to know them. I always said I don't want to get to know somebody too well; it's disappointing and shit.

I said I was going to quit at forty-five and I'm still here. I'm forty-seven next week. I got three good years left. I always say when I'm fifty I'll be dead. Not literally dead but goddamn: you're fifty!

These kids, now they're smoking THC, they're melting it down and they have all these new things I don't even know about. They're really into the percentage of THC. Have you seen that? They're buggin' out. Growers are buggin' out. It ain't Alphabet City no more. You want to get some dope, it's like a James Bond movie. Before you see somebody nodding off, be like, "Yo, where'd you get that?" He'd tell you, you'd go. Now it's like foie gras and expensive bottles of wine and shit.

Now, I'm semiretired but when I was doing my thing, when I was in the zone, people would come to my house and worlds would meet. People would ask me if I could introduce them to so and so, that sort of thing. I've had meetings in this apartment, trying to get people tens of millions of dollars, and I just put it together, trying to make it happen and shit. All walks of life. That's my currency: knowing people.

I've developed relationships with these people, it's really weird. We depend on each other. They depend on me, and I depend on them to make a living. Sometimes I'm more addicted to their money. It's bugged out. I'm really good friends with big time stockbrokers. Me and them, we have a good rapport, we understand each other. We relate to each other because we always think about money. It's not a good thing. It's not good for your soul.

People say I could have always been big at something else—a producer, something. They think I could apply this to something else but, you know, that didn't happen. I'm not bitter about it. I know how to make money. I tell girls or friends of mine, "Yo, I got a lot of fucking money, you got any ideas and shit?" And everybody just does what they do. Nobody has another idea. I walk around New York, I feel stupid. I should have an idea here or there. I'd like to take the dirty money and do something with it. I'll be fifty years old running the streets.

Two or three years, God knows what this place is going to be like. It's just a different species, a different animal now, New York, since the Twin Towers fell down. That thing changed everything. That was a turning point. After that they cleaned this bad boy up and it became something else. Everything's so clean. Everything looks like the Upper West Side. There's no danger. Before it used to have some flavor, some character. Like a personality. When I was growing up, poor people, rich people, middle class, we all hung out with each other. Now you go to a place, it's either high end or it's low end.

We used to always sit on the stairs on the street; we were little kids—anything we could sit on. And on my block, if you go there now, they have little gates so you can't sit on anything. That's when I felt, wow, it's changing. They put all these gates and all these little spikes all over the neighborhood. You couldn't sit there. The jig was up.

Just old New Yorkers have that connection with their neighborhoods. There's no more neighborhoods anymore. Nobody knows each other. It's true. Look at the church where I had my communion on Twelfth Street. It used to be ten o'clock English, eleven Spanish, twelve Greek and one o'clock would be French or something. But it's not there no more. They sold it because nobody goes anymore. Now it's an NYU dorm. They tore down the church but left the steeple up in front of the new building—you see that? Crazy shit.

To call the New York University dormitory on East Twelfth Street incongruous would be generous—it's positively schizophrenic, a sight to behold. Completed in 2009, the twenty-six-story high-rise features row after row of rectangular windows and built-in air-conditioning units—it looks more like a communist-era housing block than the latest showpiece for a private institution with a penchant for capital campaigns. The entrance is set back off of the sidewalk, crouched behind pure folly: a steeple attached to a facade that looks more like a stage set than the real thing. This is the outer layer of what was once St. Ann's

Church, the 1847 stone sanctuary that dominated the block for 150 years. Now it offers little more than a whiff of history for the students on their way to the lobby. The church survived denominations and religions for a century and a half, first Protestantism (12th Street Baptist Church, 1847–54) then Judaism (Congregation Emanu-El, 1854–67) and then Catholicism (St. Ann's 1867–2003). But it could not survive the seductions of twenty-first century gentrification: the Archdiocese of New York sold the property to a developer in 2005 for $15 million and NYU demolished it to make room for the dormitory. Church, though, is not all that has vanished from Raul's life:

One of my best friends moved to Georgia. A lot of people have left. They can't afford to live here. They gotta skedaddle, go down south and get some value for their money. It's money, man. The bottom line's the bottom line. You go where you can, in life, right? Wherever you can afford.

The whole city is expensive. Before there were areas where people of certain classes could live, and now if you don't got three g's on you, pal, you've gotta get out of here. And people that are from here, they don't have that kind of loot. That's what they make in a month. That's their whole salary.

I'm an optimist. Look at the bright side and shit. That's the only way you'll survive in New York, man. You're not an optimist and you don't stay strong, this place will swallow you up. It's not a nice place sometimes. There are two things you can do now as a New Yorker: be bitter about the past or you can just go with it and appreciate it and be amazed and shocked at the new things that happen in the city. Because I do. Things gotta change, man. Things gotta evolve.

People go, "Are you from here?"

"Yeah, I'm from here."

"But where were you born?"

"I was born here."

And they grab their friends and they're like, "Oh shit, check this out, you can't believe this shit: he was born here!"

That's the cool thing, we've become the outcasts or the weirdos, the indigenous people.

I'm New York, you know? New York is not perfect. Nobody's perfect. I'm the best of it and the worst of it. I do bad things to it and I do good things to it. I'm all of it.

9.

Michael De Feo awaits his lunch at a restaurant just east of Grand Central Terminal in Manhattan, and he picks up where Raul left off—at the moment when subway graffiti became street art:

I did five years at the School for Visual Arts and got a degree in graphic design. But my portfolio review didn't have a lick of graphic work in it; it was all photos of my street art at the time, this was in '95. And I wanted to bring my stuff into galleries but bringing my slides as a nineteen-year-old was just not going to work. I began to feel like, "Fuck them." It got to the point where it was like, "Who gives a shit about them anyway? I'll do it my own way." So I started to glue my works onto walls in SoHo. Conceptually I hadn't even an inkling of what this all meant other than I wanted to get my stuff in front of as broad an audience as I could. And that's what I began to do.

Michael is an artist but with his closely cropped brown hair, eyeglasses, and a freshly pressed shirt under his sweater he's a far cry from the ink-stained hands and T-shirt and jeans of young Raul writing on the trains in the '80s. That's because Michael's other passion is teaching art to elementary and middle school kids. This explains not just the look, but the posture, the mood: he's alert and sits up straight.

I grew up in Rye, about an hour north of the city, and when I was in middle school, seventh grade, I took a class called motors and power, which allowed us to take apart engines and rebuild them. We used tools like drill presses, spot welders, torches, all sorts of shit that today you'd never use—programs like that just don't exist any more. The teacher, Mr. Goldfarb, he invited in a high school senior who was big into graffiti to spray paint these letters over the slop sinks. They were this classic '80s bubble letter style: very legible, fun and approachable and balloon-y. He did this and I thought it was fucking awesome. Like, "This is bad ass. This guy is using spray paint in our class!" And he had a copy of *Subway Art* by Martha Cooper and Henry Chalfant, which came out in '84 so it'd only been out for a year or two. I flipped through it and it blew my mind. It was like, look at all this awesome stuff that's going on just twenty-five minutes from my house! It was the first seed: the excitement about people becoming a part of the actual fabric of the city that they live in.

Michael has a daughter and is quick to identify as a father. He grew up in the suburbs but doesn't talk about his past defensively, like many self-styled escapees. Indeed, as the details of his physical features and the facts of his life stack up, it becomes harder and harder to picture him practicing his art: plastering urban walls with glue-stained paper or photographs or stenciled images. Michael operates successfully in very different spaces but he's done a few things that link up his disparate pursuits: he published a children's book that uses street art to teach the alphabet; and he paints walls in upper class suburbs like Greenwich, Connecticut, where residents have never heard names like Banksy and Shepard Fairey before—at least not until Michael comes along. He spreads the gospel to an audience outside the usual tent.

I started with works on paper, on blueprints. I used to source my blueprints from a Dumpster on Seventeenth and Broadway. There was an architectural firm that was always filling this Dumpster with blueprints. Not only was the paper free but it created this accidental giant loop of working with paint on these blueprints and then gluing them up in the streets, possibly on the same buildings they were designed for, and conceptually it all started to snap together for me.

As far as picking locations there are a couple of factors that come into play like visibility, frequency that a spot might get buffed. I'll avoid some walls if I can tell it's going to get buffed in a second. It doesn't always stop me because sometimes it's worth it to have it up in a spot for a couple days if it's super visible. I'm attracted to things that are broken, torn, and faded, I like that, but I also put things on sparkly new things, too. It's kind of different everywhere I go.

I don't find many surfaces to put work up anymore. The city is shinier. There's a lot of glass and metal. I can do that but just take a hose to it once it dries and it'll come right down. I want something with some tooth to it.

He laughs.

I've doctored up the glue that I've used over the years. I learned something from this guy in Amsterdam when I was putting up work. This guy worked for the city and he was taking the work down behind me. He comes over to me and he's like, "Hey are you putting stuff up?"

And I'm like, "Yeah. Sorry."

He says, "If you want to make my job really difficult, put sugar in your glue."

"Wow. That's a great idea. Thank you!"

And since then I've done that.

He laughs.

The Dutch are so friendly, so cool. They're awesome.

As far as law enforcement is concerned, knock on wood, I've never been arrested. I've come very close. Not just here but in other parts of the country and other parts of the world. Cops have a bit of an attitude, a lot of them. Some of them don't. For the most part it's pretty positive. What works quite nicely is that the aesthetic quality of most of what I do is very approachable. It's very easy to understand. It's nonconfrontational. It's very easy to talk myself out of trouble.

That's not hard to imagine. Not only does Michael's work steer clear of confrontation or aggression—it can be downright bright and inviting: trees and hearts and flowers. Still he does manage to work in the occasional skeleton or set of gnarled teeth. You can find these in the kinds of places that reward a viewer eager to explore beyond the usual sightlines: low to the ground at the base of lampposts, or up near surveillance cameras capturing the traffic and the interaction and evolution of the streets.

You know the funny thing is that when I first started doing this my dad was very, very old school, more than my mom. They're both off the boat from Italy. I'm first generation. And in the beginning my dad said, "This is a waste of time. If you get arrested, don't call me. I hope you get put in jail." Shit like that. But over the years, he's changed his tune. Not just because I was getting attention but I think he started to see the larger picture. He saw what my intentions were with my work. And he began to appreciate it. By the time my book came out he was whole hog about it. He would tell his clients about my work. An interesting thing happened where he would say: "He doesn't do graffiti; he does street art."

He laughs.

And what's the difference? Maybe the greater population would appreciate what I do over what a tagger would do, perhaps, but aside from public perception they're both the exact same thing. I didn't get permission to put this here. Maybe eight times out of ten the owner of the building might like it and leave me alone but it's the exact same crime: unwelcome imagery. That's somebody's private property.

People are using this "post-graffiti" now. Like post-modernist? Post-graffiti. It's just something to use to redefine what it is we're all doing and market it. Whatever. Just let me do what I'm doing. I'm not a street artist. I'm a maker. I'm an artist. I do all sorts of things. I don't like predetermined definitions of what people think that I do. What I'm doing is my right and the right of anyone else who wants to participate.

I think people are in their own bubble going from point A to point B. School to work, work to wherever. I think this natural thing about street art is it reawakens people's awareness of their surroundings. Whether or not you're looking for it deliberately. It makes the experience of walking around a lot more engaging.

You know, we've gotten so used to advertisements being in front of our faces all of the time and people say nothing about that. That's really crazy. It's gotten so bad, a school out west, to raise money they put this vinyl advertising over the kids' lockers in the hallways. I was talking about this with family over dinner a while ago and the table was divided. I was like, "Are you fucking crazy? So at an earlier age my daughter can worry about her weight and what clothes she wears?" That's insane. The one place we shouldn't have advertising is our schools. Keep our kids safe from that bullshit.

I have some rules that I impose on my work. I would never touch a house of worship or a cemetery. I would never permanently damage someone's property. All my stuff can be repainted or washed off. Countless times my work is defaced or torn down within minutes—things I've worked on in the studio for hours and hours or days and days. You glue them up and go around the corner to take a photo of it and it's gone. Oh well.

I'm into ephemeral work, big time. Take it off the pedestal. Eff the galleries, eff advertising, eff that. But it's a little bit of a contradiction to say that. Because what you do by putting work in the street is advertising yourself. Eventually people are going to find out who you are. And although I do work outside, I happily sell my work to people that want to hang it inside. So, there are some lovely contradictions.

He smiles.

I'm a big fan of infiltrating the system. Someone like Kaws. We went to school together and I follow his career. I watched the MTV Video Awards one year because I knew he designed the new moon man. When I saw Justin Timberlake standing in the middle of a Kaws sculpture singing and doing a dance routine, I was like, "Fucking A, this is mind-blowing! He's totally infiltrated the system!" He's taken graffiti, which is what he started with, and he's found every nook and cranny of the culture to stick his shit into. Like a virus. People are like, "Aw, fuck Kaws, he's a millionaire." Maybe he is. Who cares? He's clearly following a path he started twenty years ago.

With Michael, Shepard Fairey is Shep, Dan Witz, just Dan. He's been doing a lot of traveling, working in Cabo San Lucas and Belize. On a recent trip to the West Coast "Shep's team" helped him find all the good spots.

He takes out his phone to show me pictures of some of his most recent work, a reimagining's of Manet's Olympia, *another of Caillebotte's* Paris Street; Rainy Day. *For the past two decades he has been better known for this:*

I came up with the flower later on and that was kind of an accident. I did a whole wall of imagery and that one really stood out to me. It really leapt off the wall. I made a silk screen of it right away and within hours I had hundreds of prints of different colors. And the next logical step was, well, fuck, I'm going to hang these all over town. I had no idea I'd be doing these twenty years later.

Eventually I started doing the flowers as a stencil spray as well. In a short period of time I tackled Manhattan pretty well. You couldn't go a few blocks without seeing my work right on the sidewalk. But I didn't like the idea that it wasn't as ephemeral as the paper. So I decided to stick with paper soon after that. It just made more sense for the project—the idea of a flower regrowing, renewing, rebirth, life and death, the cycle of all that.

I was driving home from work one day and got a message: "Yeah, hi, this is Jody from *New York* magazine. I love your work and want you on the cover of this week's magazine. Do you think you could come by Silvercup Studios?"

I almost drove off the road listening to the voice mail. And I went in the very next morning and I painted—all day long—this giant flower and a couple smaller things, and they were just super supportive. And they invited me back to collaborate a few more times.

Since then I think New York has become a place that is not particularly welcoming to people who are young, creative, have no money, and want to add to the cultural enrichment of what's already here. That doesn't exist anymore. The frequency of street art continues to increase because of the desire of so many people to get some quick fame. To get their work into galleries. It's become an industry unto itself. A lot of stuff, too, is designed to be successful. You have a PR agent. The more known you get, the more you can afford to have these tools, the more you can afford to travel.

It's interesting when value is assigned to it.

Over the years I've had some offers. I'm all ears for stuff. It depends. I've listened to a lot of ideas over the years and turned most of it down. The photographer who shot my first *New York* magazine cover said to me, "This image has all the makings for, like, you could stop working now. Getty will sell it for us in markets around the world forever." And so he said, "I need your permission."

And I said, "I'm not giving it to you."

He said, "Listen, just think about it because you're going to make boatloads of money and you'll never have to work again."

And I said no because of this ambiguity of when people see it. They'll have an art experience but that art experience will be replaced by a sales pitch. Here's that Heineken bottle, or here's that new Apple product, or whatever. And I don't want that. That's not what it's about.

Someone came up with the idea of launching a satellite into very low orbit and having it fixed over a metropolitan area, say New York, and it would unfurl a web of LED lights so you could then create a logo of your desire that would be equivalent in diameter to a full moon. So how fucked up is this? In the sky—the one space that should be safe to us, that should be completely protected—we'll put a big fucking logo up there.

10.

*O*n my way to Quang Bao's apartment on the Lower East
Side, I turn off Allen Street onto Stanton and see a wall
covered by a mural that extols the good times to be had
when four friends huddle together to throw back Bushmills. The
image has been executed with paint-by-numbers precision. Incidentally,
the men depicted are all vaguely thirty-something, vaguely white,
vaguely bearded—just like me, and suddenly I've arrived at that moment of self-consciousness that Ovid describes as the decent into
Hades. I cross the intersection.

I march north on Clinton Street cum Avenue B, up the middle of
the Lower East Side cum East Village known, for some period of time,
as Alphabet City, where poverty and violence and art have comingled
for decades.

Quang lives in a two-bedroom apartment just off of Avenue B, on
the top floor of a five-floor walk-up. Each flight of stairs is unusually
steep, feels longer than the last, and slopes in its own direction. Scaling
to the top calls for a moment of solitude in the hall, a chance to steady
the breathing before knocking on Quang's door.

Art surrounds me as soon as I enter—every wall crowded with canvases and large pieces of paper and slabs of wood covered in spray
paint and acrylic and charcoal. A large rectangular birdcage hangs
from the wall near the kitchen, housing four conscientious parakeets,

who keep their chirping to a calming volume. The second bedroom of the apartment often doubles as Quang's gallery or incubator called "Second Guest." If the space is not housing art it is often housing artists; currently there is a painter from Romania installed in the space. Quang, forty-four, is twisting about in his kitchen, heating up noodles while giving the painter advice on subway routes.

Originally from Vietnam, Quang came to the United States when he was five and still has memories of being wrapped in the jacket of a US soldier who helped airlift him out of his home country with his family. He has a short, wiry frame and he's permanently unabashed:

I just say everything to everyone and whoever sticks around are my friends.

The painter leaves for the evening, heading out to meet with a gallerist—Quang made the introduction. He makes a lot of connections. Deft at matching tastes and interests and resources, Quang manages a private multimillion-dollar art collection and runs the family foundation that comes along with it. The family that employs Quang adheres to a model popular in the upper strata of the art world: buy up stacks of work from an artist then decorate this artist with well-publicized (and well branded) awards and fellowships, hoping to drum up more interest—and thusly more value—in the acquired work. The ability to do this on a large scale—creating eight- or nine-figure endowments— buys sway, if not authority, in the marketplace. When Quang walks into a gallery, it is smiles all around. The informed gallerists know the buyers he represents, the stakes he represents, and they work to skillfully handle his interest in the work they are selling.

The Lower East Side has this sort of exotic exploration feel to it. The most expensive and high profile galleries are parking here. It's being in a place where there's a lot of compression and concentration, which is part of the point—you know? Bars love other bars. And in that sense, it's glomming on—likes, likes, likes. I think galleries really rely on movements of the customers. When you go to a gallery you really don't go to just one. You do a swoop of them. So you choose based on the neighborhood. And these things are actually broadcasting themselves internationally. In Dubai, the Chelsea district is something large because of its brand name that gives that gallery a certain imprimatur and street cred just for being able to be there because you have to be able to afford it. These big companies that park themselves in these places, it's like you just say Wall Street, or World Trade Center, or wherever the belly button is and then you sound immediately like a relevant player. It makes you feel not only relevant but actually driving the conversation. So everything follows itself and that's how you grow something that becomes a trend even if you're not aware of it.

As sexy as the history of art in New York is, it's still business. All the decisions that are made are business decisions. And I think the story of galleries and artists' studios is the story of commercial leases. At five years, there's a chance to renew; after ten years, obviously there will not be that chance because it will just be too expensive by that point. So with galleries and studios, neighborhoods run on the lease instead of the creative movement being over.

You're victimized by your own success, if you make the neighborhood attractive. The rents have completely gone up on the Lower East Side, there aren't any more steals. And so what you're seeing are these little gallery efforts in Bushwick where the spaces are quite industrial and big. The creation folks—the people that make the artworks, and the people who are important to filling galleries—a lot of them are there. It makes them pulsate with a certain kind of energy, which Bushwick has for real. Just look and you see the graffiti changing. You open your window and that buzz, it's you, you're a part of it. Something tunes in. It's very important that the artist be able to feel everything that's happening around them, whether it's inside the studio or way beyond in the market, because they're trying to say something about our best selves, our ideas, our thinking.

The artist's space is psychological and sacred, and you have to be really invited to go into an artist's studio. Creativity happens there but the history is there, too. You always get the detail of looking out the window and this floor was something—a sweat-shop, a factory—there's always something that they know about their space because they have to be tuned in that way.

Now you have a lot of artists who are "post-studio." They don't actually need a studio so they work in closets or they're working in environments of the city, or coffee shops, or wherever they are—they actually construct work outside the studio. You think about video artists: Where do they cut the film? So it's not so studio bound anymore.

When we say an artist loses his studio and it's tragic, it really is those more traditional forms where the painting, and the paint and the painter cannot live. They need that space—that's a long-standing tradition. But now when an artist loses his studio space it may just be a closet or an archival space as opposed to a thing that they go to every day to create things. You're even seeing this in terms of photography where people take the actual photo-graphic process and manipulate it in different ways by putting it outside and letting light do its thing. So you have a process art, which is all about trying to subvert how it's usually done. And now because the computer and the total internationalization of art influence everything, there are ways in which people can get into the art world outside the studio. It totally broadens bound-aries and collapses boundaries in a way that makes it seem almost quaint to be going into a studio to go paint.

Whether Bushwick will be participating in the notion of New York as an art market, I'm not sure. It's still confined to the people who make work as opposed to any collectors going over there. When I took my bosses to Bushwick for the first time they were excited by this notion that they were going some place that was unique and special and artist-minded and artists everywhere—and it was true. We really are talking about the people on the ground, people who make work, and people who hang out with each other in the neighborhood. That community can then become very intimate. The challenges of one artist can really bring a bunch of artists to them. Artists help artists. There's no other person but perhaps another artist who can solve the dilemma of the frame, you know, so they really do need each other. That information and education sharing always is related to the generosity of the spirit, and therefore you have to be around it because you can't do everything yourself. It's a place where, yes, your ideas, your values, are reinforced and therefore you are not crazy for making a choice that will probably not work out in your favor while you are here and alive. So they can be rewarded by all the things that go on with interpersonal relationships.

Quang is echoing mTkalla Keaton's definition of neighborhood: people. The neighborhood of an artist is not defined by place—certainly not the traditional motif with high ceilings and an oval palette that looks like a colorful Rorschach test. The neighborhood of an artist is defined by the camaraderie of others, "the generosity of spirit" that aids and enlightens and intoxicates.

One of the most popular reality shows that artists watch on television is *Project Runway*. It took me a long time to realize why. It's because they actually make something on that show.

When you go to the art stores the stuff is so specialized. Some artists will go to hardware stores for chemicals, plus tape, plus glue, plus plastic. Some of these materials are very niche and some are incredibly common. It really is like manufacturing.

I think artists remain some of the few people in New York who actually make something that isn't money. They actually don't make money.

He laughs.

They make something else, which is totally useless—it has no point, no purpose. Yet they remain the only ones that are actually making something. That's sort of amazing when you think about it. They actually work!

For me, New York City is so much in danger of becoming a place where no one makes anything. You can't sew buttons on a shirt because there's a tailor you go to. It's a service place. The art market isn't necessarily the manufacturing part. It isn't being made here as much. And for me the whole cultural tourism and seduction of New York has to do with all the creative sectors generating the kinds of things that people go to see. And if those people don't live here and make things here then we're just another shell.

Now you see Bushwick rates go up. Artists continue to go farther and farther out. Now they're going to Gowanus. So how much farther until they leave the city entirely because it's cost prohibitive? When you look at artists through the generations, from the SoHo artists going forward, none of them have been spared this movement.

What I don't understand is what it is that makes people think that we'll be in an interesting place if everything is only affordable to a certain small group of people. Who is the audience for the city as it continues to grow these towers?

What is it going to take for people to understand that while you could get higher dollar for rent, there are other factors to consider? Is there any other thing that can make your decision other than the fact that you could get three times the rent for that space? Nobody wants to bother with these things 'cause there's a line around the block for the addresses. It's like good citizenry is gone. None of us see ourselves contributing to the way a city gets built. It's like our lives are elsewhere.

When you lose an artist to a city like Berlin, they might not come back. Not because they're famous but because it's not easy to get back in to New York once you leave. So when people who are artists make a commitment to exiting the city and not participating in it any more, it's actually a subtraction that doesn't easily get made up by someone that's coming in. You're actually losing some of the history and the fabric of the city. And it's so quiet that I don't think anyone really gives a damn. There's no crisis about art, the art market is so flush and so flooded. The idea of the starving artist is almost moving into a quaint place, like "you should be successful you know." Collectors want it early and cheap. They poach earlier than ever. First-year MFA students. But the collector is not the most important person in the ecology. The artist is the most important person in the ecology. Without them there is no collector, there is no moment of frontierism, because the people who make the things aren't being supported and they will stop. And people do stop.

But at the same time there's more art than ever—and I'm supportive of everything. I've given up dreaming of utopias and commune ideals. Don't say you're happy and proud and rewarded just to make the work. Go get the money. I think everyone should go and get your money wherever you possibly can. 'Cause that's the city. Everything has come to that.

11.

*A*lan Fishman knows how to go get the money. For two-and-
a-half weeks in 2008, he served as Washington
Mutual Bank's final CEO. He received either side of $17
million when the government seized the bank, which was eventually
foisted onto JPMorgan Chase. Assuming a forty-hour workweek, this
is an hourly pay rate of $163,461.54. But let's assume Alan worked
extra hard, say sixty hours a week—actually let's just say he worked
around the clock, he didn't doze off once during those seventeen nights
in September, so consumed was he by the doomed challenge in front of
him. In that scenario, his hourly pay rate drops all the way down to
$41,666.67.

We are sitting in Alan's home office at his family's upstate compound in Columbia County, two hours north of the city. Outside the
windows that encase the room, I see a pond in one direction and a
wooded road in the other. For weeks I have been trying to get Alan to
meet with me but my requests have been beaten back by the relentless
schedule he keeps at sixty-six. So I have chased him all the way up to
the town of Ghent, twenty minutes from the town of Hudson where car-
riage houses have been revived and repainted by gallerists in whose
hands artfully distressed walls frame sold-out shows. This county is a
series of undulating fields—some cultivated, some grazed, some mead-
ows of tall grass—interrupted here and there by towns and villages

that, to varying degrees, swell in population on the weekends with the influx of part-time residents from New York City. Modern, multimillion-dollar estates, sometimes built using passive construction to limit the home's ecological footprint, share property lines with mobile homes partially covered by blue tarps that supplement their ailing roofs. Three miles down the road from Alan's house is a 150-acre modern sculpture park.

Many New Yorkers, this reporter included, live in the city with escape on the mind. A transient spirit prevails—many of us have, after all, escaped to New York, much to Raul's chagrin—and the city can be unduly unkind for several hours or days or weeks or months at a time. For those like Alan who own a second home in the Hudson Valley or the Berkshires or the Hamptons, the fantasy of escape is replaced by the routine of escape.

Alan bought this property in the 1960s and has added to it at various points over several decades. In the kitchen on the other side of the compound, his wife and kids and grandkids are making soup. My time with him is limited and this fact stays central to our interaction—he alludes to the ticking clock with his posture (shifting) and fingers (tapping) and knees (shaking) and his hands, which grab at any desk clutter within reach of his swiveling chair. Yet from his steady eye contact, it is clear that his attention remains focused.

Alan has dark, bushy eyebrows that do not match his silver helmet of perfectly parted hair. The eyebrows take their own path, jetting straight out, as if a symbol of the electricity that runs through the man. In conversation he sometimes raises his voice while accelerating what he is saying, as though we're in the midst of an argument, but he's the only one who speaks as I sit listening.

I was born in Crown Heights, obviously dominated by Ebbets Field and the Dodgers. They used to let us in, you know, as the games were going on. My bedroom overlooked the third base side so during the night games I could see the lights from our house. My parents were both born in Brooklyn. My grandparents were refugees from Russia and Hungary, so it was classic: my grandfather had a shop in

Williamsburg that made vests for high-end stores, Brooks Brothers and places like that. Fortunately I had a good education as a graduate student in economics at Columbia and I started in banking in 1969. I've been in finance and banking ever since.

Post-war, the city itself was very static. I think people were still very scared about lending money in New York City, in many neighborhoods. They were very uneasy. You still had an out of control landlord-tenant situation—you know, the owners basically didn't trust the tenants and the tenants didn't trust the owners. The city was a very static place. There was no mobility. That began to change as crime went down. You didn't really feel that change until '98 or something, during the latter part of the Giuliani years it became apparent. I think the drop in crime enabled people to move into neighborhoods. Then the mortgage business began to respond to that.

But 9/11 hit and nobody knew what the hell was going to happen, so a lot of stuff started to change at that point. The city needed a backup to Manhattan—separate power grid, separate this, separate that. And so, Downtown Brooklyn was the most ready because it was semi-baked before. And so the city decided that it had to make an investment in Downtown Brooklyn, and it needed some private sector guys to help oversee that. And just through the vapors of being a banker, I sort of knew some of the Bloomberg people and I had met the mayor once or twice: A, as a candidate, and B, just in business because I ran a trading operation. He was looking around for some people that could help him in the boroughs. And when you looked around Brooklyn there was only one private big bank left—the one I was running—and there was a public utility, the CEO was a great friend of mine. So we were two of the power structures that existed in Brooklyn.

You know, the city had underinvested in capital improvements for a very long time coming out of the financial crisis of the '70s, and Bloomberg raised so much money. Under his stewardship, the city's credit has become so stable and so shockingly strong that he was able to raise all this money and invest it so wisely. Among the unsung heroes in the city, I think, are the capital budget people. You know, nobody hears their names, nobody ever knows who the hell they are. They sit in the bowels of the budget department and oversee capital allocation. They're fabulous public servants, smart guys—and tough guys—and they have real judgment. And so working with Bloomberg and his deputies, these guys supercharged the impact of the crime reduction, they supercharged it with this giant investment system that they've put in place. What they did at the Navy Yard is pure genius.

The navy yard Alan refers to is a 1.7-mile-long stretch of Brooklyn shoreline just across the East River from Manhattan. A military site since 1806, the Brooklyn Navy Yard was a place where generations of New Yorkers made things—warships, to be exact. During World War II, seven hundred thousand workers were employed at the site. The navy decommissioned the facilities in 1966, and until the 1990s you could walk along the chain-link fence that encased the complex and see a wasteland of overgrown weeds subsuming cracked asphalt and giant, empty buildings hovering against the sky.

From 1966 onward it was essentially useless. I mean it barely survived and was really poorly managed, poorly governed, and poorly supported. You know, towards the end of the Giuliani administration they made this cockamamie deal with Doug and David Steiner to build movie studios. I'm not sure it was a real deal. You know, these things are always sort of head fakes on both sides, and nobody knows what the hell's gonna happen. So when Bloomberg asked me to go and become chairman of the Navy Yard, we had a lot to do. We had to find a CEO, and the board had to be replaced—not completely but basically from top to bottom because the board was really a politically active board that didn't know much about business. So we cleaned house and I sat down with the Steiners and took the measure of them and they of us and we made a deal. A real deal to actually do something. I think both sides got together and made a theory a reality.

The site of the Brooklyn Navy Yard is now a sprawl of various businesses anchored by Steiner Studios, one of the largest movie production facilities outside of Los Angeles. New York is a place that insists on a grand scale for all endeavors. This was the greatest appeal of Robert Moses's master plans: their seductive scale—the Verrazano Bridge was the longest suspension bridge when it was built in 1964, the secretariat on Forty-Second Street at the East River was built to house all 44,000 civil servants from 170 countries who work at the United Nations, and completion of the Triborough Bridge alone required 31,000,000 hours of work in 134 cities in 20 states. New York's economic tentacles have always had a near limitless reach—the city has always been a prominent force in local economies across the county.

I'll never forget it, we talked to David Steiner: "David, you gonna build this thing or not?"

He said, "I'll build it!"

I said, "We haven't seen any workmen here."

He says, "It's being built. Shut up. Leave. Now. I'm in charge. I'm building this thing in Pennsylvania."

And he did, and it showed up in a truck. That's pretty amazing. Big hunks of walls showed up one day.

Quang Bao told me that in New York, artists "remain the only ones that are actually making something," which is certainly true to a point—the Steiners show that even New York buildings aren't always constructed in the city. But it's also true that several businesses leasing space in the navy yard are manufacturing operations. In fact, the development corporation's initiative mandates "reusing Navy-built buildings for their original industrial intent." Tenants are making sprinkler systems, lighting fixtures, and—a direct link to the past—stainless steel air-conditioning units for warships.

Several navy yard tenants tend toward small scale, artful manufacturing—goods like clothing and textiles—and some are Quang Bao's people exactly: the artists who took his advice—"go get the money"—fast enough to hold on to that quaint, if not vanishing, idea of the studio.

There is also a small museum in the development. Here visitors can learn about the land's past and read about visions for its future, eagerly shared by entrepreneurs and real estate developers standing in line to do business with the navy yard.

These guys in the bowels of the budget department, they began to allocate capital to the yard for the first time. And we would make real economic arguments, not pseudo economic arguments. And then, you know, from there, hundreds of millions of dollars later, billions of dollars later—here's an example, this is how versatile these Bloomberg guys are: so we get wind of this crazy idea where if you're a foreign national and you invest in an approved project in America in a distressed neighborhood, you get a visa for you and your family. It's called EB-5. We went to the city and said, "We can get all this money. You guys should take this money."

And after a week of thinking about it and looking at it, they said, "We'll help you get this money." This all took a week, two weeks, whatever. You know, in other administrations this would be a year or two years worth of cogitation. And literally in days, we raised $50 million. It's Chinese people, or Vietnamese people, or whatever people, Korean people, whatever the hell, Indians, I don't know. And again, this is all with no fuss, no muss, and no memos.

Alan digresses into a swirl of celebrity investor names, all casually referred to like he's pointing to guys around his poker table:

Bruce Ratner used the program to raise $225 million. I think I'm in for a hundred and a quarter now, so that's 350, and I think Doug Steiner's in for more than a hundred, so that's half a billion dollars of money that never would have showed up. In one corner of Brooklyn!

The residency-for-capital program showcases the global sprawl of investors trying to decide where to park their money. As Neil Smith writes in The New Urban Frontier, *globalization changed gentrification: "Not only has gentrification become a widespread experience since the 1960s but it is also systematically integrated into wider urban and global processes . . . In the context of globalization, national and international capitals alike confront a global 'frontier' of their own that subsumes the gentrification frontier . . . Cities find themselves competing in a global market."*

Bloomberg did it all without any huff or puff. It just happened because he's so verbal in the language of business. The problem with politicians of course is they can't just call it like it is. They can't describe it. That's why they hate Bloomberg so much—the anti-Bloombergs—because he tells the truth all the time. He basically describes it.

He is the linguist of American business, or global business really. He invented the language of business! Bloomberg system is the language of today's modern business. The Bloomberg administration spoke the language of business so fluently, they were able to supercharge the economy without anybody realizing it. And most governments are so labored in the way they talk about business. You can see with the Obama administration, the guy's never done any business in his life. When he talks about stimulus it sounds so stupid! To be blunt. Whereas you listen to the mayor and he sounds so smart. I'm not making a political statement but a substantive statement: the contrast is overwhelming!

Both of Alan's hands are open and out in front of him, emphatic, just like his widened eyes.

Bloomberg oversaw the most successful stimulus plan in the history of time in my view. He hasn't gotten nearly enough credit for it. It's incredible. And then he goes and picks the pockets of these guys and makes them contribute to support these private sector initiatives, most recently this massive gift to Central Park.

Alan is referring to a $100 million donation made by hedge fund manager John Paulson. The money will be split equally between Central Park's endowment funds and the park's capital improvement projects. The New York Times *announced the gift underneath a photograph of the pensive Mr. Paulson looking out over the spot where he* *"hung out at the fountain as a teenager, beneath the bronze statue Angel of the Waters, which was then scrawled with graffiti and bone dry." I wonder if Michael De Feo—or even Raul—knows whose writing filled that spot and whether its absence is to be lamented, or if the statue's new visage should be treasured.*

Now I have a lot of issues about what the mayor did, didn't do, bad or worse or whatever. But in terms of his economic development plans, you gotta be in awe of what he did. This isn't by accident. This is pure genius. The city has put itself in a position to live, to compete, to continue to fight the issues that they haven't gotten on top of—and those are big issues. He certainly hasn't eradicated poverty. He hasn't turned the education system into a grand, shining example. But he certainly has allowed the city to have resources to go fight those fights. Whereas, go look at Chicago. Go look at Philadelphia. Go look all around the country and there's no money. You know, at least in New York City there's money. And if New York State was any good, which it isn't, there'd be more money. That's the easy one, to give him the super high marks for building an economy, diversifying the economy, seizing on hi-tech, seizing on tourism—you know, to really make this change in the city. And Brooklyn has been the huge beneficiary of all of that.

The more complicated stuff is having to undo the hospital system, having to undo the public housing system and remake it. Having to undo the education system and remake it. It's one thing to build a cultural empire in New York, which he's done with money basically. It's quite a different thing to have to undo bad hospitals, public housing, the education system. You know, that's been much more difficult for him, it seems to me. Basically you've got dysfunctional systems in these operations, and they don't provide the right product and they don't provide it at the right price, and they don't provide the right value.

It is hard to remember that Alan is still talking about schools and hospitals and public housing, but the language of business knows no boundaries. In Bloomberg's New York, economic wisdom can override any other public service wisdom and so should serve as a rudder in all cases.

This sensibility is evident in Bloomberg's various appointments over more than a decade. After Joel Klein's run as schools chancellor ended without, as Alan puts it, "getting it across the goal line," the mayor appointed Cathie Black to the position in 2010. Black had spent the previous fifteen years running a magazine empire and had no professional experience in education. Michael Stocker, Bloomberg's appointment for chair for the city's Health and Hospitals Corporation, was a former health insurance executive. And John Rhea, whom the mayor put in charge of the New York City Housing Authority, or NYCHA, was formerly the managing director of the global consumer retail group at Lehman Brothers. NYCHA is responsible for the biggest stock of public housing in the country—most of it is still in brick high-rise buildings.

Public housing's gotta get sorted out. I think that's way easier said than done. I don't know where you get the money for it. I don't know the answers. I'm not smart enough. I do know that the existing stock of public housing needs to be really maintained better and that's very hard. The basic tenet around which it was built as these closed enclaves is very, very counterintuitive—in today's world it's a really bad idea. I have spent a lot of time looking at the complexes themselves and they're just not built for today's society. What I would do is see whether I could gather up private capital—and public capital, obviously—and really try to build out the fringes of these entities into a more open, retail-oriented, low-rise, mixed-use, mixed-income environment so you're dealing with this in a different way. To have lower-middle-income and lower-income people in their own world is just horrible. And if you're getting into the pathologies, which are vast, those pathologies need to be changed, you need interventions there and you can't do that the way it is now. I mean, you have no traffic going through these places. There's no street life. There's only bad guys out there at night. It's just all bad. I mean, it's all wrong. Half the kids are bad kids. Not half, I shouldn't say that. You know, 90 percent of the kids are good kids, and 10 percent are bad kids, or whatever the numbers are. And it's just a bad pathology. Cops with stop and frisk, and the kids who don't want to be stopped and frisked. And the nice people that live in these places are stuck in their houses, in elevators that do or don't work. It's just a bad idea! The whole thing's bad! I have no idea what to do!

Just as Alan raises his voice, more emphatic by the moment, there is a knock at the door: lunch is ready. Time's up. He smacks his desk with his open hand, as if gaveling the session closed. We shake hands, standing in the middle of his gravel driveway, before Alan heads into the kitchen for warm soup with the family.

12.

*O*n the Sunday afternoon ride back from Alan's compound in Ghent, the train car is abuzz with overheated mobile devices, their weekender owners desperately emptying clogged inboxes before "beginning" work tomorrow morning. The Hudson River Valley passes in the periphery. We approach Manhattan by way of the Spuyten Duyvil Bridge, a rickety swing bridge built in 1900. It runs parallel to the Henry Hudson Bridge, which pierces a forested bluff at the northernmost tip of the island; the panoramic view on that green perch, once enjoyed by the seventeenth-century Lenape and whoever else might have wandered those heights before them, is now reserved for car traffic.

Northern Manhattan has a complex topography where glaciers left behind caves, ridges, and valleys. Much of this landscape is still preserved, still blanketed with trees that don't give much notice to the occasional bridge or road weaving through.

The train passes under the George Washington Bridge—the busiest bridge in the world, leading out to New Jersey and, beyond, the continental United States—and rolls down the western bank of the island. We pass several more ridges, including one to the east known as Coogan's Bluff. For over seventy years the rocky precipice overlooked a baseball stadium, the Polo Grounds, home to the New York Giants until 1957 when they bolted for San Francisco, the same year Alan

Fishman's Dodgers bolted for Los Angeles. On the patch of land where Ebbets Field once stood, shining its lights into Alan's boyhood bedroom, now stands the Ebbets Field apartment complex, an underfunded, under-maintained cluster of towering brick buildings, which grown-up, banker Alan described as a bad idea with no clear fix. Likewise, nestled below Coogan's Bluff, the land known as the Polo Grounds retained its name but was otherwise transformed: a sunsplashed green diamond became a series of monolithic brick buildings, apartments stacked on top of each other, casting shadows onto the streets and neighbors below. Approximately four thousand people live in this north Harlem complex and the president of the residents' association—the RA—is Barbara Williams.

She and her husband, Arty, live on the nineteenth floor. Arty answers the door when I knock. He takes his time—I can hear him just the other side of the door for a few moments before the sound of a series of locks being opened echoes down the empty, dimly lit cinder-block hallway. And when the door does open it happens slowly, cautiously, eventually revealing a man with blue-tinted glasses—sun? prescription? both? neither?—and a perfect two-inch sphere of hair. He asks me to name the person I'm there to see. I say Barbara Williams and he motions for me to enter.

I step into a room with two sofas wrapped around a blaring television. Just as I start to ask where I should sit—Arty seems like the kind of guy who has a usual spot—he points to a place on the couch up against a mirrored wall. He takes a chair on the fringe of the room that is straddling the adjacent kitchen. He clicks his way through a few channels while I try to think of a starting point for a conversation. Barbara enters and I stand to shake her hand. We sit across from each other and once we start talking, Arty flicks off the television. He stands up and announces he's going back to the bedroom to watch television. Only it's a short hallway and, as Arty has proven, he likes it loud, so still we hear gunfire and fight sequences playing out in the background approximately every four to five minutes.

Barbara sits at attention, wearing glasses, possessed of calm even with the sounds of violence in the background. Originally from James Island, South Carolina, she prefers to be called Mrs. Williams—Barbara requires some common ground and history and time—and she seems to reciprocate such honorifics for everyone she meets. She came to New York at eighteen, staying with family, looking to enter a work environment where a dark-complected woman like herself might still be allowed to work the reception desk where everyone could see her. She retired five years ago after a career as an office clerk cum office manager at a handful of small businesses.

I've been in New York for going on fifty years—this year I will be sixty-six. My husband's family was the first residents in this apartment. When my mother-in-law passed away we moved in—1988, I think—and we've been here ever since.

I worked most of those years so I was out early in the morning and in late. I didn't really take too much stock in the community because, trying to raise a family, you only have weekends to take care of your personal things. I have four children so it was here and there and all over the place—it was running.

As time went by and the children grew up, it was just the husband and I, and I thought, okay, it's time to start doing things a little bit differently—give some attention to your community because this is something that I've always wanted to do. I didn't know what talents I had to offer but whatever I have, I can share it. You don't have to be a family member to be support for someone—just a neighbor. If I'm out in the street and I see one of my neighbors going through some problems, I'm going to step in and say, "Do you need some help?" They're coming home with too many bags: "Can I help you with your bags?"

Today you don't walk up on a stranger and say, "Can I help you with your bag," and think that it's going to be welcomed.

'Cause they look at you like, "Why do you want to help me?" They know they need the help but, "No thank you," because they think you're going to run away with their bags.

She laughs.

People have lost trust in each other. You know when I was coming up I was told when you get lost you go to the police. Today nobody trusts the police. And they're supposed to be the guys that protect you. The children, they're like, "Are you kidding?"

I don't know what the police department is going to do but they need to do something about changing the perception that the public has of them. Like this stop and frisk thing. I never agreed with that. The police department always had the right to stop and frisk—that was a part of their duties to begin with!

She laughs.

I'm not saying that you shouldn't do it—that's a part of your job, to stop and frisk if you think that something is wrong. That's how you protect me. But don't write it in the policy so you can just—"Oh, I think . . ." Naw. There was a message that was not being said. It didn't happen to everyone. It was happening to a group of people and that was it.

My son, he was twelve, coming home from school, walking the block. He was stopped and frisked. He came home in tears. "Mom! I didn't do anything. They just stopped me, had me kneel on the ground, put my hands behind my head. Why? I didn't do anything. I'm not a criminal."

First of all I said, "Come over here. Let your mom comfort you. Let your father and I talk to you." And I told him, "It's not because you did anything, honey."

I went to the precincts. Yes, I did. It didn't go well.

She laughs.

I had my say.

They gave the same reason they give everybody else: he fits a profile. A twelve year old and he fits a profile so they had a right to stop him.

So, no, we don't need that. And now that they're stopping the policy, I fully agree with Mr. de Blasio. It needs to stop.

Bill de Blasio ran for mayor as one of the most vocal opponents of the stop and frisk policy. Shortly after taking office, he dropped the city's appeal of a judgment against how the policy was being implemented and announced that law enforcement would no longer rely on profiling for stop and frisk. And to display some ideological balance, or to demonstrate the complexities of the job, or just to contradict himself, de Blasio appointed William Bratton as police commissioner—the same William Bratton who, two decades earlier, worked with Rudy Giuliani to pioneer the "zero-tolerance" policy, which is as aggressive as the branding makes it sound. Bratton describes policing as something that needs constant attention like "weeding a garden." Small infractions—loitering, tagging—are snuffed out on each stoop to ward off the bigger stuff like gunfights and drug deals.

Reach in deep and get at the root.

Don't get me wrong: I do trust the police. I think that authority is there for a reason. There are some police officers that abuse that authority just as there are abusers of authority in every other aspect of our lives. But I've never lost confidence in our police department because you can't paint them all with the same brush. One of my sons wants to be a police officer and right now I have a grandson who wants to be an FBI agent—and I push that.

All three of Barbara's children have moved away—two back to the family's roots in South Carolina and the third to Texas. When the nest emptied and Barbara looked to support those beyond her immediate family, when she looked to get to know the people with whom she shared parks and sidewalks, markets and elevators, she started small:

I got involved with the senior center, making curtains and whatnot. Soon after that an opening came to run for the president of the resident association. They asked me to consider it but I thought, eh, I just retired, let me socialize, get to know my neighbors who I've been living around all these years. Don't know anybody other than by face, coming into the building. People on my floor, we know each other; but other surrounding neighbors, I knew virtually no one. The second time that they asked me to run it was because, unfortunately, the president that was elected, she passed away and they came back and said maybe you should do it now.

I said, "Okay, I don't know what I'm doing here, you guys are going to have to train me."

She laughs.

A lot of people who were on the board had been there for many years, so I'm thinking, okay, these are going to be my teachers. Because I know business but I don't know this type of business.

I've learned that there's a lot of politics going on so you've got to become aware of what's going on in your community, who's doing what in your community. So I just got out and shook hands and introduced myself and got to know who's out there.

And just this year I was reelected as president. Now I have a new board and we're getting to know one another. Our concern is to raise the quality of life in our community: reaching out, being good neighbors, working together to improve the entire area. We have a community center—we have basketball, tutoring, programs teaching children about being good citizens, we take them on trips.

We also have a garden club where they grow vegetables and flowers. Now I'm looking to combine the young people in the neighborhood with seniors who can teach them about fresh fruits and fresh vegetables.

You know my father used to have a small garden and he always said that the year my brother and I put the seeds in the hill we had the biggest crop ever. And as you can see I am now more than sixty-six and I still remember that. Knowing that you could share that with a child, that they'll have that kind of memory, it puts a smile on my face every time I think about it. You've put the seed in the ground and you watch it grow! How great is that?

It's another way of socializing, too, getting to know your neighbor. Maybe you saw them coming in or out, but you never stopped to talk to them, you never got to know who they are but now you're sharing this experience, you're having a common conversation where you can begin a friendship.

We're really getting to know one another and we're getting to be more of a family, working and talking and sharing. There's more togetherness that's beginning to happen here. Before it seemed like everyone was growing apart. And I came from a large family so I like people around me talking and laughing, going out in the evening and playing stickball, baseball, but in those times it was a stick—

At this point Arty emerges from the bedroom and enters the kitchen, the swish-swash of his black track pants behind me.

My parents used to say you get more flies with honey than with vinegar. And when you apply this to people it does work. As a manager I learned that technique. And now at my resident association meetings if there's a resident who has done something that maybe the board would have done and I learn about it, I highlight that person.

And you may say you're so simplistic, and I say it is simple! We complicate things! Pat a person on the back. We have schoolteachers. We have police officers. We have telephone workers. We have nurses. We have doctors. We have a little of everybody in these developments. Why are we not taking advantage of these skills? You talk to someone, you get to know them. "What type of work do you do?" And, "How can I incorporate your skills into what we're doing here?" I don't need your skills five days a week, just a couple of hours a week. A couple of hours a month. Whatever time that you can dedicate, that's what I'm asking for.

I am not a career residents' association president. I am here to make changes and once I am done I'll pass the baton. Let someone else bring in new ideas and do different things. Otherwise you're going to run out of new ideas. And the resident association board only consists of seven to eight people. They can't do the job alone. We need everybody partaking in this. The idea is to engage the residents, giving us ideas about what they'd like to see in their community.

I can tell you this: the growth in the neighborhood definitely is not serving us. I see a lot of things growing and changing but I don't see it here. We have lots of condominiums that's come up. We have all these new neighbors, all these things going on around us but nothing in our area. And I want to know why, you know? I pay taxes. I'm not just here. I want my taxes to work for me and my community just like everyone else's tax dollars work for them. That money needs to be distributed evenly. I have the same rights as you do. I live in America. If I've got to fight for a right I'm still going to get it.

We have grounds in this development that desperately need to be redone. We have seniors walking these grounds and tripping and falling because of the unevenness.

I can see Arty in the kitchen with a broom and dustpan in hand, vaguely sweeping, clearing his throat every now and again.

And other things that's needed—things like trash cans all over the place. You want to keep clean but you have nowhere to put your garbage. So guess what? You have to give people the tools to do what you are asking them to do. These are the concerns that I'm raising.

And if I have a bad neighbor we're going to be talking. A bad neighbor has no color, race, or creed. I don't want it from any-where. Has nothing to do with where you came from—you're just a bad neighbor. You need to refocus, change your ways, and redi-rect what you're doing.

And here Arty clears his throat substantially, stopping with the sweeping for the moment.

You can't destroy your building and not have some type of repercussion. For instance, every floor has an incinerator where you take your garbage. You don't have to go downstairs, they're at every corner. But instead of putting their garbage in the incin-erator, people will put it in front of the building. Why would you do that? You live here! There's children here, playing in this. All of this goes against your children and their health and everybody else's health. And it's called respecting one another. When you go to another neighborhood, where the residents appear to care about what they have and they don't do some of the things that you're doing, you say, "Oh, this is so nice." Just do what they do. Follow their lead. You can have some nice things, too! Stop making excuses. No one is coming in and destroying this. We are doing this! Your elevator continues to be broken? Somebody in your building is doing it! It's not because it's not being cared for. I live on the nineteenth floor and I use that elevator. I don't want to walk up nineteen flights. So if I see someone on that elevator doing something that they shouldn't, or allowing their child to do something that they shouldn't, I'm going to speak out. And I'm asking people just to speak out. All of this ties into accountability: the grounds, the elevators, the hallways, the doors. Everyone should be held accountable and according to your lease you are. But the people that's in authority need to enforce these rules. If they're not enforcing the rules, people are going to say, "Oh they don't care." And it only takes a few, and everybody gets painted with the same brush. "Oh, they don't care." That's far from the truth.

Arty empties the dustpan into the trash can with an angry trio of thuds.

When you come through the area you see the people who are not working. You don't see the workers. Those people are at their jobs. When they come home from their jobs they are upstairs doing whatever it is they need to do. The people that they see are doing the things they shouldn't do, so everyone in the community gets painted with that brush. So what happens is they end up saying, "Oh, we're not going to send anything over to that neighborhood. They don't want anything." Far from the truth. And that's what I'm saying about this neighborhood. People, speak up! We need to speak up and let it be known that we want.

I'm a voice in the dark crying out. I want more. And I've got people saying I don't know why you're bothering. And I'm saying I'm bothering because I want it. And I'm going to be that voice.

At this point Arty is standing still, looking out the window. I can't

tell if he wants the conversation to end, which would mean my depar-
ture, or if he's waiting to pounce on the conversation. I try to create an
opening for him to indicate one way or another. I ask about succession
rights for apartments in public housing—how they work, since Bar-
bara's already mentioned it was Arty's parents who first lived in the
home. He has no reaction to my inquiry—Barbara steps in and answers
while Arty shuffles his feet back and forth, still looking out the kitchen
window, still looking impatient about something.

We continue to forge forward to get changes. I don't know
how long it will take. Nothing happens overnight. If we are per-
sistent we'll get the change. And your agenda and mine might be
different. Our fight may not be the same because your wants and
needs in certain areas might be different than my wants and needs
but because you're my friend we're going to fight to make things
happen. No one group can do something all by themselves. Even
during the civil rights movement, I was a young person when that
started, those three boys who got killed in Alabama—two was
white! We were talking about civil rights for everybody but most
people thought we were just talking about civil rights for blacks.
That was for everybody of all races and colors.

You choose what you fight for. If you believe in something
then go fight for it. Hopefully it won't get so bad that everyone
starts running away. Areas get a reputation for a certain things.
People say, "Oh, I wouldn't go there."

"Why not?"

"Because things can happen there to you."

That's not always true. But someone may have had a bad experience. Enough of those people have a bad experience and now
you have a reputation. Now no one wants to go there. They don't
want to move in.

If you say it long enough it becomes.

So it's up to us.

I was always taught there's no faith where there's no action.
Faith is dead without action. Love is dead without action. I can

love you day in and day out but if I'm not doing anything to show it to you—

Suddenly Arty swings a seat out from the kitchen table and sits in it backwards, his arms resting on the back of the chair as he leans toward us. He asks me a question:

Arty: Writing a paper for college or something?

I am momentarily flattered—Arty thinks I'm young enough to be in college. I try to explain what I'm doing—my trip to understand gentrification—and suddenly I'm tangled, again, on what the word may or may not mean. Judging from the disengaged expression on Arty's face, the word means absolutely nothing to him. He cuts me off abruptly—

Arty: I heard you talking to my wife but my opinion is completely the opposite. The problem with us is that we are our own defeat right here. We moved back to this community right here. My kids don't want us in this community right here. My sons, they moved away from this community right here. My sister, she got money, she moved away from this community right here. We're the one's that stayed around for the community right here but community is the people, and the problem is the people. Uneducated. You have to learn to read and write and half of them don't want to learn to read or write. And they get angry with you when you know how to do it. And they get angry at you when you have two or three cars. We have more than one car and they know you live the middle-class lifestyle and they can't understand that. I was working at the office and I come home dressed up and they thought I was rich. Because they not used to seeing somebody being successful, doing what you need to do for yourself, they're not used to that. They think you have to be in the pit of the ninety-nine cent store.

I'm a businessman. I think about business. She thinks of it from the social view. I mean all the social programs you bring in here, and still they don't have the common sense to say, "Hey, I've got garbage, I'm going to put it in the incinerator." Something is wrong! It is odd! I've never made someone come to me and say,

"You know what, Mr. Williams, I don't think you should throw Pampers out the window."

But still she has to convince the people don't throw Pampers out the window, don't throw condoms out the window, don't throw food out the window.

And the elevator! They shit in the elevator. I don't want to be around them and I'm their color! We have a problem. Crack addicts on the floor in the hallway. That's everyday-common around here. Let me tell you something: that's abnormal!

Those that go to work are the working poor, and the others sit around here all day long and they want to rob the working poor. That's the way it's set up around here. The police, they know that's the deal around here. We know that if you want to live in a better neighborhood you've got to get out of here. Because you've got to survive. That's why my sons got out of here. I just had an argument yesterday with the guy next door because there was crack people coming into his apartment. That's why I took my time opening the door when you came here because maybe you knocked on the wrong door. Let me tell you, you knock on the wrong door—*and now he's pointing directly at me*—you might not be coming out the apartment!

Pointing at his wife:

This morning she says, "Honey, somebody coming by here to talk to me."

I say, "Really? Why'd you invite them in?"

He laughs.

It's safety concerns. If you're coming to my house, I want you to be safe. You could be one of the statistics. You have to think about these things. You could be on the news. People thinking, "What was he doing up there?"

I have to be honest. And I have to protect myself all the time. Because we on the different level. They don't like that she's the RA president. They don't like that I dress up and look nice. And they could get there but that takes time and effort and you got to go to school and get an education. Then you have to want to have it. You can take them to the water but they might not drink it. You have to want that.

I hate the social programs because, to me, the programs stagnate people's minds. I'm partially Republican on some things. My wife she different than me. I can't always see feeding somebody if they can't fish for themselves. Eventually they're going to get used to it and go generation to generation on welfare instead of saying, "This is just for me to get back on my feet." They don't see it that way. They see it as free money. They want to take your crumbs. They never made $50,000, $100,000 around here. You tell them you make a $1,000 a week they say you lying. I say, "Man, I'm making two thousand dollars a week. And my brother was making a half a million dollars. He was a rich doctor." They don't see that. They have never seen that type of lifestyle. So it's hard for them to get into that. It's a mind thing. If you never ate steak you only ate chopped meat you never know what a good steak is. And that's how life is. You got to improve your mind. Go to the museum. If you don't know something go see it. Nobody around here never goes nowhere.

My wife she has the programs, the trips to the theater and that's all well and good but they would never get off their asses and do it on their own. They go because it's a free thing. Only thing they'll come out to get is some fried chicken. I say, "Why do they always have to give a party out here for black folks to start thinking about their community?" I said, "Sweetheart, you've got over four thousand people over here. You don't even have one hundred people in the RA office. There's something wrong with that." If there's nothing you hand out to them free they ain't coming. You got to give some food or some music so they can jump around and clap instead of learning how they can get themselves off the ground.

My sons say, "Dad, can you please get out of there? Can you and mom go?" They're always trying to get us out of here. She knows that. They're against this whole thing right here, like I am. But we lay here and the rent is cheap. The rent is definitely cheap and it's a Manhattan address. I don't mind her being in these social programs because she likes doing that. She has her heart and soul in it.

But you can sit around all day with your social programs and it's still all about dollar bills. Because you had to have that dollar twenty years ago and you always gonna have to have that dollar tomorrow. New York City is definitely the financial capital. Anywhere you go you got to have money. You have to think on the money terms. I don't care what you say, the more money you have—you live better, you drive better, everything's better. And I keep explaining to my children, my daughters too, you got to have this—*Arty rubs his thumb and forefinger together, like he's thumbing a wad of bills*—that's what's going to solve the problem around here.

Barbara: Money is a huge part of it. But did you hear what my husband was saying: *They*. "They don't want anything." But this is my view of that: I hear that *they* and I'm like, wait a minute you live here, too. When they say *they*, they're talking about you, too!

Arty: No I didn't say everybody, I said the majority of everybody.

Arty rises from his chair, sliding it back under the kitchen table.

Arty: That's all I got to say. I had to throw something in there when I heard y'all talking.

Arty goes back to the bedroom—no television this time—and Barbara continues:

Barbara: I don't like the "they" thing. That is very dangerous to say that somebody don't want to read or write. I went to business school, I went to college. He went to business school and he went to college. We have a schoolteacher who lives across the hall and she taught right here in the school. We have another lady who's raising foster kids. We have people over here who work in business. So yeah, I got a bad neighbor next door but I don't like *they* because when people refer to me as *they*, who's *they*? Do not paint me with a brush. I am an individual and I deal with you as an individual. Don't suffer me because you have a problem with someone else. That's unfair. I never met you. I might have some negative feelings about whites—*she indicates in my direction with her open hand*—but guess what? I never met you!

Why am I going to feel that way about you when I had an experience dealing with somebody else? We've got to learn how to stop grouping people good or bad, and start learning how to deal with people individualistically. Hey, I've got black people I don't like.

She laughs.

When I came up as a girl, we weren't taught certain things because with our parents and grandparents there were certain subjects that you just did not talk about. So when you got information, you got information from somebody your age who didn't know nothing just like you. So we were all walking around blind thinking we all know something! And using that analogy, I say, go out and get the information so that when you're talking to your friends you will know what you're talking about. When you're saying something you have a reference point: "Go over here and check it out, man. See what I'm saying is right."

My mother stopped me from saying *they*. Sometimes even now I start talking and I'll catch myself and I won't say it. Or if I do say it I'll give some kind of description so you know who I'm talking about because it could be anyone.

You hear people say, "They said this . . ." And, "They said that . . ."

And I say, "Where did you learn that from?"

"Well, they say it."

"Who are 'they'?"

I often ask that question.

And I do make people a little frustrated.

13.

*R*ecently, Barbara was frustrating her state senator, Bill Perkins, prodding him about the lack of development along the waterfront across from the Polo Grounds. Over the last decade, work has been completed up and down the East River. But Harlem River Park ends ten blocks south of Barbara's building and the waterfront to the north is blocked by six lanes of traffic speeding in both directions on Harlem River Drive, another one of Robert Moses's creations, which gives the water's edge to drivers instead of pedestrians.

Barbara pays tax dollars just like the residents of the Lower East Side who now enjoy that neighborhood's East River Esplanade. She pays tax dollars just like the residents of Murray Hill and Tudor City who will soon enjoy the East Midtown Waterfront project. Barbara wants her tax dollars to work in the place where she lives. She wants to ride her bike along the water in her neighborhood. She's been working on the issue with Tom Lunke at the Harlem Community Development Corporation. They've collaborated for over three years, long enough for trust to replace honorifics: she is Barbara to him and she freely calls him Tom.

Tom's office is a subsidiary of the New York State Urban Development Corporation, which is doing business as Empire State Development, which is, in governmental parlance, a New York State public *benefit corporation, which, in practical terms, refers to a public-private corporate mash up. The entity is governed by a board of directors appointed by an elected official. Throughout his career, Tom has worked at various offices in the labyrinth that is New York City bureaucracy. He did a stint at City Planning; he worked in the Koch administration. Barbara says she clicked with him because they both like to talk. I can confirm this. Hours can zip by when either of them gets going.*

Tom wears a tie and carries a notepad and pen on the day we meet in a conference room at his offices on 125th Street, half a block east of the Apollo Theater. He shares the address with the likes of US Representative Charles Rangel and State Attorney General Eric Schneiderman. Upon entering the building and passing through a metal detector, my camera is confiscated by security. Building management nixes all cameras. Police cameras capture all activity on most of the streets that surround the building but nothing will be so freely captured by a member of the public inside the high-rise. I ask the men working the metal detectors why there's a policy of no cameras and they both look at me like they have a headache.

Originally from California's Bay Area, Tom has a wiry frame and is fifty-five years old. He has worked at the Harlem Community Development Corporation, or HCDC, for fourteen years.

I remember the first time I came to Harlem was in 1983, and I was jogging through the neighborhood, up Seventh Avenue, and I see building after building abandoned. And then there was this one woman with a little kid in tow and she said to me, "Keep running!"

He laughs.

In '89 when I was getting my masters at Columbia in urban planning, we were told about this underground meeting, sort of like the socialist movement in Harlem. I think we were the only white guys in the room—one of my colleagues and I went down. It was supposed to be 153rd and 8th Avenue, and so we took the train up to 155th and walked through Jackie Robinson Park at night—we didn't know any better. And when we got down to the bottom of Bradhurst Ave, there were these two guys hanging out and they looked at us and they said something like, "Are you guys cops?"

He laughs.

And we went to this meeting in this basement space. We were talking with all these people who had gathered and it was all about socioeconomics and the dynamics of the economy and how African Americans are not getting their fair shake. And so one of the guys tried to start a fight with us. "Oh, what do you know?" That kind of stuff. And so, you know, we were talking about how race is a construct created to divide and how we're all in the same boat and we're all trying to make our lives better and build an economic base that works for everybody. So I think we ended the meeting on a good note. But there was some tension there at the time. And then they said, "How did you get here?"

And we said, "We walked through Jackie Robinson Park."

And they said, "Are you insane?"

He laughs.

The way Harlem is structured and zoned, its place in the city is more as a bedroom community. So as the prices of Lower Manhattan escalate, people, primarily Caucasians, are moving up to Harlem. It's interesting because when I first started working here in '99, I remember getting off at the 2/3 train stop at 125th. I was the only Caucasian coming into Harlem in those days. Over the years I saw how each station, first it was 110th and Lenox, then 116th, then 125th, each station started getting more and more Caucasians. I remember counting—there's one, there's one. Now I don't even bother counting because there are so many.

There was a discussion about ten years ago that in Greenwich Village the population was decreasing but the income base was increasing. So as the bohemian culture and the lower-income people were moved out their spaces were filled by fewer and fewer people. And I believe the same thing is happening in Harlem on the townhouse blocks now.

I remember in the '80s when I had a friend who lived in Harlem he lived in a single room occupancy hotel, an SRO. And he could actually leave that hotel after a month and move to another brownstone SRO and live there for a month—he was just moving all around because it was maybe one hundred dollars a month to rent these rooms and he was a low-paid staffer at City Planning and he needed a place to live and these were opportunities for him. A lot of those SROs have been converted to one, two, three-family homes; ten units become two or three units. So the housing stock is thinning because of the wealthier people.

I was friendly with Jane Jacobs when she was alive and I asked her what she thought of gentrification and she pretty much said that gentrification is a good thing, it's displacement that's the problem: How do you engage the community in the gentrification process so that they're not displaced?

One of the things that we've noticed over the years is that not enough African Americans or Latinos are engaged in the urban planning process. In our capacity here, we're trying our best to get people to create a stake for themselves in the community, to get people educated, understanding there's more to life than just being isolated in one corner of Manhattan. You involve the kids and the adults in the planning process so they understand what's going on and can contribute, so they have a stake in the future and then they will watch out for it because they feel it's theirs.

First you have to understand how the city gets shaped. Because people often think, "Oh, isn't this always this way? Hasn't it always been?" They don't understand that people shape their own environment. We end up doing a lot of public space development. We want that public space to reflect the community, so that when people come in they feel like it's their space. If you're not given a lot of encouragement about thinking creatively, you get very shut down. This whole process of engaging the community in the planning process, it scares a lot of people but it's also thrilling to a lot of other people.

When Tom arrived in New York, in the early '80s, the city was shrinking. Public services were being cut, and there was talk—he remembers it—of tearing down swathes of Brooklyn and the Bronx; some plans, he recalls, proposed letting those areas revert to farmland. The city that Tom has experienced since then has evolved in the opposite direction—Harlem, in particular. One of the biggest landowners in the neighborhood, Columbia University, has expanded throughout northern Manhattan. Tom has been involved in talks between his alma mater and the community for a decade:

In 2004, Columbia came to the community board and said basically we want to expand. The president of Columbia had this attitude that Columbia was doing a favor to the community. That somehow all this development would trickle down to jobs for the community. The idea that, instead of giving money directly to the people, you give subsidized development dollars and free land to a development entity then that money will be translated back to the people—it doesn't ever seem to work out but people keep pushing it.

So in 2004 Columbia came to the community, and the community held back in terms of their anger but you could tell by the words they were using, the anger was just seething through their teeth. And they were basically saying, "How can you speak to us like this? Do you think we're morons?"

Then Columbia got their backs up.

So what we did was we sat down with Columbia and said okay this is what the community says it wants: meaningful jobs at decent wages. The jobs people will be losing are middle income manufacturing type jobs. You're proposing a campus. So the jobs will be student advisors, or professors, things that require a certain level of skill sets that many in the community would not have. They would not be able to transfer their manufacturing skills into becoming a professor, for example. And then they had these grand notions of interdisciplinary discussions. Like if you brought in all these engineers with artists working in the new arts center that they would somehow cross-pollinate ideas and miraculously come up with new inventions. And our argument was you could do that now. If you had the auto body shop and the Alexander Doll Company next to an engineering building you could cross-pollinate much more interestingly because you'd have people making things and people could bring ideas to them and they could create a prototype in their workshop and give it to you and that could lead to all kinds of inventions. And they were like, "Oh, no, that's not the type of cross-pollination they want."

So then we got into this discussion: I had just finished this 1960s movie *The Time Machine*; it's an H. G. Wells science fiction story about how this guy in the 1900s creates this time machine and he goes to, I don't know, the year 2500 or something like that, and the world has changed so much you have these very white, blond-haired people populating the ground and you have these monsters underneath the ground, doing all the hard labor so the blond, white people up above could live comfortably. And so Columbia wanted—and they still want—to have all of the infrastructure below ground, where all the people are doing all the hard labor so that the students can lollygag up top. And so I posed that parallel to the architects and they were sort of stunned by the comparison.

He laughs.

But their rationale for doing condemnation of the whole four blocks was that they needed the land underneath to put this infrastructure, because they didn't want trucks or normal things that happen in cities to invade their campus-like setting. So that was their justification for grabbing all the land.

At the end of the day, the Columbia campus was approved in 2008. If you look back and say did we benefit from all these years of work, I could probably say the one thing we benefitted from was to educate the community in urban planning. The community was then poised to have serious and meaningful discussion about what benefits it. The community became more knowledgeable about how it can affect change—but also mindful that there are times when you come up against a power structure that is so large you can't infiltrate it in the ways you want to. You can in small ways but the power structure vision ends up getting pushed forward.

City Planning Commission is thinking more in terms of urban design—you know, having a skyline that has crystalline towers rather than focusing on the ground-level impact of all this.

Manufacturing zones end up suppressing the value of the land because manufacturers' whole business is set up to put their capital back into their business, not into real estate. The real estate industry pushes city planning to rezone all these manufacturing areas for residential because it's a higher rate of return for them.

The problem is that as the economy moves forward it becomes more and more geared toward the service sector because you don't have production going on in the city. The whole period from the 1930s to the 1970s, where we saw a growth in the middle class, that was because we were producing things. So if you get rid of production all we have is paper pushers at the top and service workers at the bottom. We don't have that middle class anymore. And that's what you're seeing in New York City, this stratification, because we don't have this middle class. Or we're losing it. And government workers such as myself, we're holding on to that middle class but aside from government workers, where is the middle class?

I live in Chelsea and I used to be on my community board, from '96 to 2003. That was during the period where the Chelsea Plan was implemented and the rezoning took place.

The centerpiece of the Chelsea Plan became the High Line project. A mile and a half of elevated train tracks had fallen out of use in 1980, after the final three cars—loaded with frozen turkeys—passed overhead. Developers initially tried to have the tracks taken down to make way for new buildings but a coalition of residents, activists, and railroad enthusiasts challenged the demolition. The unused elevation re-

*mained structurally sound but covered over in wild grass and rugged
trees that grew up in the gravel along the tracks. In 1999, an organization was created by Chelsea residents, Friends of the High Line, and
soon proposals began to circulate for converting the elevated tracks
into a space that would be useful and appealing for the neighborhood.*

The High Line started out as a grassroots effort and then the
major developers got on board and that shifted the focus. The City
Planning Department was listening to the major developers while
still trying to be community friendly. So the designer that was se-
lected put the native grasses in and things like that but it wasn't
made for the community. It was made for the investment opportunities adjoining the High Line. There was an economic development analysis that determined you could invest in the High Line
and make it a park without changing any land use along the corridor. The naturally occurring rate of return would be enough to
justify the investment. But City Planning wanted to put that area
on steroids and really capitalize on rapid large-scale development
and that's what they've done.

Needless to say, I was in the minority when we were trying to
protect the manufacturing base in the community. Part of the whole
discussion was saving the Meatpacking District, so we came up with
this plan for the High Line where the adjoining properties would
remain manufacturing up to the third level, and then above that
you could build residential housing and other service-type businesses. But we wanted the base of the buildings to remain manufacturing because we felt that would keep the neighborhood at least
somewhat dynamic in terms of income characteristics and people
who lived in the lower-income buildings would still be able to walk
to work and things of that nature. We even asked that the High
Line be connected to the new buildings with a commercial first level.
So you could go into the building and down to the street and you
would have this connection in the neighborhood. And City Planning
said, "No, we want the High Line to be a floating park." So, disconnected from the neighborhood. And that's what it is today.

When you go over there you see tourists from all over the world but you don't see local residents because it's not really a place for us. It's an iconic structure for people to point at and look at and walk through. So that, to me, is probably the bad side of gentrification because a lot of the rich people that have bought these lofts or luxury apartments over there, they're not going to hang out on the High Line, they're going to jet-set to wherever points in the world and this is their pied-à-terre. That doesn't really do anything to build up a sense of community.

I'm reminded of the vacant lot across from Paula Segal's apartment in Brooklyn—"that big hole in the neighborhood," as she called it. Sometimes the literal hole, the empty lot, gets filled with a condo high-rise and the units are sold to buyers who visit a few weeks a year; at once coveted and vacant, these homes produce a new, more figurative hole in the neighborhood.

Ninth Avenue in Chelsea, for example, used to have the hardware stores and the shoe stores and now it's got the boutique stores and the fancy little restaurants—my neighborhood is overrun by tourists. I hardly see my own neighbors any more because they're so lost in the tourist shuffle.

14.

iko grew up in Chelsea. His Greek father owned a Greek diner on Seventeenth Street and retired in 1995. As Niko puts it, "You know, Greeks, they own diners." He worked behind the counter but the business wasn't his speed so he aimed higher with law school. He remembers the High Line as that abandoned, rusted railroad track running overhead.

The High Line was something that was looked down on by developers. But in retrospect, the irony is that now any building next to the High Line is like any building next to Central Park: it gets immediate 50 percent increase in value. So it was an interesting thing to happen, not just for Chelsea in terms of the community, but also for the real estate developers.

It brings up the question: can you artificially accelerate gentrification? Did the High Line—artificially, to some extent—accelerate the gentrification of the far West Side?

You know, there's a story about a parking lot in Downtown Brooklyn, in the middle of an area that no one would go to. The developers who owned it didn't have the financing to build, and they wanted to sort of accelerate the progress of that neighborhood. So they created a flea market and it became really cool and artsy. For a whole year, you had a bunch of people coming to a community that they normally wouldn't see because of this artificially created destination. After a year, the developers started building a hundred rental units. And the people who'd been going to the flea market were like, "Hey, maybe I'll live here, too." So that's interesting. Can you artificially gentrify a neighborhood? It's a process that I think is better done organically. A natural process seems to be better because it gives people time to change. It gives them time to save money. They can retrain themselves. But when the acceleration happens too quick maybe they're caught off guard. And maybe that's the role of government. To provide that safety net, that time for people to retool and adapt to that change. Because you don't want it to happen overnight.

And it's going to happen. You can't stop it.

Niko is now forty-one years old and works at a private firm with a specialty in real estate transactions. Sometimes it's a purchase, sometimes it's a rental agreement, sometimes it's a landlord buying tenants out so they'll vacate an apartment—always a first step toward increasing the value of the property. Niko is the man who is at the table when the dotted lines are finally signed and checks are finally, finally handed over. He finesses and bends and demands according to his client's interests and he finishes the job. Because he is good at what he does and because his services are in demand and because he sees no reason to assume any risk with his career, he will only talk to me on the record about gentrification—a "sensitive topic," he reminds me again and again—if I grant him a pseudonym and so, indeed, I have.

His contact list is a complex of real estate agents, banks, developers, and investors. Once a month he hosts a networking breakfast for invited clients and contacts. Forecasts are shared, maybe some leads materialize, and there is always a featured guest: the manager of a $100 million investment account, the president of a construction company carrying out 100,000-square-foot projects, the senior broker specializing in turning around distressed properties. The meetings take place in the Madison Avenue offices of a national real estate investment services firm. One recent breakfast was focused on investment opportunities in the Bronx—the next big thing, the borough of double-digit *returns, according to Niko's invitation. Every meeting takes place at 7:45 a.m. and at 7:45 p.m. Niko will likely still be at his desk answering the phone.*

He works in a neighborhood labeled NoMad—a name devised in the late '90s for a five-block stretch just north of Madison Square Park and east of Chelsea. The area has been oriented toward wholesale business for decades. Though Niko dresses for the job, the buttons on his suit look like they want to pop off and free the tough guy inside. His hair is slicked back, his skin is tan, and his deep voice channels a hard New York accent. We are on our way to lunch.

Here's an example of gentrification right in front of you.

First, focus to your left. There you see Broadway, all this wholesale stuff, dingy looking buildings. Turn around now and see what's happening. It's a salad shop that prides itself on the fact that everything is local. They get their stuff from Ulster County. They just opened. And you see the line?

Niko indicates the chain of people extending to the end of the block on this muggy afternoon. He points out one of the newer hotels along this stretch of Broadway.

Obama had a fundraising event here and it was like $40,000 a plate.

We bypass the salad fetish spot for the Bánh mì fetish shop, opting for different bastardized versions of the Vietnamese sandwich. Niko's sandwich shrinks in his fist before vanishing in his mouth.

Chelsea has a lot of projects and sometimes when people look at neighborhoods they're concerned about what impact public housing is going to have in the neighborhood. The city built these vertical housing projects that became a sort of infestation of crime. They were isolated. There was not integration. There was no access to work or transportation. Those were the failed experiments of the 1970s.

And maybe twenty years ago when someone was considering buying an apartment in Chelsea, they saw public housing and thought how can you have the projects across the street from million dollar homes? It's not going to happen. But it did. It happened in Chelsea, it's happening on the Lower East Side, and in parts of Harlem. Definitely seeing it in Downtown Brooklyn. Now I have investors looking at the Bronx, because they're not seeing the kind of return they want in Brooklyn. At least from the New York point of view—again, I'm sort of limited from my sort of middle white perspective—but I think for New York, the experiment is going pretty well. So is that a testament to the fact that you can have gentrification and have people of different socioeconomic categories living in the same place? Sure.

But now the projects are underfunded because there's not the revenue anymore. And there is a proposal out now that they should be selling either the retail space or the parking lots to private developers in order to raise revenue, because maintenance in the projects sucks. But sometimes organizations see this as the first step to privatization. If you privatize the retail and privatize the parking lots, tomorrow you're going to privatize my apartment just like Stuyvesant Town, where MetLife came in with other people's money and deregulated everything and privatized one of the largest public housing projects in the city. That's the resistance.

But in terms of gentrification and housing projects, I can't think of a neighborhood, if my spectrum is from 1970s to today, I can't think of a neighborhood that has regressed and become a poor neighborhood again. I mean, one might argue, "Expand your horizon, Niko—let's go to 1920s." In 1920 there were neighborhoods like South Bronx and Bushwick that were flourishing neighborhoods and then the '60s and '70s occurred and for a host of reasons those neighborhoods decayed, but those neighborhoods are now back to their peak.

All this talk of gentrification, there is another underlying principle that—nationally, I think—people want to live in urban environments and walkable communities. No longer do we have the risk, at least in New York, of white flight. No one wants to live in the suburbs anymore. No one is saying I'm going to start in Brooklyn, get a good living, and move out to the suburbs. Brooklyn and Queens are the new suburbs. And I think that has an impact on gentrification.

Now I'm doing a lot of stuff in Bushwick. This is a neighborhood with a lot of rent-stabilized product, and there's definitely a lot of transition going on. So there's a lot of people buying there now. But if it's rent stabilized the tenant has the right to stay in their apartment as long as they're paying the rent, so you have to do a buyout. And you definitely have community organizations in Bushwick that are informing the tenant community of their rights—and they should. Just because a landlord comes knocking on your door and says you've got to get the fuck out, you really don't. And if you're going to consider a buyout, be smart about it.

The buyout has to be negotiated. I've seen buyouts for $100,000 and I've seen buyouts for $10,000. I'm doing a buyout right now where the tenant is getting $100,000 for something they really didn't work for. There is an irony here that capitalism drives such a transaction but yet it is not an exchange between labor and wage. It is a transaction whereby an individual's rights are acquired.

Public policy shouldn't be dictated by the effect it's going to have on one person. What's the impact of that policy going to have on a larger community? If you ask one group of sort of laissez-faire capitalists, when you deregulate the one million rent-stabilized apartments in this city, you're going to flood the market with supply, so you're going to lower rents throughout the city. That's their opinion. So maybe there's an argument for privatizing everything. But the alternative side is, well, that's false. You're going to have to evict people from their homes, and that's going to cause a big disarray and the sky's going to be the limit in terms of rents.

I can tell you rent-stabilized apartments will not be privatized by legislation. It's political suicide because there's more tenant votes than landlord votes. But it is happening from the market side. Because every year, even a small percentage, the number of rent-stabilized apartments decreases through buyouts, and that once-stabilized apartment is probably getting deregulated. That's what's happening: the efficiencies of the market. It's happening at a very slow pace. And maybe that's how it should happen so there's less of a shock impact on the tenants.

Put the frog in the water before you turn up the heat.

15.

*T*oussaint Wortham lives alone in a three-bedroom apartment
in Crown Heights, Brooklyn. One bedroom has a deflated
air mattress on the floor; the second has a weight-lifting
machine and various free weights; the third has a full bed, which is
unmade. The hallway is empty and looks to run downhill. Toussaint
is a bachelor and points out—correctly—that the apartment is entirely too big for one person. It makes him think the place might be
haunted.

He takes me to the big windows in his bedroom, looking out onto
the street. He points at a building in the distance. It is roughly ten stories high, much taller than the surrounding brownstones, and all the
windows are boarded up.

The whole building: gentrified. You see what I'm talking
about right? With the plywood? I knew about two families in that
building, and they're all gone. Probably in the Bronx now, or Jersey or something.

That's what's going on.

They're saying most of these rent-stabilized tenants are depre-
ciating the values of these buildings. A lot of them are, you know,
and some politicians are saying we could probably do better without them. Send them down South. Send 'em to the Bronx. Send
'em to the outer most parts of the city—East New York,

Brownsville—let's put you out there now. It's not like we're saying you won't have a home, we'll just put you out there. And when we're ready to gentrify that neighborhood, we'll move you further. I got friends living in East New York and Brownsville. And I asked them, "Are you experiencing this problem?"

They're like, "Naw."

They don't even know what gentrification means.

I tell Toussaint I don't think anyone really knows what it means, which prompts him to try for a definition of his own. After a minute of contemplation and a series of aborted sentences, he gives up and insists he doesn't need to describe gentrification because he knows what it feels like.

This word gentrification, *incidentally, is not the first time language has failed to capture the phenomenon Toussaint is trying to pin down: Australia had* trendification *and in 1971,* The New York Times *tried out* brownstoneurbia, *which doesn't exactly roll off the tongue. The descriptors come and go but the patterns remain—Toussaint's description of Crown Heights, for example, sounds a lot like Friedrich Engels, who noted two centuries earlier: "The bourgeoisie has only one method of settling the housing question . . . The breeding places of disease, the infamous holes and cellars in which the capitalist mode of production confines our workers night after night are not abolished; they are merely shifted elsewhere."*

"We'll just put you out there," says Toussaint.

We move into the kitchen, bright with sunlight that streams through the apartment's biggest windows. Toussaint offers me water. I accept, and he opens the refrigerator, which has nearly nothing inside save for several large shrink-wrapped bundles of twelve-ounce bottled water. He grabs two of the chilled bottles and joins me at the table.

I have to ask about the refrigerator full of water. When I do he laughs it off, almost sheepish, and apologizes for the pile of empty bottles pouring out of a cardboard box behind my chair. He tells me that they await the recycling machine—Toussaint's not going without his nickel returns. His warm, earnest smile reveals gold-plated front teeth.

He wears a baseball hat and a large black T-shirt that hangs nearly to his knees.

Toussaint drives an Access-A-Ride bus—paratransit for travelers who qualify under the Americans with Disabilities Act. He hates the job. His routine experience: get a call from the dispatcher with thirty minutes lead time for a pick up that is an hour away; endless traffic; an angry traveler; and thus one unkind interaction after another. Calm and soft spoken, Toussaint seems to like keeping things civil.

Though Access-A-Ride is a public service, the city subcontracts the job to a private company and, by doing so, gets the job done for twelve dollars an hour instead of having to hire a higher-paid employee who belongs to a public union. This is another reason Toussaint hates the job. He says the word hate *calmly and thoughtfully, despite the raw emotion it carries. He missed his shift yesterday to go to housing court. Unsure where to begin, he shakes his head then points to the sink area near the window:*

These are the cabinets in question that they want to evict me for.

These cabinets were installed before the new owner took over the property. The previous management was aware of these cabinets and the previous management even gave me money toward these cabinets. This was five years ago, they gave me $1,000 toward them. The judge said that she would look into it.

I looked the landlord up but of course all these landlords hide behind these management groups. They do all of their dirty work. They initiated the case about three months ago.

There are four cabinets in the kitchen—two below the counter and two above. They are made of wood, painted blue, and sturdy when I thump them with my hand. They are clearly insignificant—they have no impact on the structural integrity of the apartment. In fact, aesthetically, they are the best feature in a room otherwise defined more by the thrashed flooring and peeling wallpaper.

It's been thirty-five years with very little repairs. I've lived here since 1979. I was in first grade when we moved. We moved around summer, around the time that Reagan was campaigning. I remember all the stickers and flyers. We started school that year.

My mother passed away in 2000, and when she passed away the succession rights kicked in. The apartment automatically went into my name. We'd had the same cabinets since '79 so they were deplorable. I told the previous management that I want to make a change and they agreed. I told the landlord's attorney yesterday, "Look all this could have been avoided. All you had to do was call the previous management."

And she said, "Well, I didn't know."

I said, "At least you could call prior to going through this extreme action, taking me to court. I had to take off work."

And once I mentioned the word gentrification she looked at me like, its absurd! The minute I said the word gentrification, the landlord's lawyer started interjecting and went on with something else. They don't even recognize that that's even a remote possibility. It's so obvious to people who see it but to them—it's like a scientist, right? Scientists only like to deal with the facts. We want hard-core facts—period. That's how she came across to me. Don't come to me with this theory of gentrification. To them[3] it's a theory. It's not facts. That's something that people are just saying. She didn't want to hear that. And I didn't override her. I didn't want to get into a fight. So she took the conversation somewhere else.

I asked the judge, "So if it's proven that these cabinets were installed prior to this management taking over this case should be thrown out, right?"

---

[3]   Toussaint's switch from *her* (the landlord's attorney) to *them* (whoever that may be) sends Barbara Williams flashing across my mind. I hear her voice telling me to cut Toussaint off and ask him about *them,* ask him who, exactly, they are. But then he backs off, perhaps aware of the switch, and reverts back to *she.*

And she said, "Not necessarily. It's depending on what type of deal the previous management made with the current management."

"That, I don't understand. So I'm still in hot water even if I can prove these were done with approval? What's the worse case scenario?"

And she says, "Well, you can be evicted."

I didn't really think the cabinets would equal eviction. But that's the case now.

My victory yesterday was that basically they agreed that I could start paying my rent again—*he laughs but he is serious*—they haven't been taking my rent for three months now. They've been saying they can't take my rent until the case is resolved. They bank on the idea that you'll mess that money up. These are the tactics they're using. It's been three months so they figure I might see a nice coat that I want, or nice pair of jeans, and I'll spend it, which most people do—they'll spend it. But he's got me misconstrued. I'm not that kind of person. I've got one pair of jeans.

So when I went to court yesterday, we wrote the stipulation that they'll take the money now. Today I'm going to make out a check to pay the rent.

He beams with pride. I ask him about the door at the entrance to his apartment, which is plastered with flyers: invites to events, lists of phone numbers, lists of tenant rights.

I'm always putting up flyers for the Crown Heights tenants protests. And the landlord's attorney brought that up yesterday. She said, "My client says that you're putting up flyers, you're harassing the tenants."

I said, "Look, if trying to start a tenant association is illegal, let me know now and I'll stop doing it."

She said, "No."

And I said, "I'm trying to start a tenant association."

Then she implied that I'm harassing the tenants and no tenant gave her any information that I'm harassing them. No tenant would have done that. I'm simply talking in the hallway when I'm passing by, I'll inform them about certain things that I know, especially newly renovated apartment tenants. They really have no idea that they're being overcharged. A lot of them don't understand the formula. They don't understand that Department of Homes and Community Renewal has rent regulations. And a landlord cannot just arbitrarily say, "Three thousand dollars for that." He has a standard that he has to go by.

So I'm trying to inform them. But you know, a lot of tenants in the newly renovated apartments, they don't really communicate with the old tenants. For whatever reason. I don't know. I really don't want to put a theory out because I don't know what they're thinking.

Across the hall, apartment 21, there are three girls in there, I think they're roommates. When they first moved in, they gave me an invitation to go to their housewarming, which I did and I bought them that mat you see outside their door. I had them gift wrap the bag and stuff because I didn't want them to think that I'm some, you know. So that was cool but after that we don't even—I guess if we see each other, passing in the hall we'll say hi, and that's it.

They're probably saying we're not going to be here very long. And I noticed that. There's a lot of turnover. It's not their fight I guess.

I mean, I try to put myself in their shoes and maybe they're saying, "We don't have no problems, we don't want trouble with the management. We're okay with what we're paying—we have it." It's not like it's a family that moved in. Most of the people that got these apartments are roommates. They're obviously dividing it up. So it's not significant on them. It's not like they're a mother and father with kids.

When I had two tenant association meetings only the old tenants came. None of the new tenants. And I guess the new tenants are saying that doesn't involve us. But it does, in reality. They could probably get their rent reduced—plus get money back. They just don't care. I don't know what their reality is. Do you have money you can just blow like that? You could be on Park Avenue, guy. You don't have to be in this neighborhood. What are you doing here?

He laughs.

After the meeting, management had the super put No Trespassing signs where we enter the courtyard. But trespassing is something for people who don't live in the building. How are we trespassing? We all live in the building.

I did two meetings back to back. I had one Saturday and one Sunday. On the first day, only two people came. Those two days were kind of cold and I told everyone from four to five and I didn't want to keep them out there, talking their heads off. I had a table, some chairs, and some waters. These are the remnants of the waters I had.

These are more than remnants, and now I understand: the refrigerator filled with bottles indicates the low turnout for the meetings; it indicates that Toussaint's hospitality at the meetings—never mind the information he wanted to share—went unreceived by his neighbors.

Many people identify displacement as the central characteristic of gentrification. And the idea of displacement is often tethered to physical space—someone must vacate a storefront or apartment or park because the forces of capital drive her away: she could not renew the lease, she could not resist a buyout, she did not have the money to purchase the lot. But Toussaint understands that there's another kind of displacement—one unrelated to physical space. His displacement is figurative, more subtle, escaping the statistician's graph. Toussaint still clings to his apartment but he is disconnected from the neighbors across the hall despite the gift-wrapping for the doormat. Little by little, he has become more disconnected from the community that exists in the building where he grew up. He has been drinking bottled water alone for weeks. "No Trespassing."

I have a little knowledge about what's going on. Knowledge

is power and a lot of people don't have that. That's why I wanted to share it. I should have had one thousand people here in total in two days.

The ones that did come, they were there but they wasn't really there. I kind of pressured them to come. You know: "Come on, come, please!" It's a good cause but I don't think the fight's going to build the momentum that the people really want. It's like the 99 percent crew, when they did all of that, at the time they caused a lot of ruckus, got a lot of media coverage. But it was defused. Everybody went back to their respective places. All they have are memories. "Oh man, I was a part of that crew, I was at city hall— I was!" But overall we lost. Bloomberg, he's a strategist, he says let them stay out there. He said the weather will soon get to them. People don't have the spirit that's really necessary to fight the powers that be and the system knows that. They're well aware of your spirit.

One girl at the meeting really stood out and she had the same situation I got. And so I'm telling her now, don't go into the courtroom without an attorney. Even as knowledgeable as I am about the situation, I don't go into court by myself because it's my personal issue and I could go in there and get choked up. You need someone there with you who can be objective and can speak for you and convey what you want to say. It's not to my advantage to go in there by myself. And I told my neighbor the same thing.

Toussaint brings to my attention a white piece of paper on the front of his refrigerator. Printed on the paper is a rudimentary table, off-centered and thrown together, and it looks to provide pricing for various items: $1,100 for bathroom tiles, $3,100 for kitchen appliances, $55,000 for a general contractor. The total at the bottom of the table is $69,400.

The landlord gave me that paper a few years ago. He told me that's what it would cost to renovate my whole apartment. The contractor is charging him $55,000? I've seen the contractors he's got.

And if you'll notice, it's just a piece of paper. It has no name or nothing on there. 'Cause he don't want to stand behind that. He don't have his name on that piece of paper. He was smart. He knows what he's doing—$69,400, bro?

You times that by 2.5 percent, you get a rent increase number: $1,735. So I would be paying that amount in addition to the $800 I'm paying now. I'll be paying approximately $2500. Tripled.

A while back they offered me $30,000 to move out. Originally they offered me $20,000 to leave and I said to the property manager, "Get me thirty and then call me." So he went and came back and said, "I got thirty for you. I'm in Manhattan now. I'm coming back to Brooklyn and I'll have a certified check in my hand."

And when I hung up there was a lot of emotions going through me. Thirty thousand dollars is a lot of money but at the same time this is significant life change. This is a life metamorphosis. And this guy is saying I'll be in Brooklyn tomorrow, I'll bring you the check. He's telling me March 15, I want you out of there, broom swept. And mind you this is a week before March 15. And I'm thinking a week from now? Where am I going to go? I'm homeless. So I'm kind of having an anxiety attack. Ultimately I decided I don't want to. And I never signed anything.

This happened in the midst of all this with the cabinets. All at the same time. They probably think we've got him in court, maybe he'll take the $30,000 just so he don't have to go to court. So they're really blatant about their purpose, they're willing to give me $30,000 for something that doesn't even belong to me. That speaks volumes. That $30,000 is on the table right now. I can call the lawyer and she'll get it done. That's what's really unbelievable. Because in reality they know that these cabinets are not really going to ultimately be my eviction. If they really thought that they wouldn't be willing to give me $30,000.

Yesterday at the court building, when we were going down in the elevator, the landlord's attorney was still talking money. So I said, "Look, tell your client to give me one hundred grand and I'll be gone in two days." I told them my bottom line would be $80,000.

She said, "He's not going to do it."

And I said, "There's no sweat off my back and I'll stay."

It is imminent that I may take this money, but it's a matter of how much.

If we let history be our guide we know that, ultimately, the landowners are going to win. I don't want to fool myself. You know they're winning this fight. In San Francisco, in Harlem. In cities all around the country. They're winning. They have the money. They have the tenacity. And you know, us being impoverished, what do we have? We have a voice. And I'm willing to fight that fight, but I can't even get a tenant association together.

I was even going as far as saying, we'll do a rent strike. I was reading online, people hold on to their money, as long as you don't spend it, or if you are concerned that you will spend it, then we'll put it in escrow until these landlords act. We'll go to court and he'll say you owe such and such amount of money, and you have it, and you'll pay it—it's not that you're not paying, you're withholding. And that will probably spur them into doing something for the tenants, like repairs. And my last and most extreme idea: I was going to do a hunger strike. I was going to stay in that lobby with a cardboard box and not eat anything and just have a box of water nearby.

This is a drastic situation. It requires revolutionary action. These landlords are not playing. They're taking extreme measures, as you can see, and we're not on our end. We have to fight fire with fire and we don't have money. All we have is our livelihoods and we have to put them on the line if we're going to make a significant impact. Other than that I don't see much changing for tenants in these gentrified neighborhoods. I don't think I can win. But if they offer more money I can say at least I got something out of it.

This might be a far-fetched idea but maybe some of us tenants, we need to become landlords ourselves. The last couple of weeks I've been looking at some properties, mainly in East New York and in the East Flatbush section. They have some really cheap properties. Banks got a bunch of houses in foreclosure and they want to dump them. They'll short sell all of them. So we should take advantage of these opportunities and start buying up some of these houses.

If the rent-stabilized tenants become landlords then maybe enough of us in the future can balance it. You know, me going through this situation, I can be more sympathetic towards tenants. I'd stick to my guns.

Now, it might be unrealistic because once tenants become landlords—*he laughs*—they might be as harsh as their landlords. But I'm not a money-hungry person. I'm not like that. If I have a property and the mortgage is being paid and the property taxes are being paid, I'm happy. I wouldn't charge you the market value of this apartment. Even if this apartment could go for $1,500 in Brooklyn. I'd say, "Yo, give me eleven hundred." I'd be willing to accept government programs, work with you. Maybe I'll be living in the basement but the tenants are paying my mortgage, I'm living rent-free. If I'm working I'll save my little money. I'm not trying to get rich. I know you're a struggling family, you don't have much, and maybe that can lead to a tenant thinking they can take advantage. So worst-case scenario I'll go through the eviction process. But I think more of us need to become property owners. I think that's really the solution as opposed to trying to fight the landlords.

So I'll be standing right next to my current landlord. How gratifying is that to be standing next to the guy who is trying to gentrify your home? I'll probably become his rival in the real estate market in New York.

He laughs.

I think that should be the ultimate goal. Instead of trying to bicker with somebody. Instead of fighting them, we'll become them. How do you say it? If you can't beat them, join them. And if we get in there, side by side with them, then we'll have a much more significant impact, like at rent guidelines meetings. You'll have landlord opposition to the injustices against tenants. How significant is that? That'll speak volumes.

That's really how I look at it.

I did tell someone recently that if I sell this place I would avoid coming through this block. I'd feel something. All my life I been here. I would feel some type of connection. I wouldn't look up because I'd be knowing that I sold out.

But that $100,000, that would even it out.

16.

*E*phraim sends a text message suggesting we meet at "17 Irving." I look up the address on Google Maps to get the cross streets and I see that there is actually a coffee shop bearing the name of the address just east of Union Square Park in Manhattan. I arrive ten minutes early and order a coffee, so that I can stake claim to one of the tables, for which there is fierce competition. Ten minutes goes by, then half an hour, and I try calling Ephraim. He doesn't answer but texts back that he's outside the building. I tell him I've got a table inside. This confuses him, which leads to a frantic series of texts over the next ninety seconds, at which point I realize that the 17 Irving Ephraim has in mind is an address in Bushwick, Brooklyn. Of course. Google has yet to learn that Manhattan is not the default—and I didn't question its assumption.

I bolt out the door, and as I go over the Manhattan Bridge on the subway, Ephraim texts me again saying he had to leave that building. Now he's at another building and he sends along that address. This happens a couple of times as I explore various subway connections, until I'm finally in the right place at the right time—and at a familiar address: I see Ephraim sitting in his car, which is parked in the long driveway of one mTkalla Keaton, also known as Martin, also known as TK. I walk around to the driver's side window, which is down. Ephraim is on the phone but interrupts his call briefly and asks me:

You don't care about the smoking, do you?

I note that he is not, in fact, smoking and tell him I don't have a problem with it.

Good, get in.

I hop over to the passenger seat and Ephraim turns the car on. As we pull into the street, the phone conversation plays out over the speaker system so I can hear mTkalla's voice on the other end. Ephraim is getting mTkalla—he calls him Martin—prices from his floor guy. The connection is inconsistent and they keep talking over each other in fragmented sentences. They give up and a few moments pass while Ephraim looks to be contemplating his next call, his finger hovering just over his dash-mounted smartphone. Suddenly he asks:

So what do you need from me?

Caught off guard, I stammer through a request to hear what it's like to be a landlord in so many evolving Brooklyn neighborhoods. Ephraim nods and stares out the window, as if he lacks the will or energy to answer such a broad question. So I keep talking. I ask about his family. His father fled Iran during the Islamic Revolution and moved to Israel where he met Ephraim's mother, who had arrived around the same time from Russia. The two married and moved their young family to the United States when Ephraim was four or five—he doesn't remember, exactly, or maybe he doesn't want to remember. Ephraim, a Hasid, is reluctant to get specific about his age.

That's classified.

He makes me guess. I throw out thirty-eight—admitting that I always get these things wrong, knowing privately I always guess low for fear of offending the aged—and he tells me I'm close. Still he won't tell me a number, and now he's got a mischievous grin. He wants me to keep guessing. So I start listing numbers until, finally, he nods at twenty-six, which is not at all close to thirty-eight. I was way off—I think most people would be, and I think he likes it that way. Perhaps it is the thick beard or his heavyset frame but something about the man makes him seem much older than he is. Most of all, it must be his demeanor—he is cool and reserved and circumspect, which automatically

*earns him authority beyond his age and his experience. He only started
buying buildings a few years ago.*

After the mortgage crisis we went into investing in property.
We started out small, me and my business partner. There is a certain—*he pauses, awkwardly*—I can explain to you a little of how it
works on the insides but—

*And here he short-circuits and stops talking altogether. He sighs
and asks me if I'll be revealing his name when I write about him. I say
yes and he sighs again, tilting his head to one side. If he's going to talk
frankly, he says, he doesn't want his name to be used. We settle on a
pseudonym and he continues, reluctantly:*

Do you know anything about property? There's a deed and
there's a note.

Like with a car, if you have a lease, the title is in your name
but you don't actually own the car. The deed to the house is the
same thing. If you have a mortgage, the actual thing, the house, is
the bank's. So they have a note, and they can transfer it to other
banks, they can sell it to big companies, they can make packages
of notes. You still own the deed—that's yours. And if the bank
wants to take it from you, they have to go through the process of
foreclosure. If the house has a small mortgage, that's fine—you
can sell the deed—but if the house is underwater you can't really
do anything with the deed.

So we came up with the idea: the bank takes a long time before they take the property away. It can take them up to five, six
years, and we know how to push them as much as possible. So
we go to the owner, buy from him the deed, which means ownership—it's our property, even if it has a mortgage it's our property—and then we rent it out and we get the rent until the bank
finally takes it away.

It's not 100 percent—I mean, it's legal but sometimes in the
mortgage there's a clause that says if you sell the deed you have
to notify the bank and if you don't notify the bank they can take
the property. But even if you didn't notify them, the bank has to

go through the whole process of getting the property and that takes some time.

And the banks don't care. They actually like when people take care of the building. Because it will actually cost them $100,000 a year—people breaking in, pipes busted. As long as everything is good, everything running, they just leave it alone until they're taking it.

People that have small mortgages they're going to want a lot more for their deed, to give over ownership. But if they have a $500,000 mortgage and the house is worth $100,000, they're broke, they don't have money, they have no job, they don't have nothing, and they can't even pay the mortgage. A person that sells a deed with a big mortgage usually wants to get $5,000. They don't care. They'd didn't pay the mortgage for, like, two years—the property's shit. So we would give them $5,000, $10,000, and they give us the deed. They know the bank is going to take it so they don't care. They move out and we can do whatever we want.

We started out with this, buying over one hundred deeds, all over the place, and we collected the rent. So when the market went up a little bit, about 10 percent of the mortgages were almost at market value so we'd pay them off and keep the building. If it's a big mortgage, I don't have any choice, I just sit until the bank takes it away. I'm just sitting, collecting rent. And that's it.

I used to love it. But the bad part was, come Monday, I used to go to the buildings in my car, and knock on every single door. This was like five years ago. And they didn't give me payment. One out of ten, one out of twenty, maybe. And they were yelling at me, "You fucking Jew! Leave me alone!"

I got used to it. And I understand it. Not all Jewish people are nice people. Every tree has a bad apple. Some of them are really nasty and can trick their tenants. But some of the tenants put up such a fight that you have to trick them. I used to do that—but I don't do that any more. I did that once four years ago. I told someone, "I'm going to give you twenty grand to move—just move out first, and then I'll give you the money." And then I screwed them. It was only a tenant who didn't deserve the money. They wanted $150,000 and it didn't make sense. They're using drugs in the house, and doing all kinds of nasty things, prostitution and stuff. I had no choice, I had to trick them. I gave him something but not the money I told him. And he couldn't come back to me because he wasn't even legally supposed to live there.

Some Jewish people they're going to come in and they're going to try to rip off the black tenants—and the tenants know it, there's word of mouth. So it's like, "Oh a Jewish guy again?" There's a lot of Jewish guys moving around. Like a lot, a lot, a lot of investors who are either Hasidic Jews or a little bit less, but they're Jewish. They're holding Bed-Stuy like this—*he squeezes at the air in front of him, strangling it.* So sometimes it's like—*he taps his chest*—"Hello, this was our neighborhood. What are you doing here?"

Eventually I was burned out, so I couldn't do it anymore. It was just way too much insult. I got a different guy, a bishop guy, he actually knew the community so I had him go around with me. When I started getting busier I let him go alone but, eh, no results. Because you have to really work.

So this is actually how we got a big portion of our properties, from grinding, grinding, grinding. Really hard. Every single dollar we earned with sweat. It wasn't easy.

We did it alone. When we started I could have gotten a deed for a grand. They were like, "Take it, I don't want it, take it for free, just make sure you maintain it." It was nothing. And I got 'em and got 'em and got 'em. All of a sudden people—my friends or people that used to give me deeds—they started to say, "Hey, what's this guy doing?" They started looking into it and they wanted fifty grand for nothing. It became more expensive.

And some other Jewish people started. We have Jewish heads, so sometimes those things catch. The black people, even the white, sometimes they don't make the connection. We're always jumping, not all, but some of us have jumpy heads. So we're trying to get an edge.

Now buying the deeds is a new thing with lawyers getting into it. Lawyers take over the deed and they start fighting the bank. And the loan wasn't done right and they're hoping after a while the bank's just going to say, "You know what? Fine, leave me alone, just give me something small and you save the property."

We started in East New York but we sold everything we had. We didn't want to be there. First of all, I'm really not a racist. I love black people, most of my contractors are black. But East New York is mostly, people who are—you know the "47 percent" that Romney got kicked for? This is the real truth—the 47 percent is a real thing. I don't know why he got kicked for that. This is hitting it on the nail. This is what happens in East New York. Most of them are either Section 8, other government programs. So most of it is programs, and even the person that pays with cash is too much headaches. They're not paying, they're yelling at you for every simple thing.

When I rent a house here in Bushwick, I come in to collect rent, the first thing they say is, "Can I offer you a glass of water?" Or, "Sit down on the couch." When I used to go collect in East New York, they didn't answer the door or when they answered they started yelling, or the dogs were coming out. It was just a whole mess. It wasn't worth it. Because the profit was very low. Fifty or 40 percent of them, we had in court. And when the court process finishes in five or six months they just leave. They go from one house to the other house and they just try to suck up everything.

I couldn't even sleep. They used to call me at twelve o'clock at night for cockroaches on the floor. It was really, really low class. Very low class. So we sold everything over there and we came out all the way to Park Slope. Then we started backing up, backing up, slowly, all the way to Bushwick. This is one of the houses we're finishing now.

We pull up in front of a three-story brick building. Having shed the deed-buying business, Ephraim's now involved with acquisitions and development. And he prefers to hold and rent buildings as opposed to renovating and flipping them. mTkalla calls back to continue the conversation about his floors. Just as they start haggling over numbers, mTkalla gets a call on his other line so Ephraim hangs up and continues:

It's mixed in Bushwick. But the black people that are here, if they didn't get bought out it means that they're upper class. I can't explain it to you without sounding like a racist. But there's a big difference between black and black. Like Martin is upper class. He's a classy black guy. He's not from the 'hood. He's not going to—he's a normal guy. You can talk to them. You can have a conversation with them. But the people over there in East New York, it's like everyone is trying to rip you off, everyone is trying to get away with something.

Another call comes in and a voice asks if Ephraim if he can spare two minutes. Ephraim balks—Two minutes? Okay—drawing out the last word as if to say you can't actually mean 120 seconds, can you? The rest of the exchange takes about half that time and Ephraim continues:

I have a serious ill-condition: I rarely can sit and look at the sky. I'm always jumping; I always want to do things. I'm out in the morning and when Saturday comes and I can't touch my phone and I can't do work, sometimes I get very jumpy. I have so many things going into my head. When I'm talking to you I have things running into my head! I have to! Because there's so many things I have to do. It's like I have maybe a million gigs, but my head's full all the time so I have to delete, delete, delete just to make new memory.

We had one property on 64 Hancock and we bought it almost

three years ago. It's a beautiful, nice brownstone. Today you could sell it probably for $2 million, or $2.5. But when we bought it, it was probably $800–$900,000. And the mortgage was probably only like a million, 1.1. But it was SRO tenants and that's a whole—I don't know if you even know the shit we go through with those tenants. They fight, they fight, they fight and then the bank took it away like a week ago. And that was the only one that we lost. I never lost any property, I never lost in the real estate market. This is the first loss I've had.

SROs are unreasonable. The problem is the people that make $5,000 a week pay $400 in rent. It just does not make sense to me at all. I mean if you make $500 a week: okay, fine, I understand. If you make two, three grand a month and have two, three kids, I understand. But if someone that makes that much money can just live off of you without . . .

And if you have a building that's rent stabilized, it's messed up: I have a building down on Dean Street, it's almost a $3 million building and my tenants live over there like animals. Sometimes they rent it out to someone else and we can't do shit because you're allowed to have a roommate. That's the part that bothers me the most. They pay $250 in rent when I could get $2,500 or $3,000 for that apartment. I offered them $100,000 to leave and they said no, they want $500,000. And when you go to court with one of them, or you start messing with any of them—oh, god forbid. They start new lawsuits. If I buy a building today and it's rent stabilized, I could all of a sudden find myself in a lawsuit for a million dollars. Why? Because the old landlord overcharged the tenant, let's say, $100 or $200 dollars a month. Now he comes back and sues me for all the rent the owner used to take. That's why we don't usually buy buildings with tenants because if you do you have to go talk to them. They actually bring down the value of the property almost 60 or 70 percent.

If there are rules, I understand. Someone doesn't make money, or they've lived over there for five generations and he wants to stay—that's okay. No problem, that makes sense to me. But if you make so much money—I had someone who was an airline pilot! He was making $200,000 a year, and he wasn't even living there. And I tried to explain it to a judge. It took me a year.

Ephraim stops the car in the middle of a residential block to roll down his window and light a cigarette. The street is lined with brownstones, most of which are in various stages of destruction and recreation, rented Dumpsters stuffed with shards of demolition and pallets of new Sheetrock passing by. Smoke shoots out of Ephraim's nostrils. There is a young Hasidic man standing across the street. He and Ephraim make eye contact: Ephraim waves casually, if not reluctantly, prompting the young man to cross the street with inordinate enthusiasm in his step. He stands just outside the car, slouched over with his hand resting on Ephraim's car door. A long silence follows then finally:

Ephraim: Everything okay? You haven't gotten me anything yet.

Young Man: I'm still stretching—it's early.

Ephraim: Bring me something. You have my number, right?

Young Man: Yeah. *(Pause.)* You don't have anything for me?

Ephraim: No. What do you need?

Young Man: Multi-families.

Ephraim: Ay—you do multi-families? I thought you were selling multi-families.

Young Man: No, I'm buying also.

Ephraim: No. No, I don't have anything. For now.

Young Man: You don't have anything, huh?

Ephraim: No.

More silence while Ephraim makes a point of his disinterest, playing with his phone. Then:

Ephraim: If I have something, I have your number.

Young Man: Okay.

Ephraim tosses what's left of his cigarette and moves his hand toward the button to roll up the window. The glass emerges from the door with an electric hum and the young man takes his hand away. Apparently everyone's buying.

They're like the new kids coming in.

He laughs.

He breaks for a few more phone calls—many are carried out in Hebrew, though the profession-specific words seem to be stuck in English: brownstone, skim coating, Prospect Park. There are a couple of minutes of silence in which Ephraim first seems as though he's contemplating his next call but soon I realize he's just fiddling with his phone. I ask him what the first thing is that he considers when deciding whether or not to buy any given building.

We're small, a couple properties here, a couple properties there. We don't do mega, mega, mega buildings. So we look into places that haven't caught on—we just did a place on Nostrand Avenue. People are not even there yet. We put in $600,000 and everyone was laughing at us. "It's crazy, you're over there. A building for yuppies, white people? It's not going to work." The building was full of tenants—$1,300, $1,400 tenants. We paid every tenant the average of twelve, thirteen thousand dollars to leave. I actually went to meet them—lawyers are not going to help you. And we got them out of the building and now we have tenants paying $2,700, $2,800, and they're all white. So this is what we do.

My saying is—again I'm not racist—every black person has a price. The average price for a black person here in Bed-Stuy is $30,000 dollars. Up over there in East New York, it's $10,000 dollars. Everyone wants them to leave, not because we don't like them, it's just they're messing up—they bring everything down. Not all of them.

Most of them don't believe you at first. Oh, you Jewish people you're a bunch of thieves you're never going to give me my money. But once you start actually having a base of people who know you, who you actually gave the money, it's better. Sometimes it's really tricky because you'll have one person willing to leave for

$2,000 and another wants $20,000. And the second this guy finds out that guy is getting twenty he says, "Hell no, I'm not leaving. I want twenty, too."

They don't know—*here he lowers his voice*—that even if they get the money and they left, they could always come back. They don't know that part. And it's so scary sometimes because they could come up in the middle of construction and say, "It's my property, I didn't understand what I was signing, and I want to come back."

But they don't know that—their brain doesn't work that way. But some blacks have an attorney and everything. So I try to make them happy, even if they're going to go for $7,000 or $8,000, I'd rather give them an extra grand so they're happy and they're not going to think about it too much.

Again, I don't want to be a racist, but when I have a building—I can't even say it because it's not going to sound right.

He lowers his voice again:

If there's a black tenant in the house—in every building we have, I put in white tenants. They want to know if black people are going to be living there. So sometimes we have ten apartments and everything is white, and then all the sudden one tenant comes in with one black roommate, and they don't like it. They see black people and get all riled up, they call me: "We're not paying that much money to have black people live in the building." If it's white tenants only, it's clean. I know it's a little bit racist but it's not. They're the ones that are paying and I have to give them what they want. Or I'm not going to get the tenants and the money is not going to be what it is.

The scary part about doing this is if they start realizing, if the black guys start to realize how much the property will sell for. This is a new thing now, the past year. A million, two million dollars—it's crazy, crazy numbers. None of them realize yet—some of them do—the amount of money you can get. The scary part is they're going to realize they can get the same exact house in East New

York for $400,000, $500,000 and they can get paid $1.5 million for their home in Bed-Stuy, they're going to start dumping houses on the market and the market's going to be flooded and it's going to cool down. It's already cooling down.

While Ephraim has shown that he does not let tenants disrupt his business model, sometimes there are other considerations—things more important than the drive to maximize a building's capitalization:

It's so hard to get empty buildings. When you have an empty building it's like gold. So we never flip buildings. One building we sold because in the Jewish religion there's a weird thing where you don't cut down a fruit tree. Some people really don't give a shit about fruit trees. But most of the Hasidic Jewish people will not cut down a fruit tree. There's one house in Borough Park where they cut down a fruit tree and there was nine fires over there in the last two years. Sometimes weird stuff happens. So we had a building, and the only way it's working for us is if the fruit tree comes down. We spent $50,000 doing the plans and then found out there's a fruit tree. We didn't know about it. So we had to sell the building. It's the only way I'm going to sell a building. A building is not really a selling thing. Buildings are for keeping.

In Ephraim's world of landownership and land development, buildings, ironically, do not always have a price tag but the people who live in them do.

I live in Borough Park. I have three kids and one on the way. I don't even have a house there. I rent. It's weird. It's just so comfortable to have a landlord. Something's wrong, come fix it. No one understands it. My wife doesn't understand it. Every once in a while she wants to see the properties I'm building, and she's like, "I wish I could live here, I wish I could live here."

I'm always thinking about buying but it's so expensive. You pay for a simple house, 1.1, 1.2, and for me it's so hard because I'd rather take that money and get a building and get $10,000 rent a month. It's not greedy. I'm a simple man; my car's not—it's a normal car. For the money I make, I could have a Porsche, a Lamborghini, driving around all day and I'm not even going to feel it. But I don't want people to look. I was going to try to get the Audi, I don't know if you know the Audi S? Nice big aluminum. I like speed, I like feeling the rush, I want to go fast, but I couldn't buy it because then people are going to look at it, and the attention—we're very simple. Everything we do is simple.

17.

At any given moment on the streets of Bushwick, you might find Ephraim's Nissan sedan zipping through the intersection, or Quang Bao emerging from a noodle factory–cum-artist studio, or, as it happens, a sixty-seven-year-old man walking to the subway, his steps fast and quiet. His name is William Hernandez and he is whistling; it's a rich sound but soft, too, so it stays close to his chest. He grew up in Puerto Rico on a mountaintop farm. His grandfather owned one hundred acres and William worked the coffee bean and sugar cane fields.

He has a compact frame and a shiny, bald head; he smiles even when his face is in the resting position, and that smile is framed perfectly by his close-cropped, gray mustache. William is retired now, living on a fixed income in Bushwick for the last fifteen years. He has moved four times within the neighborhood, always in pursuit of lower rent.

Bushwick is the second half of his New York existence.

He climbs the stairs to the subway tracks hovering over Myrtle Avenue, catching a ride to the Lower East Side—the first half.

I came from Puerto Rico in '81. I was trying to look for a job over here. I had a brother who used to work in two apartment buildings. He called me and he say, "William, I have a job for you." So I came and he was happy because he was by himself here and wanted to have somebody. Because you can be with whomever in the world but you miss your family and you want your family to be close to you.

Nearly every day, William waits for his daughter, Nanette, outside of Amalgamated Dwellings, the Lower East Side apartment building where she lives with her mother. It is the same apartment building where William lived until he divorced Nanette's mother in the '90s, and the same building where he worked for thirty-four years. The building originally housed Amalgamated Clothing Workers, one of the first unions to organize and sponsor building cooperatives—co-ops— through which all occupants could own shares in a newly established corporation, which acted as owner of the actual structure. That first generation of cooperators—"Pioneer Cooperators," as they pre- ferred—worked on community development beyond housing with edu- cational and cultural programs.

Today Amalgamated Dwellings is noticeably diverse—the ortho- dox Jewish community is strong but shrinking (though the bike rack is still removed every year to put up a walled structure covered with s'chach for Sukkot), and there are many recent arrivals, working pro- fessionals with infants and toddlers. Notices of sitting shiva are often followed by open house flyers a few weeks later. Pioneers often bought apartments for less than $10,000, and their mourning families sell them for upwards of $650,000.

On the other side of the Williamsburg Bridge are the Baruch Houses, a sprawling public housing development with 2,194 apart- ments spread out across seventeen brick towers.

Amalgamated is a brick, Art Deco–style building, only 6 stories tall, with 230 units that wrap around a courtyard with a fountain in the middle. Approximately four months out of the year the fountain, which is swimming pool blue, shoots water into the air under a cloudless sky; the rest of the year it is dry as a bone and stained with dead leaves. One feels cold just looking at it.

After he and his wife separated, William couldn't afford to live in the building—or the neighborhood. He moved around for a bit before settling in Bushwick. His bed and belongings are kept in Brooklyn but the rest of his life remains on the Lower East Side. "You want your family to be close to you," he says. Nanette is due home from school within the hour.

The guys at Zafis, the luncheonette next to Amalgamated, still recognize William when he walks through the door. He sits across the booth from me and checks his phone to see if Nanette has called. He tells me about her high school graduation and college applications and chemical engineering aspirations and with each ascent his smile expands. He drinks black coffee and speaks like he whistles, in a soft but rich voice:

Maybe in the beginning I didn't know English. I had English teachers before but I never went to their classes because I never needed it before. It's funny at those early ages we don't see the importance of a second language. But I studied when I came to New York and I got to speak a little bit, learning from tenants. So I catch the language a little bit, which I like now—I have a great respect for the language.

When I came to New York I started to work as a porter, cleaning the buildings and doing snow detail, maintenance. That was the way of the job, which I like very much. You know one thing, when you live in a farm, you spend all day in the farm and the labor, it never ends. And here I get to put in my eight hours and then I go home and I forget about it. That's what I think I like. Also I was working with people from different countries, and it's nice because you learn more about all the people's culture.

I used to get offers for other jobs. But I was making more here. For me I don't care if you going to have a nice job and you're going to be well dressed in the office. They're paying me more here. I'd rather be cleaning where I'm making more for the family.

When I come to New York, I put in an application to live in the city projects on Jackson Street and Madison Street over here. What happened was that in the beginning it was only me working but when my wife started to work the rent went up. In the city projects the rent's according to the income. So I decided to put in an application over here—*pointing at Amalgamated Dwellings*—where I used to live. So we put in the application and got the apartment. We were renters but then we become shareholders of the co-op. We were very happy with this. My wife went to work and my kids stayed here. They loved this site. My kids tell me, "Hey Papi, we like it over here."

I went to Brooklyn but I still like it over here. I have been all over. I have been in the Bronx, I have been in Brooklyn, but nothing compare like this community for me. I think it's good. This is good neighborhood for me. My family, they are happy over here.

At the beginning this neighborhood was nice and it's only better now. We have different peoples. When you have only one race, you don't feel comfortable with these different people, but when you see people from around the world you say we are human beings, we can get along. It's more kind. More comfortable. I think it's nice. When I used to live in the city projects and we have all kinds of people, we all different. We have French. We have American, we have smart people, English, Russian, Polish, and we used to get along like brothers and sisters and we used to visit each other and say, "Hey, come over to my house and have a cup of coffee." And we used to get to know each other. I like that, I feel much better.

There is perception that it has been not safe over here but for me that's nonsense. I think safety is the same. That hasn't changed anything. Since I came here I used to like to walk at night and any time I can walk in this neighborhood. You always have a group of people, they may be a little bit, you know, not good, let's say, but they don't mess with the people in the neighborhood. I think they go someplace else. They go out of the neighborhood, maybe to Brooklyn. And those from over there come here. So when something happens I don't think it's from this neighborhood. It could happen—anything could happen—but for me this is a nice place. And that's why my kids like it over here.

But there is one different feeling: people used to have better communication with each other. Now we live in a different world with these cell phones. Everybody is busy talking to somebody. And sometimes they're talking and you think they are talking to you and you say, "What did you say?"

And they say, "No, I'm not talking to you."

And you don't know! Everyone is busy in their own way. And I'm not used to that. But a little bit we get used to it and it will be a part of the society more and more. Even with the family members. Now it's a different world like with the cell phones.

Just then his phone rings—I think it's my daughter—*and he takes the call. But the connection is bad and the call ends.*

She'll call back. Now I see the grown people now—*his phone rings again*—this is my daughter.

He picks up and tells her he's at Zafis. He hangs up and continues unfazed:

When I came over here, it was mostly moved-in old people, maybe they were born here. There were only a few young people here. Now we have young people here because the old persons pass away and they sell the apartment. And we have young people and if they have the money, they have the apartment right here. People like cash money. It's good for the people that have the money.

In Brooklyn it's becoming like the Lower East Side.

Where I live now, before it was only Hispanic and Black American and Arab and Hindus but now we have many, let's say, white people coming to the neighborhood. They're building houses, they're fixing things. They buy lots of stuff. They looking for apartments. They come and they talk to you and ask questions and they want some information about the houses. And you see this now: when the rents go up, the family moves two family in one apartment—they could be friends or brothers or family. I'm thinking maybe that this happen in the entire city. As rents go up and up, sometimes salary stays the same. I think that rent should be less or the salaries should be more. Rent is expensive. Clothes is expensive. If you go to a supermarket now, things are so expensive. So that in a few years maybe it's too expensive. When I came here I wasn't making that much money, but the money I got I used to pay rent, buy food and clothes, and it was okay. In my last year that I worked, even though I was making much much money, I was doing worse because things are going up.

The rich is becoming more rich and the poor people more poor, and something that I've been saying to myself: "How does my son, or my daughter—how going to be their future? How will they pay their rent? How are they going to eat?" It's so expensive. And I'm worried now. I've been asking myself this question: "Oh man, what's going to happen with the family?"

The future is insecure.

I have a little house over there in Puerto Rico. I have five acres of land. I could go over there, and I live myself many nights, quiet nights. But I like to be with the neighborhood. I play guitar a little bit, I have a few friends and we get together and we go places. I like to see many people, that's why I'm here. I was trying to live in the New Brunswick, New Jersey, and it was too quiet. I like to be in the noisy places. I like to be in a place with a lot of people, many people who are different than me—I feel good when I see that. I have family here, and they like it over here and I cannot leave my family by themselves. Especially my daughter, she's very close to me, she say, "Papi, I love you but are you going to move back to Puerto Rico?"

And I say, "No, no, no, no, I'm going to stay over here until the end. Until, I don't know—"

Just then Nanette walks in and takes the empty seat next to her father. He squeezes her and her smile is almost as big as Papi's.

18.

*T*he influx of capital into William Hernandez's old neighborhood has marched west, to the Bowery, a neighborhood anchored by the street with the same name that was known throughout the twentieth century for flophouses and shelters. The Bowery Mission at 227 and the Salvation Army at 229 have operated in adjoining buildings for over one hundred years. In the 1970s they began sharing the street with a few commercial enclaves—mostly lighting and wholesale restaurant supply shops—and with the city's music scene. Punk and new wave found their epicenter at 315 Bowery, at a club called Country Bluegrass Blues and Other Music for Uplifting Gormandizers, better known as CBGB & OMFUG, still even better known simply as CBGB.

CBGB is now a retail spot for the clothing designer John Varvatos (vintage music posters on the wall; $1,298 leather vests on offer) and in either direction, the street is crowded with restaurants, bars, and—increasingly—high-end boutique hotels. Polished, black SUVs idle outside shops and restaurants, ready at a moment's notice. The Sunshine Hotel, which used to rent ten dollar rooms with ceilings made of chicken wire, has been replaced on the ground floor by the Bowery Diner, which serves grilled branzino with ratatouille and tapenade for thirty dollars a plate (no substitutions).

But still the Bowery Mission, which anchors the drag, bursts with *homeless New Yorkers. The sidewalk in front of the building serves as a gathering spot for men who are freshly showered, rested, and fed— and more men seeking the same.*

The New Museum of Contemporary Art, the Mission's neighbor to the north, inhabits a much newer building that was opened in 2005 and was funded by a Carnegie Corporation grant made possible by Michael Bloomberg. It has seven stories that look like six differently-sized steel blocks casually stacked atop one another. The museum is instantly captivating—and radically incongruous. It has nothing in common with the brick facade and stained glass windows of the Bowery Mission.

The Mission facilities require twenty-four-hour staffing and Matt Krivich is the director of operations. At forty he remains bright-eyed and approachable. His smile is boyish, and the earnest tone in his voice transports me to a black-and-white television show.

He greets me at the building's reception desk. As we walk back to the dining hall, nearly everyone we pass knows Matt, and many have a question to ask or a message to give—someone is always vying for his attention. We sit at a table, and men come and go—an ongoing series of fleeting conversations, most of which prompt Matt to jot down reminders to himself.

I grew up in Ohio, just outside of Cleveland. Had a great upper-middle-class life, had everything I wanted, probably spoiled. But because of a situation in my family—the family unit broke up. I was young, probably about twelve or thirteen, I was very angry. I became rebellious, met new friends who were also angry and rebellious, maybe didn't have both their parents in the household, maybe weren't going to the right schools. We rebelled together and I started a fourteen-year drug addiction.

It started off very innocent, I thought, just weekends with LSD. But then it gradually built up. When I last stopped using I was addicted to heroin. I was homeless. I was in trouble with the law, with various agencies, and at what I thought was the end of my life. I attempted suicide. I wanted to pass. I wanted to be away from this life, away from that pain. I wanted to get rid of myself.

And there had been a pastor who found me on the street through a family connection, and he looked me in the eyes and didn't judge me, didn't see me as I was, as I saw myself, and told me that he cared for me and wanted to help me if I was ready. It was one of the first times I really saw pure, honest love. It made a lasting imprint on my mind, on my heart. In a sense, I'd never felt that before.

Momentarily I was able to embrace it. He wanted to send me to rehab in Fort Meyers, Florida. But he gave me the money instead of buying me the ticket so I went and used that money to purchase heroin. Ended up back in the streets. The next three months were probably twice as hard. I think I was carrying a little guilt but I also think there was a reason all the doors were shutting around me. It was either death or life and I had to make a decision quickly. And he found me again in the streets. He looked me straight in the face and he laughed and he said, "Matthew, you schooled me but I'm going to help you again. This time I'm going to buy you a ticket. And I'm going to put you on that bus and pray for you and I'll wave as you're going down the interstate."

And it was the beginning of my life being transformed.

I had an amazing experience in Fort Meyers. I spent a year down there. I didn't know where I wanted to go but I knew I didn't want to go back to Ohio because that's where things had fallen apart and I felt that if I went back there it would be too hard or it would be too sad for me. I checked a number of places and the only opportunity for me was an interview here at the Bowery Mission. A friend of mine bought me a one-way ticket to New York City. I had a place to stay for about five days in Garrison, upstate. So I came to the Mission and at the end of the six-hour interview the director said, "We'd love to have you here. When can you start?" And that was great news because if I didn't have an opportunity I'd have to find a new place to stay in two days. So that's when I started my internship at the Bowery Mission.

And slowly, gradually, as I've been here over eleven years now,

I've learned more about the Mission and the ministry in New York City and I've been given the opportunity to take on additional roles.

Every aspect of the Bowery Mission, in one way or another, seems to fall under Matt's domain—or perhaps it's more that he seems willing to take up just about any responsibility in the name of the Mission. He oversees the kitchen, which serves three meals a day, every day of the year, through hurricanes and blackouts. He also oversees the endless maintenance required by a building constructed in 1876, in use twenty-four hours a day.

Matt is usually on the premises for most of those twenty-four-hour cycles—he lives in staff quarters on the property. After ten years alone in the city, he recently married. He and his wife are hopeful children will be in their future.

I think it's a good example and a good testimony for the men that are in the program to see a healthy family. I want my wife and I to have a healthy relationship but it's also for the men to see. It's a continuation of my testimony to them.

I usually start work before seven. I do my rounds throughout the building.

I want to start work before anyone else is really moving so if there's any issues or anything that needs to be addressed I can get ahead of the day a little bit. There have been fights. There have been days when I woke up and we've had people that came at the end of their day and they're cold and in the morning they don't wake up. So we've had people pass here.

You know, I used to come to New York from Ohio for things that weren't very productive—and you think of Times Square, you think of Wall Street but you don't really think of the Christian community. There's a deep, deep feeling of support in the Christian body here. But also the need is so great in New York City. There are so many opportunities to serve and I can't imagine myself anywhere else.

We've got great relationships with this community. We've got

a great relationship with the community board. Amazing relationships with the fifth precinct. If we have an issue here and have to
call 911, they're sensitive to the situation. They're sensitive to who
we're serving here, but also they want to help the person.

My first winter here we had probably 165 men sleeping in our
chapel and it's a small space for 165 men. The fire department
came in and I was the only staff member on duty and they looked
in the chapel and the captain turns around, he closes his eyes, and
he says just make sure there's a clear egress. He could have easily
said you know this isn't good, we've got to count the people and
then three people have to leave. But they understand.

We've got great relationships with the city agencies. We work
with the mayor's office on a regular basis, various projects. Our
first big project was through the mayor's office, they painted our
roof white. It keeps the building cooler and helps us save on elec-
trical costs—heating and cooling bills. All these relationships are
what help us do what we do on a daily basis.

Over the last couple of years the neighborhood's been changing a lot. You know, initially, we weren't quite sure how that was
going to look. What's it going to look like when we have a museum next door? What's it going to look like when there's a Whole
Foods on the block? When they start building condos and we have
a whole influx of community that don't know the Mission, that
don't know the history. But what we realized quickly is that it's
an opportunity to share what we do here and an opportunity to
share that we can't do it alone.

We've been able to place a number of our men at Whole
Foods. There's a local company that's just recently started called
Heart of Tea and they've employed two of our men full time and
one of our men part time. I mean our guys are not always the eas-
iest to employ because they've got job activity for a couple years
and then there's a five-year gap and then you've got job activity
for six months, and then another gap. So it's hard to explain that
sometimes. But if the employer knows who we are, they know the

staff, they know our programs, they've served our men, they're more willing to take that chance because they understand.

The museum next door, they've been supporters as well. They've allowed us to use some of their space for one of our events before. They're currently working with some of our guys. There's an artist who has a project next door and they've invited our guys in to work with them, learn about art, learn about photography, film, and then they're also receiving a stipend.

In the last five years I've seen a drastic change in the rise of homelessness in New York City. I think the latest statistics, and these are statistics put out by the mayor's office, were over fifty-three thousand people in New York City are homeless. Of that fifty-three thousand around twenty to twenty-two thousand of those are children. And this number is a low number because they're counting people that are easy to count: people in beds when they do a roll call. But they're missing people who are in the subways; they're missing people who are in the tunnels. I know men who come here every day, who live in the tunnels. They're missing the people who are doubled up, tripled up, quadrupled up, fifteen people in a small apartment. They're missing a lot of people who are couch surfing and almost invisible. New York City is so energetic and there's so much going on it's sometimes easy to forget about that guy who's on the sidewalk. Or forget about the guy that's in the park.

For us the need has been growing. Since Hurricane Sandy we've seen a drastic rise in the number of people coming for food and shelter. And that's put a little bit of a challenge on the Mission because this building wasn't built to do what we do. So we're sort of busting at the seams. It works but it puts a challenge on our staff and it puts a challenge on the building itself.

Matt suggests I take a tour and gets up from the table. Just as he does there is a man behind him. He is wearing a blue jacket with shiny gold buttons, and he whispers something into Matt's ear. Matt asks me for a minute and the two of them step away for five. Lunchtime is ap-

proaching and the dining hall is abuzz. A dozen or so volunteers from Kentucky bring out stacks of plates—almost all of them are in New York for the first time and they have come to serve.

Matt returns and apologizes because he needs to attend to timely matters. He has brought along a coworker, Julian Padarath, to give me a tour of the building. Julian has a portly frame and smiles immediately. We shake hands. Matt apologizes again and disappears around a corner with a cluster of people trailing him—one of them is the man in the blue jacket, out of place with those shiny buttons.

Julian leads me down to the basement and we enter a room filled with boxes and shelves and racks of clothes. It is Tuesday, which means that after lunch, approximately 150 men will take a shower and then come down to this room—"Blessingdales" to those who know it best— and pick out the clothes they need. If they have an interview they get a suit. In his three years at the Bowery, Julian has noticed a change in the clothing donations that come in:

Now with all the artists and the gentrification and the museum, it's like a trendy hip place to live. With the neighborhood getting better, the donations get better. We're getting Armani suits and Versace—it's crazy.

Julian is in charge of requesting, receiving, and storing all in-kind donations—two thousand pounds of bread a day and beyond. Originally he worked in finance. In 2007, his company relocated to California, and Julian was asked to make the move but opted to stay in New York with his girlfriend. He was happy and in love and worked in finance, so jobs were not hard to come by. Then the financial system crashed and Julian couldn't find a job; his savings ran out, his engagement ended, and, eventually, he needed a place to live. Friends suggested the Bowery.

I worked fourteen years in corporate finance and I get more gratification since I've started working here. I work twelve, fifteen-hour days and I don't care. I love it here.

Originally from the Fiji Islands, Julian grew up on the Upper East Side, the son of a diplomat.

I had a privileged childhood, I'd never even come down here. This was skid row.

He shows me the chapel, the barber chair, the classrooms where men study for a GED. He shows me the conference room lined with pictures from the Bowery Mission's 135-year history, including an image of President William H. Taft speaking to over 600 men and another of Willie Randolph serving a meal to likely as many—in fact, pictures of celebrities and politicians and big-time donors wrap all the way around the room. In the corner is the piano of Fanny Crosby, composer of over eight thousand hymns, who played at the Mission when it first moved into the building in 1910.

We step into the food pantry where inventory is stacked on shelves extending to the ceiling. Julian's favorite donation is lobsters and he estimates the Mission gets five hundred to one thousand pounds of live lobsters every month, mostly seized by the Department of Environmental Conservation for being served too small, or taken from illegal poachers.

Julian makes sure I notice there are few sweets in the pantry.

Matt's real big on nutrition. We used to have Magnolia Bakery donate tons of three-dollar cupcakes, we'd get bags every day. Matt told me to cut it off. And I was like, "What do you mean?"

He laughs.

He's all about nutrition. Because guys get too comfortable. When you think of a soup kitchen you think of slop. But we're able to provide a well-balanced meal with meat and fresh vegetables.

Julian's eyes widen when he tells me about Thanksgiving, "our Super Bowl," when tents are erected and the whole block is closed to traffic.

On a regular day we serve nine hundred to one thousand meals, on Thanksgiving we'll serve nine thousand, so we'll cook for about four to five days before. We'll go through about eight hundred turkeys, about four thousand pounds of potatoes and yams. In here it's filled—you can't even walk. It's awesome.

Julian takes me by the nurse's office, the social worker's office, the administrative offices. He shows me the quarters for the men who live at the Mission. Eighty beds spread out over three floors.

They are bunk beds, well designed so that the top bunk exits to the right, while the bottom bed exits to the left and each man has one sliver of privacy.

The guys who live in the program, they all have different job functions. Some work in the kitchen, in clothing, in the laundry room, cleaning, mopping—everyone has a job function because we do put a roof over their head, we clothe them, and give them a meal. They live in New York City for free. All we ask is that they do a little work.

We help anyone. We try to keep it structured and have rules in place but if someone comes in and they're really in need we'll help them. If they need a shower, are stinking things up really bad, we'll take them down for a shower. So even if there's rules, we'll bend them a little bit.

We ascend the last staircase, narrow and steep, to the roof.

We've got Landmark status, did Matt say that? Historic structure. So we're not going anywhere. In the neighborhood for good.

We emerge outside and are surrounded by rows of barren garden beds, still awaiting warmer temperatures.

Sitting here and watching everything grow is amazing. We've got all kinds of stuff, strawberries, vegetables, and kale. It's funny because there are so many different cultures in the building—a lot of West Indian and Caribbean, and they love their hot peppers so we take requests and have all different kinds of peppers for them.

We walk toward the front of the building and look out at the street below. Julian points halfway down the block at a recently developed condo building whose large box windows dominate the facade.

That building, 250 Bowery, that's ridiculous. There's a three-bedroom penthouse on the top going for like $6–$7 million. It's funny because, when their website went up it crashed because people were trying to get in. And someone blogged, "Gimme a

break with the six million dollars. The Bowery Mission is a block
away."

He laughs.

I mean if you're going to raise a family you don't want homeless men sleeping on the front of your building. But people are
buying them outright. That's crazy.

Julian turns in the opposite direction, toward the Salvation Army
building, which flanks the south side of the Mission.

The Salvation Army was for the Chinese elderly because Chinatown is next door. There's ten floors but eight of the floors have
been vacant for years. We tried to buy the building. Three years
ago when they were first trying to sell it, we offered them $14 mil-
lion—market value at the time. They wanted $24 million, ten over.
And they just ended up getting $30 million for it. That's crazy,
right?

I consider the extraordinary range of activity crammed into the
building below us, and how much more might be accomplished if the
Bowery Mission had acquired the Salvation Army property immediately
next door. I wonder how much the Bowery Mission's building is worth,
and how many hovering investors are poised to venture a guess. Julian
escorts me down to the building's entrance. Before we part ways he in-
vites me back to volunteer next Thanksgiving.

I see Matt just as I'm leaving and I stop him to ask about the sale
of the Salvation Army next door. Instead he tells me about the new fa-
cilities they are opening in Harlem, since that's where they were able
to successfully buy a building. But I press him on the building next door,
which they wanted to buy for $14 million and use to expand services
in their neighborhood.

The building next door to us was recently purchased and it's
going to become part of the Ace Hotel group. So that will be a little bit of a change for us because of our new neighbors. Right now
we work with Salvation Army: if they have resources, they share;
and we share if we have. Their staff will come over and do a
chapel service and our staff will do the same. We've been working

together over the years because we've been shoulder to shoulder and have similar values and goals of serving the less fortunate. So we're going to miss them.

People ask us, "Are you moving? Are people going to want you to move?" But we've been in contact with the hotel developers and they well realize what we do and they've actually said as they're developing, as they're under the construction process, "Let us know whether there's anything that we can do, or if we're becoming a nuisance for you," so they've opened up that door.

We're hoping that the people who are running the hotel are open to working with us. We work with a number of hotels here in the city. Sometimes it's picking up lost and found, sometimes it's working with their kitchen and we can take food they're not able to use. There are a number of ways that we've worked with hotels in the past and I don't see there being any difference with our new neighbors.

Things evolve, right? I remember when I was younger we had a forest behind our house. Huge trees that were amazingly tall and over the years I realized that the tall trees were all gone because they had all fallen, but there were smaller trees where the taller trees had fallen and the forest was thicker. When I was a kid I could run straight through it and look up at the canopy. It was amazing. Years later the canopy was gone, there were still trees, but you'd have to wiggle your way through it. That was the evolution of the forest behind our house. And that's happening here in the city as well. Neighborhoods evolve and I think if you're willing to be a part of that process you're really able to enjoy that process and enjoy your city.

Again the man with the shiny gold buttons appears and this time Matt introduces us, passing along my name but not his. The man smiles at me, smiles big, and looks away, presumably distracted by something in the distance, which he follows out of the room. Matt tells me that the mysterious man is one of the developers for the hotel next door.

First-name basis, loves the Mission. You can see their heart for what we do here. You know, yes, he's thinking about making money but he's also thinking about the neighborhood.

I tell Matt I'd love to talk to the man with the gold buttons about the hotel and how he sees it fitting into the neighborhood. Matt suddenly looks mildly worried and asks me to stay in place while he chases after the man. When he returns his boyish grin has yielded to a grimace and he tells me that the man with the gold buttons wishes to remain anonymous. Something about that phrasing—"wishes to remain anonymous"—told me these were the man's exact words, and not Matt's own, and instantly I admire the framework of seeking anonymity: it makes it feel as though a gift has been humbly bestowed.

Later when I call to ask the Salvation Army about the sale of 225 Bowery, they respond to me as they do to all inquisitors: no comment. When I ask about the previous market rate offer that the Bowery Mission made, they do not respond to my question, or illuminate what factors, other than cash on offer, were considered when choosing a buyer for the building, which has now begun the transition from a shelter to a hotel that is plugged into a chain with locations in Portland, Palm Springs, Seattle, Los Angeles, and London.

19.

*J**ust around the corner from the Bowery, Barbara Shaum shuffles
over to the stool in the middle of her shop. The whole place is
swamped with leather. Everything else in this narrow space—
shelves, chairs, cabinets, workbenches—peeks out from behind leather in
one form or another: sandals, bags, belts, big sheets of it rolled up and
stashed in overhead wooden bins, scraps of it gathered in drawers and
corners and jars. Guarding her recently shattered femur, Barbara settles
onto the stool. At eighty-four, she is short and slender and fits perfectly in
this sliver of East Fourth Street. The empty-handed mailman is at the door.*

Barbara: Hey, Jimmy!

Jimmy: Barbara!

Barbara: You don't have any mail for me?

Jimmy: Nothing. No bill. I only give you check, no bill.

They smile at each other.

Barbara: I know, darling, I'm waiting for a check.

Jimmy: Don't worry, I pay attention for the check. I don't give
you bill; I throw it away.

Barbara: Okay.

*She smiles and watches him go. She watches until he's out of sight
so it's silent for a while. Then:*

His name is—well, Jimmy is his American name, right? And
I said, "Stop—that's not your Chinese name."

He said, "I can't tell you my Chinese name."

I said, "Oh come on, Jimmy."

He said, "Nah, in English, dirty word."

"You can tell me."

He said, "Fuk Yoo."

Barbara laughs, which leads to a throat-clearing cough. Her frailty cannot be overstated. She is a collection of bones beneath a magnetic smile and lucid, engaging eyes. With her sharp nose, pale coloring, and short auburn hair, she sits like a wise bird. She sips a large coffee and tosses small pinches of a pumpkin muffin into her mouth. She looks around constantly—searching for thoughts and tools all at once. Though most of the hammers in the shop seem to outweigh her, including those she made herself, she does not hesitate to raise any of them over her head—or to bring them down with authority. Another sip of coffee, another pinch of muffin, and this time it lodges in her throat. Her assistant, Jessica, emerges from behind a sheet of leather hanging in the back and begins patting Barbara on the back. Barbara, still doubled over with the choking, screams despite her disappearing voice:

Harder! Harder!

Her voice always sounds faint and broken but now it's nearly imperceptible:

Harder!

Jessica thumps her in the back—wincing immediately, fearing what her blow might do to the old woman's rib cage. But the impact is just right and suddenly Barbara rises, clearing her throat. She takes a sip of coffee, shakes her head, thanks Jessica, and reaches for a different, bigger hammer.

Above one workbench, phone numbers cover a wooden shelf, some written on scraps of paper, others scribbled directly into the wood. For every number Barbara recalls a person and a story:

That's Sebastian. Sebastian's gone. He's a monk. And he used to come down here on Saturdays to make sandals for the monks.

Most of Barbara's leatherwork is handmade sandals. Wednesday through Sunday, she kneels before customers and grabs hold of their feet. They might get embarrassed; she never does. She works in imperceptible increments. Never mind half or quarter inches; in the field of form-fitting open footwear, a sixteenth is consequential.

A young stylist enters and starts asking about belts. She mentions—with a kind of false casualness—that she is shopping for a fashion shoot with Naomi Campbell, at which point Barbara becomes annoyed and passes her off to Jessica. When the stylist finally leaves, Barbara watches her go, shaking her head:

Naomi Campbell? Am I really supposed to be impressed by someone who took a diamond from Charles Taylor?

Barbara sees my cell phone on her workbench and asks a few questions about "those little machines." She just bought her first cell phone, reluctantly. The broken femur forced the issue.

I'm old-fashioned and I don't like the idea that everyone has a cell phone. When a phone rings your tendency is to answer it, right? It's very difficult not to. I don't like that. I don't like people picking up the phone in the middle of a conversation. And I don't like that people think they can talk to me any time they damn please.

Someone unexpectedly pops in to say hello to Barbara every ten minutes or so. Sometimes it is someone who lives on the block, and sometimes it is someone who's come from farther afield after many weeks or months or—in the case of one man—years. He tells Barbara he's happy to see she's still running the shop.

Man: I'm surprised you're still here.

Barbara shoots back—Me too!—as she salvages the silver buckle from the belt she made for the man some ten years ago, freeing it from the grips of the deteriorating leather.

Soon thereafter the porter for the building comes in and asks Barbara to help him with the leather pouch for his phone. His name is Neptune Baptiste; he is a lanky Jamaican, at least six-four, and he wants a hole cut in the pouch so he can feed the wire for his headphones

through the top flap. When he disconnects the headphones to show Bar-
bara the problem, Bob Marley blares from the phone with "Keep on
Moving." Neptune watches Barbara raise a hammer over her head,
driving it into the top of an awl that punctures the leather. She does so
with remarkable precision—though she does warn Neptune as he leans
toward her:

Don't come too close, I'll bang you.

She finishes the job and hands over the altered pouch. Neptune
slides the wire through the new hole, gets himself reconnected to Mar-
ley, and then leaves with a smile. Barbara blows a kiss.

We trade: I do things like this; he pulls big bolts of leather
from the top shelves there and puts them down. He's very nice.

I'm from a small town. Pennsylvania. West branch of the
Susquehanna River. Foothills of the Allegheny Mountains. I'm a
neighborhood person. I'm nosey. I don't know. I like people. I really do, you know? People always ask me for this or that. If I can,
I give it to them.

This country is full of levels of society. I grew up entitled,
right? A small town, 5,600 people, and my family was a big deal.
My parents were lawyers, both of them, always busy. And we had
maids. So I was a snob before I got cut down to size, before I
started to identify with workers. I was born in 1929 so during the
Depression I was a little girl, and people would come by wanting
to mow the lawn, do some gardening or anything for a meal. And
I used to hang out with them. They didn't come to the front door;
they came to the back door and they'd have their meal there. I remember very clearly one woman came by saying, "Oh, I'm leaving. I'm taking the bus to the next big town." I might have been
almost ten by then. And she had been a miner's wife, and not long
before that there had been all these mining accidents. And she told
me what it was like for the men who worked in the mines. So
that's where I started getting my politics, from sitting on the back
porch talking with workers.

I spent a good part of my time away from the family. Girls'

school then college. Three colleges. I was searching, I was searching, I was searching. English at one point. Theater at one point. Theater was good. I preferred doing sets. I preferred doing costumes. But I never finished a degree. Some people can take courses they're not interested in, in order to achieve a goal or something. I'm not one of those.

She laughs.

I went to Carnegie Tech, which is now Carnegie Mellon. I was in summer stock in Manistee, Michigan. Late '40s. My parents were sending me five dollars a week. The end of the season came and I didn't want to go back to Carnegie Tech. I certainly didn't want to go back to Jersey Shore, Pennsylvania. So I took a plane to New York City. When I arrived at the airport I had a dollar.

She laughs.

I had one dollar. I seem always to be able to get myself into these situations. I do things that other people won't do.

I was twenty-one. Maybe twenty. Nineteen fifty-one. I escaped. I had no sense. I had no sense at all. I didn't know what was happening. I called one of my classmates on Long Island. Couldn't have been more than a dime, or maybe a nickel—oh god, Jesus. Anyhow, he came and picked me up, told his mother, "I'm moving into the city!" And we left.

She laughs.

His name was Steve and we ended up getting married. I don't remember even where we got married. It certainly wasn't religious in any way because I've been agnostic or atheist or whatever since I was twelve.

I wasn't in love with him. I wasn't with him more than two years at the very most. His parents didn't like me. They just thought I was an interloper. I was trying to marry beyond my station in life. Funny.

Later I married again. But he was older than I, considerably, and he died a long time ago. I haven't been married for decades. But you know, I've had stints. I've had stints with gents.

She laughs.

The late '50s were absolutely wonderful days. It's awful but it was marvelous. They were still making us pretend that if somebody dropped an atomic bomb on New York City we could survive it.

She laughs.

I made sure I never learned to type. I'm serious. Typing, no. Just—no. Oh god. Earning money and that sort of thing: jobs were weird things, just awful things. I had fun working one place and that was the New York Public Library on Forty-Second Street. Going down to the stacks, right? Pulling books out. And I used to do Charlie Chaplin. I loved that.

She makes her finger a short mustache over her lip and shimmies her shoulders, as though waddling down an aisle with bookshelves on either side.

And I came out of work once and there was a news kiosk, right? There was *The Nation*. I looked at it and I said, "Gee, there are people that think the way I do! I'm not the only one!" That I remember really clearly, and it sort of wedded me to this city.

Those were the days with the Korean War, the War Resisters League—all that stuff, boiling all through the East Village. And I was involved with all of it. Anybody who was even half liberal was very much together on these issues. And there was a lot of creativity—a huge surge of new kinds of creativity: John Cage, modern dance.

I paid $21.45 a month for my first apartment. That was at 242 West 10th Street. Cold water flats. I used to pass by this leather shop and the guy that owned it was Walter, Walter Humphries was his name. He was wonderful. And he was sleeping in the back of the store. And Steve, my ex—I have to give him credit for this—he said, "Eh, she's wonderful. She can do anything with her hands. Can she come in and work for you?" So that's how I learned this stuff.

I was a natural. And I opened a shop on Seventh Street, down away a piece between Bowery and Second. Nineteen sixty-two. Seventy-five dollars a month rent. The Bowery was really the Bowery. It was. Bums would come by for a buck and they'd put a chalk mark outside. It meant, here's a good place to ask for quarters. And I'd have more people coming all the time. And god, I got taken. I got taken so many times. Somebody would come in with a vacuum cleaner for twenty-five dollars and it would work for about a half an hour.

She laughs.

Stuff like that.

For twenty-four years, as a matter of fact, I had that shop and I lived in the back for a while. Had a huge backyard. I used to give barbecues. It was wonderful. It was next door to McSorley's Ale House. I was a good friend of the pub. They would borrow my hose in the backyard to clean out the ovens, you know, that sort of thing. It was the only pub in New York that still didn't allow women inside—they never had. But really I'd been stopping in after hours for a long time. Doc worked as a bartender there and he played the violin. He was a gypsy—a real honest-to-god gypsy—and he'd be playing music, sometimes threw concerts after they closed. And if I were passing by, he would say, "Hey Barbara," and wave me in. Funny. They had a cat that wouldn't stay there, it insisted on coming over to where I lived. It was family.

Dorothy Kirwan—she was a friend of mine—she inherited the place from her dad, and when he died she promised him she would never go inside so long as she lived. That was way back in the '40s and even in 1970 she wouldn't do it. On the day the city passed a law allowing women in the bar, Dorothy asked her son, Danny, to be her surrogate and so he asked me to walk in with him. I was on Danny's arm. And my friend Sara—Sara Penn, she had a shop in the neighborhood, too—she was on somebody else's arm behind us. I said, "Sara, I'm putting on a hat."

She laughs.

So she did, too. We both had big hats and pretended it was afternoon tea or something. Although I think it was the morning. They had cameras and all that. It was a civil rights thing, you know? Everybody got very excited. The whole block was very excited.

I don't think I actually had a drink. Maybe a wee little sip. I came back to work. Really it was a small thing when you think about it, drinking at the bar with the men. Equal pay, when we get that, now that will be something big.

She laughs.

Shortly after that I was living in an apartment on Seventh Street. That was a sublet—perfectly legal but when the landlord found out it was me subletting the place, he said, I don't want that woman in my building.

Because I was active.

Suddenly she breaks into song:

> Banker and boss hate the red Soviet star
> Gladly they build a new throne for the czar
> But from the steps to the Caspian Sea
> Trotsky's great army brings vic-to-ry
> So workers hold your ranks
> Stay sharp and steady
> For freedom's name raise your bayonets bright
> For workers' Russia, the Soviet Union
> Get ready for the next great fight.

I was fighting for some kind of—I don't know what you call it. People who had Laundromats, for instance, they would be paying $600 a month. And you have absolutely no rights, so suddenly they'd say, $5,000 a month. You can't change from $600 a month to $5,000. You can't do that.

I was fighting that.

Miriam Friedlander—great, great, great congresswoman—she came into my shop one day and said I should start organizing. So I did. And in those days you couldn't just email and say, let's meet at so-and-so place; you went and got them—you had to physically go and gather everybody together.

A lot of us, we fought. We didn't go far enough though. We didn't have enough billions of dollars, I guess. It didn't work. It worked sometimes. On Avenue C there was a bakery and I did manage to save him. There were two older ladies that lived in my building, and they tried to get rid of them. I got them a lawyer. There were times I had goons come by my shop and threaten me. "We know who you are and where you are . . . lay off the boss." That sort of thing. It was happening all over— Brooklyn, too.

I think it started to really change in the '80s. Suddenly I began to see people in suits. And there were briefcases! That's when I knew things were different. See there's a whole area here around the Bowery that is "in rem" properties. It means that the landlords didn't pay their taxes, they just abandoned the properties. So the city was selling those off and people were coming in to buy them up for nothing.

I got kicked out of my shop next to McSorley's. The owner of the building died, and his wife couldn't keep it. She moved out to Astoria. So some investors bought the building and they wanted me out.

I went to court in 1980 and I guess you could say I won the case. The first time I went to court, the owners said, "She has parties in the backyard!"

"What kind of parties?" the judge said.

She said, "Barbecues!"

Which I did, four times a summer, at least.

And the judge said—*in a sarcastic voice*—"Oh, she has barbecues in the backyard in the city in the summertime?" And then he turned to me and said, "You never asked me over?"

And I said, "I did not know you, your honor."

She laughs.

So the first time going through court it was heaven, you know.

But that was the beginning of the end. I was back five years later. And finally they won. My lawyer had said, "Whoa, we're in luck, we got the same judge."

Oh, no, no, no. The judge looked at my lawyer and said, "The politics have changed."

Which means the landlords are on top now. The tenants are not on top anymore.

The politics have changed.

So in 1985 I got a shop through Cooper Square, the community development committee. The place had rubble this deep on the floor—*she reaches down to tap her knee.*

I was fifty-six. I didn't have money because I hadn't worked for six months. And some kid on the block came in, right? And he said, "Give me that broom." So all we needed was a shovel and a broom and garbage bags and you know, there was nobody on the streets in those days so we packed these garbage bags full of rubble and we'd go down to the corner and . . . shhh.

She pantomimes surreptitiously dropping a bag and laughs.

I paid him what I could. And other kids came by, too, and started helping out. Now, would that happen these days? I don't know. Now people are so isolated in some strange manner. I don't know.

I don't want to be done with the shop. I guess I'll have to be at some point. But I have tools—tools that I've worked with and changed and made. All kinds of stuff like that. It's been so much a part of me, who I am, that removing myself from it, I would really—I don't know what I'd then do. I probably shouldn't even worry about it but smashing this femur was really a wake up. I mean I thought I would be rolling around, scooting down on the floor and fitting things. I can sort of work around it, but it's not, you know, it's not like it was.

I quit smoking three years ago. After sixty-two years. I just decided I didn't like smoking any more—I'm done. And I don't drink a couple of vodkas and tonics a day anymore either. Just one here or there. I have a squished vertebrae, and as I work, here, this one spot—*she points at her lower back*—give me a vodka tonic, yeah, no more pain.

That's the other thing: I don't like to hang out with old people. I really don't. They all talk about their injuries.

She laughs.

Just lately, oh my god, every which way I turn is, it's tough. My next-door neighbor, suddenly she's in the hospital somewhere. She fell out of bed and I guess she broke her hip or something. Shirley, my neighbor, she's getting dementia. Every which way I turn it's rough. It makes me older! And I'm trying to stay young so I can work.

This block is still incredible. There is a community. But NYU started taking up all the space. They just rip out everything and anything. Beautiful things. Destroy everything. They build huge monstrosities all over the village. And Cooper Union, the art and engineering school, now they've started doing the same thing. You see these big buildings they paid for? And now they want to start charging tuition. They have never charged their students tuition and now they're talking about doing it for the first time in their history. She's going there now—she'll tell you.

Barbara nods in the direction of Jessica, the twenty-four-year-old assistant from Williamsburg, Virginia. Jessica has a crew cut and wears overalls. She's been working in the shop for roughly eight months. She is an art student just around the corner at the Cooper Union for the Advancement of Science and Art. The school was set up in 1859 by Peter Cooper, the industrialist and presidential candidate who wanted to institute a model for free higher education for those who qualify "independent of race, religion, sex, wealth, or social status." The highly coveted, tuition-free education on offer keeps the school's acceptance rate at 8 percent.

Jessica: I definitely came to New York with nothing. I worked my ass off for a couple years. I was a waitress for a while. And then I just tried to get into schools. I applied early to Cooper Union. I didn't get in, got waitlisted. So I went to Parsons for a year and now I'm in an incredible amount of debt from that. Then I applied to Cooper again and got in. It was so interesting to go from Parsons to Cooper. Luckily at Cooper I don't have to pay for education and I'm able to just go to school. Well, and pay for my expenses through working for Barbara.

Barbara: She doesn't make enough here to really live in the city.

Jessica: I live Crown Heights, Brooklyn. Six hundred and fifty-five dollars a month. I have two roommates. And we have a studio. It can be pretty dirt cheap out there. Props to Crown Heights.

She pumps her fist in the air, keeping at her task of unrolling and measuring a large swath of leather.

Jessica: Now everyone is in Brooklyn. Bushwick, specifically. Some of the richest friends I have actually have an apartment in Bushwick and I just don't understand why. You're living in these really awful homes, the architecture's terrible, the neighborhood's not great. It's not even about what's actually there, materially. It's really weird. There's the perversity of being on the edge—I don't know. It's like farm-to-table food: it sounds so nice and it sounds like you're really being close to something but it's really about this ideal. People want to belong to something, or be a part of a new art scene in Bushwick. But they're not. They're paying $3,000 for a two-bedroom apartment in Bushwick.

I'm a junior. Trying to not graduate ever, that's my goal—ever.
She laughs.

I could just stay at Cooper and live in this little wonderful, creative fantasy world. Why not? The community that's there is so unlike anything I've ever had. Everyone is there for a reason and knows that they're there for a reason, and it's all about collaborating and being open and trying to formulate new ideas. You can't beat it. I've never been anywhere where the faculty really treats you as a part of this democratic experience instead of an authoritative situation. It's all based on merit and hard work so you get all of these different people. Like my friend Marina is from Berkeley, pretty well-to-do, middle-class family; there's a kid who lived in the school without anyone's permission last year; and there are these two twins that go to my school that lived through a bunch of different adoption homes and are still sort of very wayward. The professors are always willing to help out where they can. In different ways, too. But that's starting to happen less and less. There used to be this thing, a Cooper loan, and any time you needed it you could just go and borrow $500 on the spot—whenever. They don't do that anymore. Financially they can't do it.

They voted against charging tuition for this year but after that we don't know. A lot of the seniors are heavily involved trying to keep the conversation going for those of us who will still be around but we all just feel like it's inevitable. It seems like they've made up their mind to start charging tuition. So we've slacked off. And now maybe we're fucked.

Barbara: It's all money, money, money, money. We flee to New York because we know it's the place where there's freedom. But it's not going to be free for too much longer.

A few months later, Cooper Union's board of trustees votes to begin charging tuition in the fall due to the institution's financial shortfall— against the mandate of the institution's founder and the will of faculty, students, and alumni. The announcement is made in the school's famous Great Hall, just across the street from a brand new academic building, 41 Cooper Square, one of Barbara's "huge monstrosities." While the necessity and financial feasibility of the building were being publicly debated—it had a price tag of $165 million—the trustees approved a range of expenditures that included $350,000 for an inauguration party and $50,000 for a guest speaker.

In his review of 41 Cooper Square, the architecture critic Nicolai Ouroussoff said, "We'll have to wait to find out exactly what the end of the Age of Excess means for architecture in New York . . . The new academic building at the Cooper Union for the Advancement of Science and Art is yet more proof that some great art was produced in those self-indulgent times." The aluminum and glass building looks a bit like a boxy spaceship, and those who were protesting the tuition fees have all been cleared out of the lobby.

20.

T *he blocks immediately surrounding Cooper Union fall under the domain of the Cooper Square Committee—a group of residents who work to prevent private capital from dominating their neighborhood. The committee has had some success doing so, and it's been at it a long time—in the 1960s, members hung banners from fire escapes: "Cooper Square Is Here To Stay—Speculators Keep Away."*

The Cooper Square neighborhood is composed, roughly, of the four northernmost blocks of the Bowery before it splits into two separate streets at the entrance to Cooper Union's Great Hall where, 152 years before the school announced it would charge tuition, Abraham Lincoln was propelled to his party's presidental nomination after giving a speech asserting the government's authority to limit slavery.

In addition to the school, the Cooper Square neighborhood includes a building that houses The Village Voice, *several theaters— the Public, La MaMa, New York Theatre Workshop—and Barbara's old haunt, McSorley's. After the judge informed Barbara that the politics had changed in 1985, it was the Cooper Square Committee that helped her get a new space for her shop.*

Still fighting off outside capital in 2012, the committee won a decades-long battle that gave them approval for an expansive co-operative housing plan that allowed tenants to buy shares in their apart-

ment buildings for as little as $250. The Cooper Square Committee is studied and revered—in large part because its sustained success is a rarity. It is challenging enough to get two neighbors to agree on the optimal volume at which music should be played; how much greater is the task of getting a building or a block—or several blocks—to agree on unified interests when they all sit in the direct path of a hurricane tossing money in various directions?

Crown Heights has one such organizing effort under way. In this part of Brooklyn, a handful of large building management companies dominate the area; they oversee maintenance and billing for investment groups and other landlords who, as Toussaint pointed out, rarely seek direct contact with the people who live in the buildings they buy.

Celia Weaver has only lived in Crown Heights for two years but she's been organizing in the neighborhood twice as long. She goes by Cea and works for the Urban Homesteading Assistance Board. She can easily get revved up talking about how her neighborhood is changing, and when she does she reminds me of a twenty-eight-year-old version of Barbara Shaum—the same red hair, the same fair skin, the same socialist song in her heart. At university, Cea explored different kinds of ideology that government imposes on the home; she wrote a paper comparing two vastly different mid-twentieth century models: private development in Levittown, New York, and a public housing project in the Marzahn section of East Berlin.

We sit in a coffee shop across the street from a shuttered, stone-faced private school built in 1910 and currently covered in scaffolding. Plumes of smoke occasionally shoot out past the building's temporary cover; the sound of spinning electric blades echoes up and down the street.

The residents here really feel squeezed. There have been intense buyouts. They'll go to tenants who are paying lower rents and they'll say look, let me give you $10,000 to move out. It's kind of insulting so then the landlord goes away and comes back and says, "Okay, we'll give you one hundred thousand dollars." Value is so subjective. But that extreme financial value, it just arrived. It feels raw.

And we've started to see some really weird things you wouldn't expect in a city with a housing crunch. Landlords in this neighborhood buy up buildings that are in foreclosure and empty the tenants but don't bring in new people. My only guess could be that they want to sell the building empty but that ends up being extremely painful because it keeps the housing supply artificially low and that just further drives up rents.

If you talk to the Caribbean residents—tenants and home-owners—it's so visible on the street, and it feels raw. It's like you woke up one morning and Franklin Avenue was a different place.

So we're doing an interesting project in this neighborhood: we see the foreclosure as a weak point where there's actually more of a balance of power between the owner and the residents and we try to help residents take over the building.

A lot of the times with someone going into foreclosure in multi-family housing, it's not the same kind of sympathetic homeowner story that we're used to. They're often private equity companies or hedge funds that were buying up multi-family housing stock in New York City from 2005–2008. They're not sympathetic guys. A lot of the buildings have been sold in bulk to different hedge funds, private equity, what-have-you.

So we've been organizing against landlords of multi-family buildings that are in foreclosure. If they took out a $4 million mortgage on a six-unit building, such a risky deal can only work out by completely turning over the tenancy. In New York, generally rent is regulated so if the tenant stays in the apartment the rent can go up usually between 4–7 percent but if a tenant vacates an apartment the rent can go up 20 percent each year. So there's a huge incentive for landlords to vacate apartments. But if the tenants refuse to leave, if they don't accept the buyouts and the landlords can't bring in new people that's a problem for them. They took out their mortgage on the hedge that they are going to be able to move people out and raise rents rapidly. If tenants decide to fight back, that mortgage is not sustainable. And if they leave and they go out to East New York, wherever the landlords want them to go, they'll be able to pay back the mortgage. That's the situation in Crown Heights. In places like the South Bronx they're making the same bets but a lot of these private equity groups are buying so indiscriminately, they don't know anything about the neighborhoods.

The private equity companies don't care about the rent laws, you know—tenants care about the rent laws, small landlords care about the rent laws. People investing in commercially backed securities don't know about the rent laws. Who knows who these investors even are? So the larger the gap between people who know about New York City housing and the people who own the buildings, the worse it's going to be for the communities.

New York City does have really strong tenant protection laws for when a foreclosure happens because, of course, the tenant never took out a mortgage, it's the landlord that's being foreclosed upon. So we often go into buildings that are in foreclosure with the goal of organizing tenants to use the foreclosure as an opportunity to bring in the kind of ownership they would want.

We decided to join all these tenant associations together, working with a group called the Crown Heights Assembly, which came out of the Occupy movements. Now we have the Crown Heights Tenant Union, which is a collective of tenant associations.

It's a challenge to build larger coalitions. In the past our organization has been very building-centric. And we do want to maintain a percentage of that and maintain resident autonomy over what's happening in their building.

We had a rally two Fridays ago. We have a list of demands around notifications, around illegal rents in the buildings; there's a lot of evidence that the rent guidelines board, which sets the rents in New York City, has been letting rents go up faster than wages and faster than oil costs in response to the landlord lobby. So we're calling for a rent freeze in the neighborhood.

Some of our demands may sound crazy, but there's a lot of

evidence that points to the fact that they're actually fair. We're really excited—there's a lot of energy in the neighborhood because the displacement and gentrification pressures are really palpable here and they're really racial. It's easy to recognize. The neighborhood has been under attack and there's a lot of energy and anger and desire to fight back.

I think the problem around all gentrification dialogue is this false dichotomy between a changing neighborhood and what was happening before. So a lot of real estate people will say, "Ten years ago there was a race riot in Crown Heights, it was so dangerous you couldn't walk down the street. You wouldn't really want that. What neighborhood are you fighting for? Are you crazy? This is so much better."

But the tenants, especially the tenants who have been here a long time, they say, "We lived through it being shitty, we want to stay and enjoy what's coming."

There are ways to have a neighborhood have less crime and more economic justice that don't include displacement. And I think that's kind of the crux of what we're organizing for. We want the good things. We want the coffee shops. We want the safety. We want the better schools. But we don't want that to be at the expense of the community who's been here a long time. And that's the problem with gentrification. Even with the anti-gentrification folks it becomes Us vs. Them, and that's really what we're trying to combat and talk about.

Gentrification has obvious symptoms—new residents, new shops, displacement, sometimes less crime—but I think that often these symptoms become conflated with the definition of gentrification.

When a lot of people think about gentrification they think about artists moving in. But cultural critiques about gentrification are less interesting to me than capital and real estate. The other thing about the artist thing: are the West Indian people who have been living here for years not artists? They probably are and so when people say artists and gentrification they kind of mean white artists and that's not helpful.

She laughs.

In the '70s a lot of the gentrifiers coming into Brooklyn—Park Slope or Clinton Hill—were people who were maybe two-earner households and commuting from the suburbs wasn't an option since there was this desire for the women to work outside of the home. You needed to be in the city. So in those days it started as a socially progressive movement with people looking for diverse communities and equality of gender, which I think is really interesting because now I think it's taken on a more sinister capital driven lens.

I tend to think about gentrification as a sort of structural process where real estate capital sees growth opportunity in neighborhoods and comes in and tries to do neighborhood turnover. Real estate developers see a difference between what the neighborhood is currently making in rent capital and what its potential is and that gap is something landowners can sort of exploit and that's where gentrification happens.

This idea of the "rent gap" that Cea is describing was first conceived and narrated by Neil Smith, the urbanist: "Building owners and developers garner a double reward for milking properties and destroying buildings. First, they pocket the money that should have gone to repairs and upkeep; second, having effectively destroyed the building and established a rent gap, they have produced for themselves the conditions and opportunity for a whole new round of capital investment. Having produced a scarcity of capital in the name of profit they now flood the neighborhood for the same purpose, portraying themselves all along as civic-minded heroes, pioneers taking a risk where no one else would venture, builders of a new city for the worthy populace."

The people moving into this neighborhood—I wouldn't say across the board but just generally—maybe don't have that different of an income than the long-time residents but the income potential is different. So there will be students who are content to be living on a lower income now but don't intend to be doing so later on.

There are race differences, there are age differences, there are social capital, if not actual capital differences. So even if you still live in your apartment after many years, if the neighborhood is unrecognizable to you and you're not welcome in a coffee shop, it's totally different. And if you walk down Franklin Avenue right now there is a total difference in who shops where, and what businesses are welcoming to which sort of race and class of people. That's an unquantifiable human cost. And the costs of groceries go up. Neighborhood amenities go up. Even if I could afford to live in an apartment on the Upper East Side could I afford to shop in the grocery stores on the Upper East Side? Probably not.

I think one of the painful things about gentrification is that people say, "I don't know my neighbors anymore," and that they don't feel connected to the neighborhood anymore and the only way to mediate that is to talk to people around you. And the racial divide ends up worsening when people are afraid to confront their privilege or confront what's happening. There are good ways and bad ways, you know, to do these things.

I think a lot about my race and class while I'm doing this work in Crown Heights and I want to be sensitive about it. I don't want to take on a leadership role in what I'm doing and part of that is because I want to be sensitive to the racial and class issues that are happening in this neighborhood.

In avoiding a leadership role, Cea strikes me as a welcome evolution on the theme of "three white girls in their twenties, teaching old black women in their sixties how to cook," as Shatia Strother put it when lamenting the lack of diversity in our prevailing paradigm of leadership. Cea is happy to organize and assist and wear out the soles of her shoes under the leadership of someone with an older, deeper relationship to the neighborhood.

The way the previous administration went about economic development in the city left something to be desired in terms of community input. It was sort of like Bloomberg considered himself a benevolent dictator. If you wanted to effect development in New York City under Michael Bloomberg you had to stand in front of a bulldozer. If not, there wouldn't be anyone who's willing to sit at the table with you.

Community boards are sort of rendered impotent. Their votes are only advisory. It's not like if the community board voted no that would mean that the project goes back to the drawing board. It goes all the way to the City Planning Commission, which are all mayoral appointees, before voting actually affects the process at all.

And that puts us in a really bad position with this false dichotomy: developers are saying I'm making your neighborhood better and the community is saying get the hell out of my neighborhood. What we really need is a more participatory urban planning world where residents have a say in what's going to happen. It's wrong to say that New York City is static, New York City has always changed, but the question is who's going to be driving the train?

21.

*O*nce a month, the Crown Heights Tenant Union gathers in *the atrium room of the Center for Nursing Rehabilitation on Classon Avenue. At first glance the meeting looks like group therapy of some kind—and, in a way, maybe it is. Clusters of three or four people sit in chairs, talking, loosely forming one big circle around the perimeter of the room.*

A white man in his thirties and a dark-complected woman in her fifties stand in the middle of the room, trying to corral the smaller discussions and bring the entire room together. As the man occasionally takes a stab at speaking over the din, more people come in and each person gets a chair from Cea. She is happy in the shadows—more effective in the shadows, pulling chairs from a stack to make sure everyone is comfortable at the meeting. The man standing in the middle of the room gets everyone settled enough to hand the floor over to the older woman standing at his side. When she speaks her voice booms:

New tenants and people who have lived here for a long time should not be pitted against each other. That weakens us—and empowers the landlords. Break the cycle! Break the cycle!

The sound of agreement rumbles across the room—either side of fifty people, nodding and shifting forward in their seats.

The woman in the middle of the circle goes on:

We are not a union in name—we are a union in deed and action.

New York was the birthplace of the labor movement, and it will be the birthplace of the tenant union movement.

She opens the floor with a question:

What's going on in your building? Any improvements?

Silence. So the woman brings a new question to the room, asking if anyone has recently experienced harassment or encountered new problems. Hands are raised all around her—and then a few overlapping voices:

They're not housing people, they are housing cattle!

I am not an animal!

The woman reestablishes order by pointing to a young woman who stands to speak. Her name is Nefertiti Macaulay; she is thirty-two years old and she begins by giving the address of her building:

1059 Union.

Everyone begins by giving their address—it's a tag, a badge, it is the piece of crucial information: 1159 President Street, 1580 President Street, 1045 Union Street.

Nefertiti tells her story of living on the third floor with her deaf, diabetic grandmother, caring for her for a decade until she passed in 2007. She has rats in her kitchen, visible water damage in multiple rooms, and her apartment has not been painted since her grandmother's passing.

I can remember her there in her chair by the window, watching TV.

My grandparents moved in when I was born, and I moved in to take care of her when I was nineteen. The super knew me. The landlord would come in and sit on our couch and have conversations—he knew me. But still I got a note of eviction saying I am squatting. We were in court for a year, every month. I had a lawyer and we went through trying to prove I lived in the apartment. All my bills were at my mother's house so the only proof we had were the people who knew me. I went around the building and got them to sign, saying that I lived in the building. We even brought neighbors and medical caregivers to court to say that I live in the building. After a year the judge said, basically, "You don't have any proof that you live there so we're going to have to give you fair market price." And my rent went from $750 to $1,156.

She passed away and it was thrown at me. As a young person, you don't prepare for these things. I think they wanted to scare me so I said, "I'll take it." And sometimes I take three jobs to make it work.

I have nowhere else to go. It's scary. The system is not on our side. We need to get everyone on board. This is not fighting for one person's rights—it's fighting for everyone's rights.

Each person who speaks is asked to yield the floor before she has told all there is to say, because there are always more tenants waiting to speak, more stories to be told. There are common themes that run through the testimonies: lowball buyout offers, threatening lawyers, unsanitary living conditions, and unsafe construction sites.

During a break in the meeting, two politicians running for the same office in the same upcoming primary work the room, sympathizing, handing out business cards.

Representatives from various nonprofit organizations are here, some offering advice, some just listening.

One in-demand, frequent visitor, Brent Meltzer, is not present to hear these testimonials because he must work deep into the night. So I go looking for him in the Downtown Brooklyn building where he works. He greets me at the elevator and takes me to his office. The filing cabinet has broken: stacks of folders and pieces of disassembled drawers are strewn across the small room; miscellaneous hardware and tools have been dropped in frustration onto every surface unclaimed by the folders and busted drawers. There is barely room for Brent, let alone visitors, so we convene in the conference room down the hall. Everyone has left and all the lights are out. The room is lit by the last traces of sun coming through the windows. Brent, forty, has a knee that won't stop bouncing. He leans back in his chair and tries to wipe the exhaustion from his face:

I saw one building where on the main floor the landlord

punched a hole through to the basement. You go down and there are rooms. No certificate of occupancy. So someone's not supposed to live there because there's no windows, and it's a fire hazard. Two young guys rented it. Got it for $2,300 bucks and thought it was a steal, and they don't know it's a firetrap.

Brent has worked for South Brooklyn Legal Services since 2002. His office, which is a UAW union shop that provides free legal advocacy for low-income people living in Brooklyn, is part of a consortium of offices throughout the city, which began in the 1960s using federal funds provided by President Johnson's War on Poverty. Brent has been the manager of the housing unit since 2008.

I come from Canada so with that alone we have different cultural backgrounds. There's some mistrust at times and you want to try and get past some biases. I'm not super judge-y. I tell my clients this all the time: "You need to tell me everything because I'm your lawyer I'm not your parents. Whatever you tell me is pretty much fine." They can tell me they've killed someone and I can't disclose it. The only thing I can disclose is if they're going to kill someone. Clients love that one.

He laughs.

It's just a good way of breaking down barriers.

We do have stronger tenant laws here compared to other cities but the pressures are also much, much more here than other cities. I lived in Portland, Oregon, for a while and there's a lot of housing. The vacancy rates in New York are under 5 percent. If you get evicted you can't just go down the street.

A lot of people are precariously housed in New York at the moment. So while we do a lot of housing work, we also work with tenant organizers. I work with this group FUREE, Families United for Racial and Ethnic Equality. They had a big fight with rezoning Downtown Brooklyn and our office helped them with Mama Joy. She was a homeowner and she believed that her basement was used for the Underground Railroad over here on Duffield, and they were going to do eminent domain and take away her home and create a parking lot. So we sued and, lo and behold, it looks like it might have been used for the Underground Railroad. So they stopped the eviction.

Mama Joy appears in a photograph clipped out of a community newspaper. She stands in her basement, her braided hair poking out from under a bright orange gele. In the image, she points at a portion of the wall that was clearly once an opening—a tunnel of some kind, which has been covered over with bricks. She died a month ago and a street near her preserved home, not far from the office where Brent and I sit, has been renamed Abolitionist Place.

I moved to New York in 1999. So I've only known Giuliani and Bloomberg. And I wouldn't say Bloomberg was hostile to us but he wasn't necessarily friendly.

He laughs.

And Giuliani was definitely hostile.

He laughs again.

Bloomberg made the government work. But the question is for who? When I think of the Bloomberg administration, they're modernizing, computerizing—you can go online and check stuff and it's great. But it didn't happen in any of the agencies I work with, the poor people's agencies. For instance, lots of tenants that live in public housing, they're on public assistance. And there's just not communication between those two agencies. It's shocking when you think that's what Bloomberg was all about, getting government to be more efficient and there was no efficiency for poor people. It was all for the Upper East Side and can they call 311 and, you know, get the snow removed. But meanwhile we're paying so much money for people in shelters because these agencies just weren't talking together. You know lately that's what's been on my mind a lot, how can we make this government reactive for my clients?

No doubt there's going to be changes with de Blasio, even the access that we're getting. But what's shocking to me, talking to people I know who are connected to de Blasio, it takes time to get up and running. Yesterday I met with Vicki Been, the head of the Housing Preservation Department. And Vicki is my old law school professor. She is really smart, but we're having this meeting and there was a lot of stuff she just doesn't know. This is a bright professor. It's not her fault, she doesn't know about everything and she needs to get briefed on it. The head of the Human Resources Administration is Steven Banks who was the head of The Legal Aid Society but even then he doesn't know everything—and he's one of us, literally he's one of us. So it's going to take some time.

We're taking some different tactics with this administration. We'll reach out to them and say we're about to do this, and give them the benefit of the doubt, and say, "Will you work with us on this?" And if they don't, so be it. We'll shame you all to death.

He laughs.

I'm not trying to stop gentrification, I'm just trying to stop my client from being evicted. I'm not opposed to change. And yet there are some that say, "Well yeah, if we allow the neighborhood to start changing it's going to remove long-term housing and that might be something we should be concerned about."

And I say, "Well, yes, but if there's more affordable housing and it's real affordable housing, I'm alright with that."

Neighborhoods are going to change. Even people who say, "Oh, gentrification is horrible," it's sometimes rooted in that, "Oh we like these black neighborhoods, these Latino neighborhoods and now these white people are coming in and ruining it all." And it's not necessarily the case. There are definitely neighborhoods where black middle-class professionals move in—is that gentrification? I don't think if you ask most people in Harlem or somewhere else they'd consider that gentrification.

Then it gets complicated. You start talking about class, you start talking about race. Take Crown Heights for a moment. This is predominantly an African American neighborhood and it's becoming white. Really, really white. So what does that mean?

I think in the United States it's hard to disentangle class and race. I live two blocks from here. I moved to this neighborhood in 2003 and every year they'd have a big Puerto Rican block party and they're all old-school rent-stabilized tenants. But since I've been here, they slowly shifted out. This was a strong Latino community around here but it's just gone. I don't know what to think about that. It's problematic that we're losing affordable housing. But if it's just a shifting of ethnic groups, the romantic in me has no problem with it, you know, that's what New York's been about. I mean Carroll Gardens was an Italian neighborhood and there's still some vestiges of that but it's changing.

When you're talking about gentrification are you talking about class? Are you talking about race? Are you talking about ethnicity, language? There are all these different things. Atlantic Avenue used to be a big Arab population, now they're all out in Bay Ridge and have started up a new community out there. And that's interesting to think about, is that gentrification? I don't know.

For instance the Fulton Street Mall was the second or third highest grossing commercial strip, after 125th street and the Hub up in the Bronx. But the language has always been we need to clean this up. It used to be a Jewish strip but there's not actually a Jewish community living there so people would come in and the talk around the city, we have to clean it up. Which was code to get rid of the Jews.

And then it became an African American strip and if you went down there on the weekend it was a very black shopping commercial district. You know, Big Daddy Kane used to go down there—that's gone. I know an activist, and she had a shop down there, and they basically said you're not good enough for us. Now there's an Armani there because that was a good commercial space. And she's out of business. She couldn't set it up somewhere else because this was where people knew to come. So that, to me, looks like gentrification because it's getting rid of local businesses and putting in big box, corporate businesses.

Which I'm happy to have as well but what has that done and who is that helping?

The desire to shift a population from its neighborhood is often expressed openly. In 1929, a consortium of boosters in Lower Manhattan wrote a proposal called the "New York Regional Plan," which called for the removal of the area's existing population, the construction of residential units for upper-class residents, new shops, and the physical redevelopment of the Lower East Side highway system, so that it would link up more directly with Wall Street: "The moment an operation of this magnitude and character was started in a district, no matter how squalid it was, an improvement in quality would immediately begin in adjacent property and would spread in all directions. The streets thereabouts would be made cleaner."

Another question: who's actually getting into new buildings? Who are they developing these for? It's not my client who's on public assistance because the landlords are not going to take them in.

There are definitely some people in my field who think that we should only be working with people at 30 percent of area income and below, and we just shouldn't do anything else. But then you're going to squeeze out the middle class. What are you going to do with the teachers? Where are the police officers going to live? They're all going to live out on Long Island because they can't afford the city.

It's funny that when I first started and I was in law school I was like I'm never going to turn anyone down, that's the worst thing you can do. And honestly that's part of my job now. We have limited resources. I'm one of the biggest housing units in the country and we only have 10 or 11 full-time attorneys for all of Brooklyn—2.3 million people. That's not a lot. If we tried to help everyone that came in, gave everyone advice, that's all we'd do. We'd never represent anyone, we'd just be doing intake and nothing else. So it's these hard choices that we have to make and, yeah, it sucks. I always say we should have a therapist on staff for us because I spend half my day going out into the hallway and being very cold and saying, "No, you have to call our hotline, no I'm not going to give you any advice, I'm not going to help you." So there's that.

And they say, "But I really need an attorney."

And I say, "I know you need an attorney, it's just not going to be our office, I'm just not going to do it."

You know, I just did a training recently on unconscious bias, and it's been really interesting for me to think when I walk out into the hallway here and I'm helping someone: Who do I talk to, who do I not talk to, why do I talk to them? Also making sure that I'm not being—I mean, I'm a gatekeeper, we're an institutional player as well. We spend the day railing against other institutions and it'd be pretty hypocritical for us not to look inward and make sure that we're not keeping people out, too. It's trying to catch yourself in all this stuff, being equal to everybody.

I struggle: we turn away a lot of hard cases at times. Those are the ones that, theoretically, we should be doing. Hard cases. But if we just did those we'd never meet our numbers because we also have grants with requirements. So it's finding that balance, and I think we pride ourselves in thinking about ways that we can impact our clients' lives beyond the individual case. The person that really, really needs our help, but who's a long shot, can we justify putting resources into that? I was just talking to someone today who was completely railroaded in court. The judge was just wrong. The whole case was just wrong. But they can't afford their rent. So do we go into that case because there's a right involved? Absolutely there's a right violated. But we'd go in, vindicate that right, and then the person is going to be evicted in two or three months because they can't afford the rent. What do you do with that? I don't know.

I always ask, "What's the exit strategy?" It's horrible to say, like it's the Iraq War. But seriously, if we're going into this, how are we going to get ourselves out, because if we're just going to go in and fight for rights, that's great but we need to get out because otherwise what's the point?

So we really try to focus on cases where landlords are clearly violating the law. We have at least four or five cases right now where landlords go in and demolish properties. It used to be that they just wouldn't do repairs and through neglect the tenants would move out. Or they would bring bogus cases. There's one landlord attorney in court and he has a kind of big mouth and he was saying, "I tell my clients bring ten bogus cases, it's only forty-five dollars to file. And nine of them get dismissed but you win one and you get your money back plus so much more." And that's the reality.

Housing court is definitely an experience. Go to federal court first and then come to housing court—just to see what a money court is versus a poor person's court. Family court, housing court, criminal court—those are all poor people's courts. There's no justice. And I think a lot of people don't understand that.

Have you gone to housing court before?

You need to go to housing court.

22.

*T*he civil courthouse in Downtown Brooklyn sits amid a cluster of bureaucratic towers that border a commercial strip whose tenants include everything from a ninety-nine cent store to the kind of restaurant where bartenders prefer to be called mixologists. The Quaker-affiliated Brooklyn Friends School—$28,000 a year for preschool—is just up the block.

Inside the rectangular steel-and-glass building leased by the civil courthouse, the elevators break down year-round; the air conditioner only in summer. Before he was mayor, Bill de Blasio, acting as public advocate, put the building's landlord on his "Worst Landlord" watch list. The city's lease for the property expired last week but, unable to find new housing, housing court—ironically, or perhaps not—will stay in the ailing building.

The line to get in the door—to shuffle through security and wait in a second line for the persnickety elevators—usually runs onto the sidewalk and all the way down the block well before eight in the morning.

On the tenth floor, the elevator doors open onto a crowded hall filled with the strident din of heated conversations. Clumps of three or four people are staggered from wall to wall: always a landlord, always a tenant, usually a landlord's lawyer, occasionally a tenant's lawyer, too. They are all haggling, trying to reach a settlement; when and if they do, the details are immediately written on a piece of paper and *taken into one of the court rooms to receive a judge's approval. There are dozens of courtrooms; some for hearings, some for trial—all of them with long waits.*

In room 505, Brent Meltzer is grinding his way through the trial of a client named Noelia Calero. He is cross-examining an engineer, and Noelia's landlord's lawyer, with the landlord at his side, interrupts every question Brent asks—every question. He is relentless with his objections and words them for the judge with a sarcastic tone. Unexpectedly, the judge tolerates the lawyer's behavior and, what's more, upholds the majority of his objections. Brent does not mask his disappointment but he is impossible to rile, which is all that the other lawyer is really after. Noelia sits at Brent's side, her stoic expression concealing a complex of emotions. After the hearing, she suggests that I see her home for myself. A few days later I pay her a visit.

Her apartment is on Linden Street in Bushwick. The closest subway stop is nearly a mile up the street. Most of the blocks between her apartment and the L train are lined with three-story apartment buildings, some private developments, some public. American and Puerto Rican flags hang from several windows; in a couple of spots, banners of small flags are draped across the street from one lamppost to another. There are Laundromats and barbershops and delis—Sea Town Supermarket occupies two separate buildings across the street from each other, so the smell of fish hits you from both sides. Two live poultry shops, Kikiriki and Pio Pio, operate right next to each other. Three men are standing in front of Pio Pio—each holds a briefcase and wears a dark suit on a hot, midday sidewalk. They point at the building, discussing its facade, trying to hear each other over the clucking chickens.

When I arrive at 98 Linden, Noelia, thirty-two, greets me at the front door and escorts me down the hall to her apartment. The first room we enter is mostly filled by a bed where her mother rests, watching television. Noelia's husband is at work, repairing potholes across the city. Noelia is currently unemployed. She has several years of clerical work experience, mostly with a construction company, where she became versed in building permits and city agencies.

Originally from Nicaragua, Noelia has a calm, sober demeanor. Her hair is brown with honey-colored highlights and pulled back into a tight bun. She takes me through her narrow railroad apartment, requiring passage through one room to get to the next. We sit at the dining table in her living room. It is a small, cramped space, and it is packed with boxes stacked to the ceiling along every wall. It feels like sitting in the cleared middle of a storage unit.

Since I was six I've lived in Bushwick. Before it was a lot of Mexicans, and Puerto Ricans, and Dominicans. Now there's a lot of Ecuadorians and Colombians. We lived here for twenty-three years in this apartment.

All the owners that I've known, four or five, haven't been good owners. They don't want to repair, they don't want to fix up. The previous landlord, when he bought this, he tried to kick us out, too. At that point the entire building was rent stabilized. He tried to kick all of us out. We had to go to court. We've always gone to court. We've never had a good landlord here. We've always had problems in this building—always. We've always paid our rent on time for twenty-three years. But every time we have to paint or fix something we've done it out of our pockets.

But these owners have been the worst. They bought the building last year, January of 2013. The previous owner sent a letter in January saying that he sold the building. And we didn't hear from these new people until March when they sent a letter saying they wanted to fix up the building. After the letter we were like, "I'm not going to say no to fixing up the building."

They didn't show up to introduce themselves until a few weeks after. They were actually very polite. They were like, "We just bought the building and we want to make it look nicer." They told us they want to change the floor tiles and put paint and fix the bathroom. Basically he said, "Happy tenants, happy landlords."

And I was like, "Okay that's different."

So we moved all our things from the kitchen and the bathroom to this room and the backyard. He said it was going to take a couple weeks.

And we believed him.

And we're going to have a year now with no bathroom, no kitchen. Completely demolished.

Both owners came—two brothers, apparently. They brought one worker with a sledgehammer and electric saw. They took out the walls that divided my bathroom from the neighbor's kitchen. You could just walk right next door. They ripped the walls open and the floors. They completely destroyed the sink that was in the kitchen. In the bathroom, too, they removed the toilet and the sink. There's no tub. You can't even tell where the bathroom was. It's completely destroyed.

It took them less than two hours and they left. It was very chaotic. I didn't realize they were gone already. I opened the door and saw that it was completely destroyed. I could walk over from my bathroom to the neighbor's kitchen. It's my uncle next door. From there it's even worse because you can see straight into the basement.

The landlord came two or three days later and I asked him what's going on and he said, "The work, it's bigger than we expected."

"You didn't say you were going to break the floors or the walls."

He said, "We want to fix the whole thing, we just want to get work permits."

A few weeks passed and I called him several times to follow up and he didn't get back to me. So one day he shows up with a work permit. And my husband said, "The landlord's here and he says that we have to move out."

I said, "That's not what we agreed upon."

So I looked at the work permit and it's an old work permit— and it was for the third floor. I was upset. So I ripped it off the wall and I told him this is not for my apartment. That's when he got rude and he said, "Well, I need you guys to leave."

What they want is to get us out and fix the apartment and raise the rent. The minute you leave your apartment you don't have your rights anymore.

So I said, "That's not what we agreed on."

And he was basically like, "You're just going to have to go."

"No. We're not moving. And you'll be speaking with my lawyer from now on."

At that point we'd already seen his intentions. It had been a month and he didn't respond, and he didn't come see us, so we'd lawyered up at that time.

We've met other tenants from other buildings that are going through the same things. So we've come together a couple times to help each other out. We know a few of this landlord's tenants that were evicted. His workers destroyed the electric meters and the piping so the Department of Buildings actually evicted those people. Right here on Central Avenue, one of the ladies there, she went out one day and when she returned her apartment had been destroyed. From what I know of other buildings, that's his tactic. Destroy the kitchen and the bathroom and people just give up and leave. That's been his way of operating in this neighborhood. But too bad for him he met with the wrong people. Now he has to deal with us. We're not giving up. We're just not.

In the living room where we sit, Noelia has set up a hot plate and a small refrigerator. There is no running water in the apartment.

My aunt lives upstairs with my uncle. And that's where we use the bathroom. We started using the kitchen there but as you can see we have a little electric burner. I try to avoid going upstairs as much as possible because I wouldn't want someone invading my space all day long. We're very grateful to her for letting us use her stuff. Even though she's family she didn't have to do that.

A hodgepodge barricade of scrap and plywood closes off the entrance to the back half of the apartment, to what were once the bathroom and kitchen. Noelia is not allowed to enter that space, much less show it to me.

Sometimes we hear rats and we hear cats fighting back there.

One of the channels, Telemundo, they have a Nicaraguan and I actually met him once, so that's how we got the media to come here. They were horrified to see how we were. So they took it on themselves to help us. I've been very grateful. At first I was like, no, I don't want to be on camera but then I think about other people and other Hispanics, a lot of them don't speak English, or maybe some of them are illegal and they get scared and they leave. But I'm not illegal, I'm a citizen, and I do speak English and you're not treating me like this so I'm not leaving.

The landlord wasn't happy we were showing the media. He got a partial vacate order so nobody's allowed to go back there because it's unsafe. Of course he destroyed it while we were here and he wasn't concerned about our safety in the beginning. But it's not convenient to him for us to show people. So we can't go back there.

One of the last times the landlord came he brought a guy to live on the second floor and basically harass us. He basically said he's the security guard. He was hired to be here. So we're like okay, as long as he doesn't touch me, I don't care. But when he first moved here he used to walk around with bats, with a sledge-hammer. He's always screaming. He puts loud music on and it's annoying but I don't let it show that it bothers me. I just sing along to whatever he's playing and I walk around like it doesn't bother me. His friends come over and they're yelling at two or three in the morning. We call the cops and they don't show up. We've lived here for twenty-three years, we've paid our rent on time, and, you know, you're not going to kick me out of my apartment. Not in that way.

The other day I was thinking: my cousin lives next door and we're like sisters, we have such a great relationship. But I think this has put so much stress on all of us that we're all moody and sometimes I don't even want to talk to her.

My husband and I were planning to have a baby and things haven't worked the way we planned. It just hasn't happened. And I think I've just been stressed out. Sometimes I cook here and this is my little pot where I have to put my dirty dishes so I can go upstairs to wash them and sometimes I have to go up there three times a day and I just want to grab it and throw it and, "UGGGHHHHH!"

There are days when I think we should just leave. We visit family in Pennsylvania and they're so comfortable there. And I'm like, "God, I want this." But I grew up in New York. This is home. This is where my heart is. When I look at the New York skyline: "Ah, beautiful!" There isn't any place like New York. As much as I hate the situation and used to hate Brooklyn because it was so ugly and there was a lot of drugs—this is home. When I walk down the street I know where everything is. This is where my friends are. My family is here. My neighbor, Anna from the third floor, I've known her for twenty-three years. She's seen me grow up. In this building I know everyone. So I could walk up and down the stairs and I feel safe. You don't get that in many buildings.

When we first moved here I was eight years old but I remember it was ugly.

She laughs.

It was ugly. Down the block there are those new houses. But they were empty lots. There were a lot of drugs and people yelling. I used to know the code for "police coming"—it was just ugly. I used to want to move. I hated this place. Before they didn't care about cleaning up Brooklyn. Then they started to build things and it started becoming nicer. There's less drugs. There's still crime but not on this block. I feel safe walking around my neighborhood. And I thought finally they're fixing Brooklyn. But I didn't know it was at the expense of the people who were already here. Before it was a lot of Hispanics and a lot of blacks. Now you don't see a lot of them. You see a lot of white people. It's not for us to live in.

It's for other people. But I'm like, "Ooh, I want to try that restaurant. It looks nice." I like organic stuff, too!

She laughs.

My cousin and I, we love Starbucks so I say, "I can't wait to have a Starbucks right by!" Everything that's in Manhattan is coming in here—I like that. But I don't like that it's so expensive. I think change is good when it's for the better. I just wish it were in the way that we could all live here. Until this happened to us I didn't realize that people were getting kicked out of their homes. Even though I'm still here, it's happening to me, too.

There are days when I want to throw in the towel but when we leave this building or have to leave Brooklyn it has to be when I want. Not when someone wants to kick me out like an animal. We have to stick together to be forceful. So I say no. I say we're going to do this. We're going to be treated with respect until this is fixed. And then I can decide whether we stay here or move—on my terms. I'm not going to be kicked out of my neighborhood because it's not just the apartment. It's the neighborhood, too. Rent is very expensive. Where would I go? It would mean I move out of New York and that's not something that I'm willing to do.

Who can I complain to? It's just frustrating. We used to have a backyard and right now the door would have been open. And I would have been cooking or cleaning and my dog would have been in the backyard. Sometimes I don't even know what the weather looks like because the only window we have is in my mother's room. And I have to be in my room or this room—the living room, slash kitchen, slash storage. So it's very frustrating.

Housing court is horrible. Slow. Helpless.

Housing court, to me, is all about landlords and whoever has money and forget everybody else. I feel like they prefer to help people who have money rather than people that don't. There are a lot of laws to help and protect tenants but the courts aren't doing much to enforce them. That is the problem. When people go into court they come out without getting the help that they deserve. We just feel like we're helpless. What's the point of even going?

Brent has been incredible. He's been so good to us. We used to have the Department of Buildings coming in here and telling us that they were going to evict us. And any time that we call him, Brent is there to be like, "Hold on, let me see what's going on." We've been very lucky and so grateful that we met him. I'm sure he doesn't sleep—just like us!

We first went to court late July of last year, early August. At first they're like the landlord can't do this. They have to fix this. It's an emergency. Blah blah. Emergency? Almost a year! Look, somebody step up! If I could fix it I would have already fixed it. But then I would get in trouble because I'm not allowed to fix it. But then they didn't force the landlord to fix it.

The trial finished last week. We're waiting for the judge to make her decision; it could take two or three months. They're trying to settle with us, giving us some offers to consider. They tried to settle before but it's always been to delay the process. It feels like déjà vu. I don't really believe them. Why don't you just start getting the permits so we can tell that you're serious? We aren't stopping you. You should have been on that months ago.

Eventually something has to happen. I try not to make myself think, yeah they're going to fix it. Because I've been there already where we think that they're finally going to fix it and then it doesn't happen.

That's why we feel like we never win. I mean, yes, once we get the rest of our apartment back—thank God—but then we still have to deal with him. Go away already! Why did you buy a building that was like this if you don't want to deal with it? Who does this to other people, other human beings? You're a horrible person.

It always seems like regardless of whether we go to court or not we're always losing. We contacted the media. We contacted the government. And it always feels like we're the bad people. But we've lived here for twenty-three years. We work. We don't mess with nobody. We've paid our rent on time. And who's helping us? Who's there to help us?

23.

*T*he government's answer to Noelia's question—"Who's there
to help us?"—is someone like Daniel Squadron. He is the
state senator for New York's 26th District, which includes
all of Lower Manhattan—Wall Street, Tribeca, the Lower East Side,
Chinatown—and many of the waterfront neighborhoods in Brooklyn,
just across the East River.

*His grandfather immigrated to the United States, passing through
Ellis Island, which, as Daniel likes to point out, is in his district. After
living and working on the Lower East Side for much of his life, Daniel's
grandfather moved the family to the Grand Concourse in the Bronx,
leaving Ludlow Street for "life in the country," as Daniel puts it. His
father was a leader for the American Jewish Congress delegation and
marched in Washington, DC, with Martin Luther King, Jr.; his mother
went to Mississippi to march during Freedom Summer in 1964.*

I grew up in a house with parents for whom a basic sense of
fairness and opportunity in government was really a mission. This
says a lot about why I do public service. That drives me in a lot of
ways. There are individual and community issues that inevitably
get left out, that get left behind, that are overlooked. They are the
orphans of the system.

*Daniel has glasses and a closely trimmed beard—he looks serious
and studious. He likes to point out that the crowded metropolis of New*

York qualifies by multiple measures—population, economy, etc.—as a "large state or even a small nation." His chief of staff is at his side, scrolling endlessly through her inbox on her phone. She looks at her watch every few minutes so that Daniel doesn't have to.

We sit on a park bench between events on a sunny Saturday afternoon. Daniel steers clear of the word gentrification*. It is not a helpful word for a politician speaking on the record—and it's risky: too many implications, too many donors who might not like what they hear. So Daniel does not talk about gentrification, opting instead for many murky references to "it." He uses language that's bright and optimistic, that verges on empty*—equality, democracy, opportunity. *This is the mark of the politician. Squadron, like Alan Fishman, is more comfortable with the macro, the big idea, the framework, while the micro—the intricacies of self, the apartment shared with rats and feral cats, etc.— is avoided altogether. At a certain point in the conversation, you hear* The Vision—*the kind of thing that's better suited to a speech than a conversation. In Squadron's case,* The Vision *is intelligent and generous and sounds like a magical place I'd like to visit, where democracy reasserts itself to share power equally with capitalism:*

We've seen some of the ways in which as much as things change the challenges stay the same. If you look at the Chinatown community you still have a lot of the same challenges you had before with folks who don't have basic protections because they are undocumented. On the Lower East Side, sometimes one of the big fights is to have people realize just how much need continues to exist there. More than forty thousand public housing residents, a number of immigrant communities—and so when you talk about all the changes it's always really important to remember there are many things that aren't changing.

Housing is, in many ways, the existential issue for the city's future.

Having housing and neighborhoods that allow a broad diversity of people to make a life in this city is the greatest challenge, in my view, of the next decade. This issue is the most important issue and we are not doing nearly enough. We have more people that want to live in the city than we have room for right now. And when this has happened in the past, the city and state have been extraordinarily aggressive in figuring out policies that make it work. That must happen. If we become a city where you need to be at the top of whatever profession you're in, or an investor, or one of the very few who live in what's left of subsidized housing— that doesn't work. We need more affordable housing, we need more middle-class housing, we need to think about things like workforce housing. Once upon a time there were all kinds of pro- grams to help labor unions build and help artists have dedicated housing. And we were expanding public housing instead of des- perately trying to hold on to what we already have. Because of how many people want to live in the city today, we need to deal with that.

Currently 247,262 families are on the waiting list for public hous- ing in New York. And the Section 8 housing program, which provides rent subsidies to low-income earners in cities across the country, has closed its waiting list: it will take more time than anyone is willing to predict to respond to the 121,999 families awaiting word on their ap- plications in New York for that program.

The idea that it is inevitable, that the city is going to change completely and we're not going to be a city that's as diverse is ab- solutely unacceptable. And it will mean we lose the city. The great- est thing about this city is that we have the strongest collection of energy and expertise anywhere in the world. And that means peo- ple from around the world who are coming here to be part of the great engine of opportunity, it means people from around the country who want to be a part of what New York has to offer, it means people who are born here with fewer resources but still are able to get the opportunities offered—and it means people who can live anywhere in the world and chose to live here. If it's not all of that, we've lost it. And there's a real risk of that.

My wife and I are raising our son in Brooklyn. We see all

around us how hard it is to make a life here. And it's much harder than it used to be. That's true for sort of everyone, whatever their background. And I think the experience of having a growing family, desperately wanting to be part of this city that we love and the challenges we see around us, is meaningful.

As a city we need to figure out how to grow and change but we need to do it in a way that is community driven. It is possible to grow and change in a way that brings the community in instead of taking it out.

24.

*I*nterstate 278 is the de facto southern border of Daniel Squadron's district in Brooklyn. The highway is also known as the Brooklyn-Queens Expressway, or the BQE. It is yet another Robert Moses project—a long, winding traffic jam that, for many stretches, is elevated above the street. The overhead drone sends the stink and heat of car exhaust onto the sidewalk below and separates the 26th District from the neighborhood of Red Hook, which, in many ways, is separated from the rest of the world. Gita Nandan has lived in Red Hook for eleven years and talks about it as though it were a sleepy seaside village.

December, January, February are the bleakest months possible. And that's when you only see your fellow Red Hookers on the street. And then there's some huge snowstorm and you go to the bar and you know everybody because everybody needs to get out of their house. But there aren't people coming to Red Hook in December. The tourist events happen in June, July, August, September, and then everybody forgets about Red Hook.

It's waterfront and disconnected so it's not quite like Bushwick, which feels very connected.

Bushwick is where Gita, an architect, works at the Thread Collective. The firm describes its work as "sustainable architecture [that] explores the seams between building, city, and the environment." We sit in the backyard behind the collective's studio on the ground floor of a four-story, LEED-rated[4] building that they own, and which they designed and renovated. Gita's business partner, the designer for the building, lives upstairs from the studio; her kitchen features reclaimed wood from the Coney Island boardwalk. The facaade of the building, all big windows and dark ipê wood, stands in stark contrast to the rest of the block, most of which is defined by vinyl siding and Fedders air conditioner wall sleeves. The collective's building has a solar system with enough muscle to power the first two floors, a green roof, and a rainwater collection system. The garden where we sit is surrounded by young, wiry trees, just now tall enough to stretch over the fence that encases the hideaway.

We are gentrifiers.

Gita laughs, revealing dimples.

This building has been a gentrifier. We always knew in the back of our minds that there was the potential but we never really took it seriously.

You know you can be a designer and just build what I call the Fedders buildings—like what's across the street—you can build something like that, which is a very innocuous building. I think they're very unsuccessful and I don't think they do any good for the city. But at the same time they're not symbols of gentrification. Or you can build something like we did, which is special or unique or done with design in mind. So why does that become a sign of gentrification? We don't make any more money than your average Bushwicker. We may be in a profession but we're at the low end of the totem pole.

She laughs.

So to me it's very interesting. Why is poor architecture welcomed and interesting architecture isn't? It's not that it isn't—it's

---

4   A certification process administered by the US Green Building Council that verifies certain buildings "save money and resources and have a positive impact on the health of occupants."

just that it's this thing. I wish it could be wow and interesting and cool without it being the gentrifier.

We've met real estate agents that use our building to show to people interested in living in Bushwick. So that's kind of disappointing. And I don't know how you prevent that 'cause I wouldn't be willing to build something like that—*she points across the street, in the direction of the buildings defined by the Fedders units.*

I'm not interested in that at all. And we built this building for a heartbeat. We didn't even have the money. We could have spent another $200,000 easily and we chose not to because we didn't have the money. And I'll bet you that building across the street cost almost as much as this building. We didn't pay a huge amount more. So why shouldn't everybody get good design? Every once in a while they'll give an architect an award because they've done a really beautiful job on a low-income project. And I wonder, why doesn't everybody design like that?

For us, it's too bad that the design is often the symbol of what gentrification is, or that gentrification's coming. And so it often makes people not want to do design or not want design in their neighborhood because they think that it's associated with the pushing out of the sort of native culture. I wish we could kind of invert that thinking. I don't know how you go about doing that other than bringing better design to the people that can't afford it. And showing that neighborhoods can still be well designed and beautiful and accessible and still used by native cultures. And when I say native cultures I mean the people that have been there, existing.

Gita, forty-three, has blue eyes and dark curly hair that's giving way to gray. She teaches design at the Pratt Institute and she advised Matt Krivich and Julian Padarath on the rooftop garden at the Bowery Mission, thanks to a grant from the city's Department of Environmental Protection. She and her colleagues are also working on a Red Hook project called Lowlands, trying to improve the safety and sustainability of public housing built on ecologically vulnerable former wetlands.

Red Hook pokes out into New York Harbor across from the Statue of
Liberty, and in a post-Hurricane Irene, post-Hurricane Sandy world
with ever more hurricanes expected, Mother Nature has become a cen-
tral player in the neighborhood's development.

Mostly she commutes back and forth between Red Hook and Bush-
wick by bicycle. It's a substantial ride—nearly seven miles—but she is
used to it. Red Hook has limited bus service and no subway lines within
easy reach.

Red Hook is isolated, and that isolation slows down the gentrification considerably. It's not like an immediate five-year turn-
around type of situation.

When I first moved there eleven years ago, I was like whoa
this place is crazy. The streets were pretty desolate. You couldn't
get a head of lettuce. It was a real desert, in a way. Between now
and then, it's not radically transformed but amenities are much
more available.

I don't want to become too gentrified or too many amenities
but as a neighborhood it has to function and it's just beginning to
have enough stuff that it is functioning. When your only choices
to go out to eat are the local deli, and get a horrible sandwich, or
get a meal that's one hundred dollars, those are not viable options
to eat on a daily basis.

While I think gentrification is a problem, I like to think of it
as the betterment of our city, so how do you put the betterment
of our city into the hands of the community. What are those structures that we could make happen? To make things much more viable. It's hard because people would look at this as so
anticapitalist but it's totally not at all. Its pro-development, it's
still pro-jobs, it's still pro-money. I just don't understand, why
don't you want these people to make more money? Pay more
taxes, you know? I don't understand it.

My neighbors moved into Red Hook in 1939. They've seen it
all. There are people like that, in their sixties or seventies and have
lived there for forty years.

It was originally settled by really poor artists. My husband was a super poor artist. The weirdest thing about Red Hook was that they were really struggling but the houses were so cheap. A lot of them had saved $15,000, or $10,000, and they could actually buy a falling-down house, get a mortgage, pay next to nothing, and slowly fix it up.

So these artists were coming and they're probably the same income level as the people in the projects, maybe slightly higher. Then the professionals started coming in. An editor at *Lucky* magazine lives there, an editor at *Vibe* magazine lives there. Now there are all these professionals that live there that really skews the income and the census numbers.

Even the professionals that live in Red Hook, they're weird and quirky, or else they wouldn't choose to live in such an inaccessible space. They certainly don't live in Manhattan. They're not choosing to live in Tribeca, which is where you think they would be living. So even though there is this income gap, it's a different type of person that comes there, and they come together. That's the only saving grace for it.

There are an incredible amount of local nonprofits, given the fact that it's so remote and it's not a very wealthy neighborhood. There are probably twenty local nonprofit organizations that exist to help the community. It's really about trying to see how it can be more pro-mixed-income development that incorporates affordable living situations within it. Not just this is high end and this is low income but really to create mixed income projects. Or to create a community bank. Therefore there's more investment put back into the neighborhood. I think that is the good thing: as places get made to be more functional, in a way it makes for a situation where the higher property values could be used in a hyper-local situation where you funnel money back into the neighborhood. Development can be done so it creates jobs and those jobs are hyper-localized.

The small business association was doing a business survey:

what do you need in Red Hook? We need a hardware store where
you can buy nails, a measuring tape, a bucket. We just don't have
something like that. And we have to go all the way to Downtown
Brooklyn to get a pair of socks, which is kind of annoying. I mean,
where do you buy socks?

She laughs.

Red Hook is a destination spot so people will often come and
they'll have brunch or breakfast and then they'll wander around
and they want to go window shopping so that's what they'll do.

They'll say, "Oh, look at those cool bags."

"Oh, look they sell sunglasses. I'll get some sunglasses."

So you know it's like this weird little shopping thing that people do.

There's one row of shops that we call "unnecessary row," and
it's right where I live. It's Dikeman Street to Coffey Street. There's
a really fancy bag store, a really fancy jewelry store, there's a
tchotchke store. And I know all the owners, they're nice people,
and they're all local Red Hookers, but, you know, we don't need
these things in order to make a neighborhood function. It'd be
typical for those things to come later and the places you need
would come first but it's been the total inverse. These things that
you don't need are the typical symbol of gentrification. They've
managed to subsist but I don't know how.

Definitely the amenities for the local residents aren't being
considered at all.

It's a food desert so there's a really high rate of obesity and
diabetes and asthma, and it has disproportionately affected the
projects.

Red Hook is really divided. Eleven thousand people live in
Red Hook and seven thousand live in the projects—and it's the
largest projects in the city—and the other three thousand or so
are on this sort of white side—or whatever—I would say it is primarily white. There's a huge income disparity and everyone's incredibly aware of it. And after Hurricane Sandy people are trying

to address that but issues of gentrification on top of that just don't help.

On Lorraine Street by the projects there are shops, all owned by the same property owners, and they're in really rickety shape and they didn't survive the storm well and they're haphazardly put together, not to code and all sorts of things. They're pretty trashy. And there's been a desire to upgrade them a little bit. There was a deli on the corner of Lorraine and Richards, and it was one of those places where in the evening you could only order through the window and there's bulletproof glass and it was a real symbol of the old neighborhood. And after the storm they were able to rebuild and get funding and gut renovate the whole space and now it looks like a lovely, nice, typical deli. It's lit up at night. You can walk in.

That to me is like a symbol that we're in a safer neighborhood now. We don't need that bulletproof glass. Wealthier people will feel like they can live here now. It's often a domino effect and it's this vicious cycle. Right? You try to make something better, it raises the prices. Then in order to build there you have to raise the rents, and it's just this vicious cycle, and I don't know how you stop it.

I teach at Pratt and we've been doing this green infrastructure class that is about storm water management and how to get the city to deal better with these increased storms and heavier rainfalls, and often green infrastructure and beautification of neighborhoods is looked at as gentrification. And it does often bring higher property values but at the same time, something necessary like storm water capture, which is being done in these beautiful ways with these planters and these streetscapes, is thought about as beautification of a neighborhood, which means higher property values, which means that a lot of people aren't going to be able to afford to live there. So it has all these other domino effects that were never the intended consequences.

There's also this issue of transportation—transportation is

lacking in Red Hook. Obviously if you're a nurse living in the projects and you have to commute to Midtown the commute is hellacious. But the lack of transportation also creates this island, it's a demarcation: Are you going to make this commitment or not? If we were to increase the transportation, which would be helpful and necessary for all the people that live there, does that open this floodgate to transform the neighborhood? Imagine if there was a subway. Wall Street to Red Hook is actually really fast. If you can afford to take the Battery Tunnel every day, and you have a car, you can be there in seven minutes. If that were to really open up more you can imagine how totally destructive that might be.

So it's solving the problems of the residents and trying to deal with that before trying to deal with all the problems of gentrification. And you'd try to stem that with other tools.

One of my colleagues at Pratt, he was really upset that I'd even consider that maybe we don't want any more transportation. Maybe the transportation we have is okay. He feels like you can't say no because of the consequences that it could potentially bring. But I say you kind of have to control that situation.

Communities that do have some control over their own development and are doing it as a self-improvement thing—that's how I'd like Red Hook to see what it's doing, instead of seeing it as all these others coming in and redeveloping. I think that's what happened in the Lower East Side, it was all these others coming in and developing. It wasn't a controlled situation from within. And I think, ideally, Red Hook would be able to do that. But it's very hard in the United States, it's privatized, all the land is privatized, so you can't really make stipulations. That's a more socialist mentality.

The rebuilding required in Red Hook after Hurricane Sandy has expedited a collision between the socialist tendencies Gita is describing and the various bundles of private capital vying for the chance to do the new construction.

It's funny, you'd expect real estate prices to plummet after the storm but they've actually gotten higher. Building more in flood zones doesn't really make sense but at the same time we need millions of new houses to satisfy the population.

There was this huge fight in the spring because the Environmental Protection Agency has been studying the Gowanus Canal and after two years they've decided part of their remediation plans need to consider local economies. And they had a willing participant in John Quadrozzi who owns a lot of the waterfront, he's a concrete manufacturer, and he was willing to use part of his property to house a remediation facility that would take toxic sludge and use it as aggregate inside these concrete blocks that can be built into piers and all sorts of things. There were lots of open meetings, lots of yelling and screaming because Red Hookers really don't want the toxic sludge there. There was a big push to say, "No, we don't want your toxic stuff, take it somewhere else," which I think is okay and I understand. My problem is that then it just makes for environmental exportation because all that toxic sludge has to go somewhere. It's going to go to a community that can't say no. So it will go to West Virginia, or Florida, or Georgia—it's going to travel and get put somewhere else. Which I don't think is a great solution.

I'm the co-chair of this city neighborhood revitalization zoning board. Governor Cuomo created these twelve zones around the city, specifically to have community input into how the city will be reconstructing and so the committee meetings start this month and we'll see how much they actually take the community voice into account. In the planning process, I have to say, the state and the city have realized that they need more community input.

There's a lot of talk with all this funding coming down the pipeline through the community block grants and the federal millions of dollars for the post-Sandy construction, there's a lot of talk about how to use that for community good. How do you create a sort of off-the-grid Red Hook? Or how do you create a community banking situation? It will be interesting because Red Hook could develop in this really weird way where it could attract all these wealthy people, or it could attract these really do-it-for-yourself and scrappy worker people who could potentially live side by side in this interesting way. And I don't think that type of model exists in New York City right now. I think it exists in other places like Portland where there are really wealthy people but also starving hippies, and they sort of manage to live side by side because they have this singular notion of living off the grid whether you're a millionaire or you're not. And it's almost the same in Vermont where everybody's there because they want to be close to the land despite how much money they might have. Ideally there might be something like that that emerges out of Red Hook. We'll see.

25.

I *'m curious about this inextricable link Gita identified—and lamented—between design and our most negative assumptions about gentrification, so I ask her for examples. She doesn't hesitate:*

NYU has money coming out of its ears and they have the ugliest buildings going up across the Lower East Side, and instead of making it a beautiful place, it's the opposite. They could have at least made it a really beautiful neighborhood. I even know those architects who build that stuff—it's bad.

In recent years, criticism of New York University's expansion has come from several places, including its own faculty. Sitting in a former arms factory that the university acquired in 2004, Andrew Ross, professor of sociology and an uncloseted working-class revolutionary agrees with Gita:

There are many people who are in opposition to the university's expansion plan—like myself. I don't think it's necessary development; it's debt driven. It's a debt-driven growth machine, NYU, like many urban universities. We just seem to be that model on steroids. I don't think there's a need for it in terms of academic space, and I'm much more in favor of the dispersed campus anyway, I don't like campuses that are a concentrated cluster. In fact, I think the way that NYU has been quite dispersed and integrated in the city is one of its virtues and more urban universities should be like that.

I think it's a very good thing that students are exposed to the variety of urban life and that they don't live in a bubble. From the point of view of the residents I think it's better to have exposure to students in small numbers than on one whole block.

He laughs.

The more dispersed they are the more they are treated like human beings and fellow residents.

NYU is one of the three biggest landowners in the city and that's one of the reasons there's so much controversy over their expansion plan. Spending $5 billion to put these towers up south of Washington Square in an area that was really ground zero for someone like Jane Jacobs. It was really Jacobs and her peers that saved Washington Square. That's often seen as a turning point in American urbanism. And NYU had a part to play in all of that. The upshot was NYU took over the area south of the square.

Universities are being asked to play a much greater role in this city. You know if you think about some of the formulas for turning around urban economies in the last couple decades there was a period when downtown managers were building new sports arenas or convention centers or museum complexes. And every city had to have that downtown. And they weren't very good economic drivers, at all. Then there was the period of the creative city, and there was the "meds and eds" formula. It's one that is focused on the kinds of jobs that aren't likely to disappear. Urban universities and large hospitals aren't likely to relocate overnight. They're not going to relocate at all, in fact. So they're much less risky than recruiting corporations or hi-tech industries. They attract a lot of young creative people who are likely to stay. They bring in a lot of money in terms of research grants. And in return, I think city managers increasingly turn over ad hoc responsibility to universities for their neighborhoods. They're often the biggest employer in the city—they're so large, they should be stewards. They don't often behave like stewards, but they could be stewards of urbanism. I don't think my university has done a great job of that. But it could do—it's ideally placed to be a steward of urbanism.

The problem is when you hand over de facto planning powers, they become so big and powerful that they get anything they want in terms of zoning variations, or permissions for all sorts of expansions, new buildings, and that's essentially what happens around the country now. Quid pro quo. And so universities have become part of the urban growth machine. It seems counterfactual if you consider that the prestige of the university, the degree should be predicated on a scarcity, not its proliferation.

With his earring, uncombed shoulder-length hair, and jean-blazer combination, Andrew's more record producer than academic. He tends to have the energy of someone who just woke up from a nap—slow moving, no wasted movement—and he takes time to slink back into his thoughts before speaking them with a deliberate cadence, marked by a soft lilt from the lowlands of Scotland.

I'm thinking about my own patch of Manhattan, which is on Hudson Street south of where Jane Jacobs lived, but which is actually a block that sits on a square that has been through many, many different phases of settlement. Some of them residential and some industrial. It's undergone gentrification several times. In fact, St. John's Park, which is now basically a traffic complex where the Holland Tunnel exits, was a very elegant park in the late eighteenth century. It was originally a plantation that had a tobacco house on it actually. Trinity Church took it over under a patent from the crown in 1705. They still own some of the land there. They're one of the biggest landowners in New York. So they built a church, which, at the time, was an anchor for gentrification.

He laughs.

You build a church and churchgoing people congregate around it. And then they made this private park and it was intended to spur residential development all around the site. It was privately held; there was a board of trustees. They would flood the park in the winter to make a skating rink and open it up to the public. So there was this sort of noblesse oblige.

Then, of course, the price of land went up and they sold it to this central Hudson River Railroad, to Vanderbilt. He built a huge railroad terminal there, a freight terminal, which was the main freight terminal for his line. The gentry weren't going to hang around near a freight railway station so they're moving farther uptown. And if you go and visit now, of course, you'll find the Holland Tunnel exit has taken over, but it's surrounded by very affluent converted warehouse loft spaces—some of the most expensive in New York once again. So it's actually undergone two waves of what some people might call gentrification but of course it's a term that has a very broad spectrum of interpretations. You could do a whole history of that block and come up with shifting land uses, shifting populations, the whole history of New York in that one block. Who knows, in fifty years time it may once again be a park, or something else—a moon port.

He laughs.

People often talk about gentrification being formulaic at this point. Now it's really studied and cultivated and monitored by the real estate industry and I think that it's true in certain neighborhoods, you can pretty much see the signs, "We're at stage two, we're at stage three, we're at stage four." But not all neighborhoods are on the same path of development. I think that's true of my neighborhood, even though people consider it the home of the gentry, or one of the homes of the gentry in New York.

I haven't always lived in Tribeca. I used to rent a loft in SoHo—the spice warehouse is where I used to live. One of my old neighbors, who is a little crazy, claims that she can still smell cardamom in the summer time when it gets too hot. Maybe she can?!

He laughs and smiles.

Eventually it became too expensive so I looked for the cheapest loft I could find in downtown Manhattan. That's the reason that I bought the loft that I currently live in, twenty years ago. And at the time I joked to my friends that if something bad happened to Lower Manhattan, I could just run through the Holland Tunnel. And in fact it was only months after the bombing of the World Trade Center in 1993, so something very bad did happen—and would happen again.

At the time, in '93, I got very interested in bombs, the history of bombs in Manhattan. Which is a very interesting history. Most people know about the bombing of the J.P. Morgan building in 1920 but in the 1960s there was a whole spate of bombings, third world and leftist groups. But actually, the real violence doesn't come in the form of explosions. It is visible spatially. It's in the slow transition—sometimes much more rapid—the slow flow of capital through the city, block by block. It's the relentless pursuit of rents, surplus capital. And that's a form of violence, some theorists of gentrification see it as a form of violence. And you can see it in a lot of neighborhoods. Did I see it in my neighborhood? It's more difficult to say.

When I moved to Tribeca there was nothing there that would lead one to believe it would be what it is today—which is a sort of residential adjunct to Wall Street. It's one of the favorite residential places for the 1 percent. At the time, there were a lot of vacant bombed-out buildings, there were still a lot of artists left living down there. I used to play soccer in the streets. I mean people talked about the gentrification of SoHo at that time but it seemed unlikely that Tribeca would follow that path. And to a large extent it hasn't because it's a residential enclave, and the commercial rents are too high now for the kind of shopping mall that is SoHo.

I never much liked living in Tribeca. I didn't spend a lot of time there actually for the first decade. Most of my life was just north, most of my social and intellectual life. There wasn't much in Tribeca that I needed. And then I had kids. If your kids go to the local school, your neighborhood becomes something that's much more fully integrated in your life. It becomes well populated with people that you not only know but depend upon for all sorts of things. So now the streets of Tribeca are filled with people that I know, mostly from the school. And that was not the case before. The place didn't change so much as my own particular needs and pathways changed and I became more of a functional resident.

My kids they go to the public school there now, and most of the families have at least one person who works on Wall Street. And that's the reality of it. I have to keep my mouth shut a lot of the time.

He laughs.

If I know them well enough, they know my politics. And they think that's cool, to have a radical or left-wing acquaintance.

He laughs.

The debate about gentrification among a lot of scholars tends to break down on the production side or the consumption side. How much of it was push, how much of it was pull. How much of it was making an offer you can't refuse on the part of the real estate industrial complex and how much of it was a "let's get out of this dirty city."

A lot of it is a power struggle, I'm afraid, people vs. profits. But within that broad terrain there are all sorts of models that do soften the conflict and can bring some reason to the outcomes. If you go to the end of this corridor you will see that the blocks on the other side are part of the Cooper Square community plan, which is the first successful community plan in the city, a wonderful example of what happens when you do community planning at the grassroots level.

Or take a city like Phoenix. There was this real effort to do downtown revitalization, and to do it in an affordable way. The reason I started studying Phoenix was because the artists were playing a role in downtown development. It was a little different from what I'd seen elsewhere. It wasn't acting as an involuntary agent of gentrification. Artists were trying to seize control over blueprints for downtown development and they'd learned how to become urbanists, and educated themselves in a very admirable way and had become full-time urbanists, urban activists. And they had bought downtown property in areas so they couldn't be evicted. They had strongholds in place. And then came the housing crash so whatever was happening collapsed. So you can draw conclusions about that. But for me it was a lesson in the unevenness of the landscape. It's by and large not very prudent to assume that the same development is happening everywhere in American cities. And the worst thing you can do from a New York–centric position is assume that what happens in New York is going to get emulated elsewhere. It just doesn't happen.

Despite the protean quality of gentrification as it moves from one city to another, one country to another, there has always been the temptation to cluster cities along ideological or geographic lines. In the early 1960s, academics and politicians presented the idea of a "megalopolis," an urban development running down the East Coast from Boston to Washington, DC. And in 1967 the Greek architect Constantinos Doxiadis took the idea even further, predicting that "Ecumenopolis," an enormous universal city with no boundaries, would cover the earth's surface—total urbanization of the planet.

Since leaving office, Bloomberg has played a big role in the C40 climate group of city managers from the world's big cities. They exchange a lot of policy knowledge. Especially the police forces, the zero-tolerance policies that were pioneered here under Bratton. These things are exchanged and swapped and shared with counterparts in different cities. It's a fairly small world and with a footprint of globalization being what it is, these cities have much more in common with one another, especially these so-called global cities. New York has a lot more in common with London or Shanghai than it does with Philadelphia at this point. And that's a kind of rupture of scale and a geographical anomaly, historically speaking. But it's the world we live in. And the world that a fraction of the highly paid creative class operates in now. So it doesn't surprise me that a consultancy like Bloomberg's would set up shop. Richard Florida did it—set up as a consultancy for creative city making—why can't Bloomberg do it?

At the beginning of the twenty-first century, when cities had tired of throwing money into new stadiums and shopping districts, the urban theorist Richard Florida suggested a change in tactics: luring what he calls the creative classes—those working in science, engineering, education, computer programming, research, arts, and media—for capital and cultural growth. These "high bohemians" represent forty million US workers, or 30 percent of the workforce. Citing places like Silicon Valley, Austin, and Seattle, Florida makes a case for these professionals as an ascendant economic force.

Richard Florida has been very influential in a lot of ways: there's been a scramble on the part of a lot of Midwestern or second-tier cities trying to turn around struggling economies. They go out and try to attract gay graduate recruits to come to Midwestern cities and the like. I can understand why it would appeal to city managers because it was a very cheap urban formula. It didn't cost very much. A few bicycle lanes here and fair trade coffee shops there.

He laughs.

But it costs nothing even remotely in the same league as what you would have to spend on tax exemptions to attract a corporation. And nothing in terms of public expenditure, nothing to match the stadium-building complex of the '80s or '90s. So a very cheap formula—and the prospect of rising land value. I think that was the most attractive thing to city managers—that the creatives would boost the rents and housing prices. Maybe they did for a while, but I don't think the evidence is in on that. And that trajectory was broken, anyway, by the housing crash.

Global cities do tend to create a certain bubble. New York and London, I would put them in a class on their own. They are much more cosmopolitan cities. The degree to which they've become unaffordable is something that has happened in tandem.

Central London is the worst-case scenario. There are whole parts of Central London that are just vacant all of the time. They are foreign-owned places and the people who own them are hardly there. Huge neighborhoods. You probably wouldn't have the same feel for that in New York City but there's probably a lot of absentee owners.

Outside of London and New York, it's pretty easy to find the footprint of globalization in cities, especially in developing countries. You go to Shanghai and you know where the expatriates will be living and you know what kind of amenities they'll be demanding—and they'll be getting. And outside of those areas you're living in a completely different city. In the Gulf States it's even more egregious because local elites and Western expatriates are living in a bubble, and they're a very tiny percentage of the population, and the other 95 percent are migrant labor workforce. In its most extreme form, I would say that's the manifestation of globalization. That bubble created by global cities.

It's uneven but in developing countries you're going to see more of a disparity between the bubble and everywhere else. But then you get to New York, a place at the other end of the spectrum, and it's more difficult to say where the edge is. And probably even more so in Central London. There's really not much left in Central London that people would consider to be affordable.

A lot of urbanists will talk about global city regions instead of simply global cities. There are seven or eight of them in the US that are talked about as global city regions, and they can incorporate three or four cities. Like the Great Lakes region, which stretches from Chicago to Toronto; and Seattle and Portland and Vancouver, which are part of the Cascadian global city region. And that's an interesting way of looking at. It's beyond the metro region, it's a whole regional cluster that can compete globally. A lot of the advanced cities have been thinking about global city regions and planning transportation patterns that make sense for those regions. Like the area between Frankfurt and London, which has been conceived and developed as a cluster in terms of transportation.

We're hoping there'll be some time of transition in the policy temperature when de Blasio takes over. I'm a little skeptical but you wouldn't have to do very much to differentiate yourself from what Bloomberg has done. Forty percent of the city has been re-zoned in this space of time. And if overall the goal has been to promote high-density development—fine. I'm not an opponent of high-density development. But it's not affordable development. How you actually create density or encourage density in an af-fordable way is the big challenge. And he had no interest in doing that, other than to pay lip service to it. But with de Blasio you have a lot more than lip service going in. And you have a lot of goodwill and the power of a lot of people so we'll see what hap-pens. But community planning is different from urban planning. It's less technical. There are people involved. It's not about the ra-tionalization of space and land use. It's about the lived experience of people and what they want in their neighborhoods, and their right not to be displaced, which is a very important part of the right to the city.

If you're elected and you want to show that participatory planning and participatory budgeting—both are ideas that de Bla-sio has paid lip service to in his campaign—if you want to show that will actually be meaningful then you have to take steps to guarantee that they will have some impact or else people won't bother to show up at these meetings.

Most of the community board meetings I've attended play out with a severe downward trajectory: there is some life at the beginning—mi-crophones are held close to the mouth, thoughts are projected, patience is upheld, despite the demands of bureaucratic procedures—but then an agenda item runs a few minutes over its allotted time, a member of the public speaks until he has said everything that he wants to say, and before long the meeting is in its nth hour and everyone has devolved into lifeless, yet still irritable, robots. One community board member described the final hour of the meetings as the "elect Hitler" portion of the evening because "everyone's so tired they'll vote yes for anything just to close the debate and move on. You could hold a vote to elect Hitler president of the universe and everyone would say 'ay'."

The drone of the meeting could provide the perfect white noise for falling asleep if it weren't for the one row of people—usually half a dozen, maybe a dozen—who are making all that racket, waving all those signs about something that, for whatever reason, hasn't riled the other 99.99 percent of people who live in the neighborhood. The school auditoriums, libraries, and public housing community rooms where these meetings are held are generally not more than half full unless there is a marquee issue reverberating in the press such as the demolition of an eighteenth century stone church or Ikea's application to build a store in Gita's neighborhood of Red Hook.

During meetings, a lot of community board members—the men with loosened ties and sweat-stained shirts, the women with furrowed brows bearing massive headaches—are visibly exhausted from a long day of work. This is their spare time. Many are small business owners in the neighborhood or working professionals who have their own interests in mind just like everyone attending the meeting. On certain micro-issues, the board's recommendations can guide state government decisions—whether or not to give a new bar in the neighborhood a liquor license, for example—but, as Cea Weaver pointed out, it is not until votes are cast by mayoral appointees and city council members that any stance has a direct bearing on the shape and composition of a neighborhood.

The people in this city have had these experiences watching community boards being overridden. The NYU expansion plan, case in point. The community board here voted almost unanimously against it. And that made no difference whatsoever to the planning commission. No difference whatsoever to our elected representative in City Council, Margaret Chin. So when people look at that process and they say, "Yes, we can spend a lot of time working on this, getting all worked up about it, working toward some kind of solution that we believe is the right one and then it means nothing"—you're going to generate apathy that way. So let's see if de Blasio is going to do it differently. So far the people he's appointed are all political hacks. And that doesn't betoken much of a transition. No new names in the Rolodex.

He laughs.

With the lack of new names in the Rolodex, with the reappointment of city officials like Police Commissioner William Bratton, an unsettling continuum emerges, one that exists above and beyond two mayors like Giuliani and de Blasio who have wildly different politics and priorities:

I think that the permanent government of New York are very wealthy people who are unelected and they make their desires known. Not to us but to elected officials in all sorts of ways. Elected administrators who are familiar with the past, who are familiar with governance, and who know how to carry a government forward. In the course of their experience they have learned all the customs and rituals of pleasing the permanent government. And that's what you get. The pressure does come from them. They expect the city to be governed in their interests. That is quite clear.

26.

*R*ob Robinson is trying to steal the attention of elected officials from the permanent government:

    I get access to all the policy and planning folks in
the city, the commissioner, but then they're afraid because I get
access to Washington—the human rights work that I do also
gives me access to high-level government folks, right? So the
policy and planning folks have to hear me out.

*Rob works with the National Economic & Social Rights Initia-
tive in downtown Manhattan. Though he sits in a rather formal conference room with large windows looking out over the financial
district, he is in blue jeans and a baseball cap. This fifty-seven-year-
old African American does not do frills. A cane rests against the
chair next to him.*

    I grew up on suburban Long Island, went to college on a foot-
ball scholarship. I went to the University of Maryland, and my
dad told the school the only way he would sign off on me getting
that scholarship was if I would still get a full four-year education
if I got hurt. And they bought into it. I injured my hip playing but
I still was able to complete college.

    So I came out of school and grew up in the restaurant busi-
ness. I was a chef, right? It's what I knew how to do, I did it since
I was a little kid with my dad, and the doctor told me my hip is

going to deteriorate the more I stand on it. So I eventually had to change careers and ended up in customer service.

The company I worked for moved me to Miami in March 2001, and in July, I was called into the general manager's office, told there's no more money in the budget for your position. I was stunned, shocked—thirteen years—but I wasn't angry. I was confident. Alright, I'll get a job. But Miami was going through tough economic times, and I just kept fighting through it. A year passed and I'm running out of unemployment, I'm running out of severance pay. Another year passes, and I tap out my bank account, then my 401(k). Before you knew it, I ended up on the streets of Miami, homeless. Spent two years on the streets, found my way up to New York City, spent ten months in a New York City homeless shelter.

When I was in the shelter, there were issues that I thought needed to change, and I started pestering. People call it organizing; I call it pestering.

He smiles.

I needed to bring things to the attention of the staff. I kept telling my caseworker and nothing changed. I'd go to her boss, nothing changed, and I wrote letters to the guy who runs the whole thing and he came to the shelter saying, "I want to meet the guy who's writing me these letters—this is a guy from the shelter?"

He laughs.

You know it was friggin' incredible. He said he was impressed because I wasn't just listing a bunch of problems—I gave him possible solutions and he found value in them.

So he pushed me into something called the New York City Coalition on the Continuum of Care, which monitors about $110 million dollars that goes into the shelter system. Sometimes I scratch my head like, you know, I just wanted to build a better shelter—how'd I get over here?

Rob is the exception on the twenty-four-person steering committee

that decides how that $110 million flows through the system. The for-
merly homeless don't generally make it to the table where the decision-
makers gather but this is where Rob finds himself. Over the past decade
he has worked with several local and national organizations—Picture
the Homeless, Take Back the Land—collaborating with groups around
the country that want to engage in direct action: eviction defenses;
breaking into foreclosed houses and moving the homeless in. He is often
ferried to DC to give lawmakers fieldwork perspective on housing pol-
icy. He works with organizations in metamorphosing cities like Bu-
dapest and Berlin, and speaks at conferences in Switzerland and Brazil
and Columbia. Despite his profile, Rob mainly lives off of a monthly
$1,600 disability check, supplemented by honorariums from speaking
engagements. He says this is the happiest time in his life.

The Department of Homeless Services, which is not far from
here, has a budget of $850 million. So that combined with the
$110 million that we oversee, in New York City it is about a bil-
lion dollars spent on homelessness. It sounds great when you hear
the number but it's problematic because when a body is ware-
housed in a shelter it's not getting into the root cause of the solution, it's a temporary Band-Aid.

So I've been able to articulate going through homelessness and
that's been valuable because it challenges power and it challenges
the solutions that government and some of these agencies came
up with.

Now there is a lot of push back on me, which I don't mind,
saying, "Well, how can you talk about us that way? You benefitted
from the shelter system."

And my response is, "Yeah, I did benefit: I got an inside look
on how you operate and how you're not getting at the root cause."

And I'm going to articulate that as widely and as broadly as
possible.

I think we've been effective because we've just had something
handed down from the Human Rights Council in Geneva saying
the United States is guilty of criminalizing the homeless. The way

they push people out from public spaces when they have no alternatives, people have to go to the bathroom and they go in the bushes and end up getting a ticket that just prevents them from getting a job because now you have a crime, or you got locked up, you can't produce bail, you got a record, that record follows you, you can't find housing, it just exacerbates an ongoing problem. The council looked at a specific case and under the International Covenant on Civil and Political Rights, they said, yes, the Unites States is criminalizing the homeless. So it's raising awareness now, Geneva is shining a spotlight. Not only that, but the Unites States is due to go through something called the Universal Periodic Review next year, where all of its peers in the UN get to ask the United States publicly, "Why are you criminalizing the homeless?"

It gives a person like me more ammunition to really expose the issue and try to make change. A former professor at CUNY Law taught me the value of using the human rights framework; it makes people focus. Here in this country, we've always tended to say, "Ah that's something international; we don't violate human rights." Even our government will point its fingers at other governments but here is Geneva saying, "United States, you're violating human rights."

Multiple incidents in cities across the country prompted condemnation from the United Nations. In March of 2014, for instance, Albuquerque police shot a mentally ill homeless man multiple times. He had been standing about ten feet away from the trio of law enforcers, and he was carrying lots of gear, including a knife, because he had been camping illegally on public property. When he took the shots and fell to the ground, motionless, the police continued to shoot at him—now with "beanbag" rounds, pelting the skin instead of piercing it. Then they released a K-9 unit to tear at the man's leg. The incident can be observed by anyone who cares to watch it because it was recorded by a helmet-mounted camera worn by one of the cops. In the video, the man does not react to the dog's bite. As his leg is yanked in various directions, the man remains as he had been before the beanbag rounds and the animal attack: motionless.

In their report, the Human Rights Committee openly questions if the United States is in compliance with a human rights treaty it ratified in 1992 and makes several sensible suggestions about how to fall into compliance—funding municipalities that implement alternatives to criminalizing homelessness, if not abolishing the criminalization of homelessness altogether. But the tendency across the country is exactly the opposite and many cities are strengthening laws that target the homeless: restricting camping, sleeping, or sitting for too long in a public space. Informal tent cities that sprung up after the collapse of the housing market in 2007 are mostly broken up now, some of the inhabitants put into shelters, some given one-way bus tickets to far away places, and some locked up for violations that ultimately have everything to do with survival: seeking shelter, food, and clothing. In November of 2013, Los Angeles politicians debated making it illegal to feed the homeless on the streets if local residents complained. And at the beginning of 2014 in New York, a fifty-four-year-old mentally ill veteran named Jerome Murdough died in a Rikers Island cell that had a temperature of 100 degrees. A prison official told the Associated Press that Murdough "basically baked to death." He was serving a sentence for trying to sleep in the stairwell of a housing project.

In defense of the government, there is a real effort now, looking at New York City and other big continuums like Los Angeles, where they are saying no more money going into transitional housing. Generally you would come off the street, go into an emergency shelter for up to six months then transitional housing where you can stay anywhere from six months to twenty-four months with the hope of you finding permanent housing. What we found is people falling off the cycle, coming back in through emergency shelter, so it was almost a merry-go-round. The care providers running these transitional facilities call themselves not-for-profit but somebody's profiting—their beds are always full—and it's a little bit of a merry-go-round. You're not helping that person get to independent living or permanent housing.

When you're in a shelter, you get a family looking for services in the Bronx, and they finally get placed around eleven o'clock at night, and they have to get on the school bus and be trucked into Brooklyn, so they get in bed at one o'clock in the morning. Then the mom has to wake the kids up at six o'clock—'cause they go to school in the Bronx—so she's got to get on the subway and take them. It's absurd—absurd!

That money being spent on temporary housing, or temporary shelters, they're throwing it in the garbage because if you put that money in permanent spaces, people have a permanent place to live. All of a sudden health care doesn't become an issue because you have stability of a home, you find a doctor, you find a school for your children to go to—so a home is the basic foundation. And home is more than a house; it's a sense of community, so when you don't have a babysitter you know the family down the street will watch your kids—all of these things that make your life work and allow you to do things every day fall into place once you have a home. HUD[5] and other government agencies finally realized that and made transitional housing the lowest priority for funding, which is a good thing. There are some other issues within HUD but I think that is one good thing that the government is doing that I'll speak in favor of.

And when the Bloomberg administration did something, well, it was only because of pressure from the federal government. Bloomberg always had this business mentality, which I get, business does do some things well. I often have to challenge the organization I work for, which will totally dismiss general corporate practices. I will say corporations are successful because they do some things well, right? We can borrow some of that, we don't have to borrow the entire picture, but they do some things well and you have to admit that. But by the same token I think they lack the compassion that is necessary, numbers outweigh morality and that's problem-

---

[5]   US Department of Housing and Urban Development.

atic. I need to get to a bottom line and I don't care who I run over to do that—that's the basic fundamental system we have in this country now, capitalism. And it lacks compassion. It's about greed and this totally dismisses you and I as individuals.

The long-term goal is to change that. In the short period of time that I've gone through this transition in life, I'll be honest with you, my thinking is along socialism-Marxist lines—I get it, you know. Capitalism is not going to work, especially with respect to housing for poor people. Poor people are never going to win the housing fight when housing is a market commodity. It just ain't going to work. Especially in this city because it's on a steady incline. You see new buildings being constructed—condos, studios starting at $2.5 million.

He pauses then laughs.

If you don't have two-and-a-half million don't even look, right?

He laughs.

That's a reality. That's what it is. And they just keep putting up tower after tower around the city. It's three thousand a month: Do you want it or don't you?

Seven towers just south of Central Park are either under construction or on their way. One is known as One57, and it aims to be the tallest residential building in the city—though after four years of construction only seventy-five of the marketed ninety stories have been completed. Two of the towers are nearly as tall as the Empire State Building—one will rise 1,424 feet. At this height it will form a monolith of steel and glass with a shadow long enough to deny sunlight to giant swathes of Central Park. In fact, the group of shadows from the larger towers will dominate the southern portions of the park throughout the year and at midday on solstice these shadows will extend half a mile, elongating to almost a mile as they cut northeast, prioritizing the views for the relatively small group of luxury condos over thirty-eight million park visitors left to experience darkened baseball fields, playgrounds, paths, and fields.

At its fundamental core, capitalism is about greed, right? How much can I get out of you, how much can I maximize from you? And it just doesn't allow room for sharing or for anything that has anything to do with morality. During the financial crisis, when our government decided to bail out the banks, that was a point, in my opinion, that there should have been revolution in this country. What our government essentially did is say that it is okay for you, homeowner, to fail but the banks can't fail. We're gonna take tax money out of your pocket and give it to the banks so that they're stable. Then those same banks turned around and said, "You can't pay your mortgage? Well, you know what, I pay an insurance policy that gives me the incentive to evict you. So I am going to evict you and take your house and put it back on the market and sell it again." I don't care that the tax money came out of your pocket, I don't give a shit, this is how it works and you got to go.

Greed, man.

And you're seeing this around this country. I'm now working with the New York City Anti-Eviction Network, but it's modeled after networks that were popping up around the country, where people are reclaiming houses and they've taken the direct action to a level of: Okay, you want to evict this family? We're gonna defend their right to be in the house. The same day that the marshal is going to come, we're going to the nearest branch of your bank and shut it down, there will be no business conducted in that bank. It's gotten to that level. So a hundred people in front of the house, a hundred people in front of the bank: showdown. Banks are like: "No, no, we'll give you principle reduction, come in and let's talk." So when you pressure them they reduce the principle on your mortgage right? But they weren't going to do it otherwise. It shows you how messed up the system is.

At Take Back the Land our theory was that even principle reduction is not a good deal, because it still leaves your house on the market. It's not transformative. If we go through another economic downturn you can go through the very same shit again. Take Back the Land forces all banks to turn over property to community land trusts. Then we have control of that house, the community governs what happens to that house, and the people get to stay in it.

It's gonna be constantly scrapping for what's left and it's not much because the banks control it all and we have to change that. We have to rise up with transformative organizing where community gets control of the land. Make no mistake about it, that's what's at the crux of the problem in this country: land. The fight for land and property rights. One percent of this country owns land; 99 percent of us are out of the equation, man. The only way I see changing that is through revolution. I never believed that before; at Take Back the Land we always talked about nonviolent civil disobedience and direct action, we called it positive action. But it's going to take something like revolution because capitalism's not going to surrender, you know? It's the old "Power concedes nothing without the struggle," right? That's real.

So how do you organize and politicize people to get to that point?

It bothers me in the city when people don't take control of their lives. The one thing that I see traveling around the world is self-determination, and that doesn't exist in the United States. I just came back from Columbia where people will find a piece of land and they'll take it, and they'll defend that piece of land. They'll build shacks to live in, to defend themselves from the elements. That level of self-determination doesn't exist in this country. It's something that bothers me. We have a sense of entitlement in this country: "Somebody's gonna fix it." I get frustrated sometimes at some meetings and say: "What are you going to do? 'Cause there's no helicopter, you know, above the building with the three-bedroom apartment asking you where do you want them to place it." That ain't happening, you gonna have to get up and do something to make it happen.

I'm working now with a lot of Occupiers and students who were in urban planning classes who identify themselves as gentrifiers and want to figure out a way to reverse that—they feel shitty, right? I often have to tell them: "I understand the situation you're in, you need a place to live, you need to find a place affordable for you." I tell them, "I wouldn't necessarily call you a gentrifier. You didn't just come in and say bulldoze this neighborhood; you did something different than the gentrifiers do, you said, 'I can co-exist with these families and I'm fine living here.'"

It's about us, right? What are our needs? What is it our community needs? We need land, we need housing, we need health care. When you organize around needs, it takes you away from self-centered values. It's using the human rights frame, which looks at human needs vs. property rights. There's been narratives spun in this country, home ownership is the way to wealth. I'd argue that anybody who is wealthy didn't get wealthy buying a home. They got wealthy either 'cause money was passed down over generations or they made investments, and poor people can't make those investments so you're never going to get it, but meanwhile we bought into this narrative that home ownership was the way to wealth.

I remember my dad moving us out to Long Island in the '60s and everybody in the family thought we were rich because we had this house. I look back now, understanding the history of housing in this country, redlining and all of that stuff, and I realize, you know, actually it was a load of shit that we were sold.

When my dad and mom went to look at houses on Long Island these real estate agents were leading them to neighborhoods other than where they wanted to go, and then the one house that they really fell in love with, the agent told them it was rented. My dad didn't trust the agent, and he asked his friend Murray, who wasn't black, to go out and inquire about the house. Murray did it, and the guy was willing to sell the house to Murray, and my dad realized that this stuff was going on. He went back and threatened the agent and ended up getting the house. It's the house I grew up in.

I'm not going back to my dad to say, "Look, you got jerked when you bought this house back then," but I get it now. And I'm able to articulate this in real terms by telling my own family story. You got to share those stories. People buy into narrative. Look at the big picture of capitalism and what it means. Maybe that's our mistake as grassroots organizers, not coming with the political education on a regular basis and having things like the MST[6] school in Brazil where all the folks and young folks come together, and learn together, talk about struggle together.

I think in this—quote unquote—the wealthiest country in the world there are expectations and people have become complacent, sitting back saying the government will fix it. My response to that is the government broke it, why do you think they are going to fix it? Them and the corporations broke it and I don't think there is going to be any attempt to fix it.

---

[6] Brazilian Landless Workers' Movement.

27.

*J*erry has been arrested ninety-three times:

Almost all political—no theft or anything like that, nothing serious, a few little things here and there in the course of it all. This started before I ever came to New York. See I refused to go to Vietnam—I'm one of those. So my very first arrest ever was for desertion when I was twenty-three.

Jerry, aka Gerald Wade, aka Gerald Green, aka Gerald Douglas Hines is a man whose rap sheet bares a long list of aliases, each with its own story. Mostly he is Jerry the Peddler and he is giving me a tour of 155 Avenue C, home of C-Squat since 1989. Jerry lives in a 350-square-foot apartment and over the last four decades has squatted in three different buildings and helped to open several more on behalf of others. He takes me onto a catwalk overlooking the basement—formerly several small apartments, now one big open hall.

This is our performance space. We've had everybody from—you name 'em—False Prophets has played here, Black Rain has played here, Leftöver Crack has played here—but half of Leftöver Crack lives in this building, so—

He laughs.

We used to do a lot of parties, like once a week. Sometimes they put two cops on each corner just to keep an eye on us when we sit back and shut down the block and party. Nowadays we're a lot more civilized than we were just a few years ago.

We're getting old, I'm a token hippie in a building full of aging punks.

I like Jerry because he reminds me of Willie Nelson. Jerry lets his beard grow much longer than the outlaw country musician but both men have a way with a bandana—they wrap them around their heads with similar precision. Jerry has the tired eyes of a sixty-seven-year-old lion and the mischievous laugh of a man who has never answered to a boss. The walls of the performance space are covered in graffiti, large pieces of work in a few spots.

There was a time when the walls in C-Squat had graffiti all the way up. Real graffiti—art and what have you; unfortunately we had to come up to code and that meant putting up all new Sheetrock in the hallways. So now in the hallways we got tags instead of graffiti.

Most of the people in this building have been here from the beginning. When I first came in the late '80s they were punks, they were all in their late teens to mid-twenties. There was no roof, there was no stairs; they had a series of cargo nets that they used to climb up to get from floor to floor, mind you. They taught themselves carpentry, and plumbing, and electric. Nowadays when they need money, they go out and find themselves a construction job.

We walk out onto the street and Jerry points at the tree in front of his building:

I planted that, '02, I guess. It's a plum tree, it produces plums every year. I've yet to have one. Just as they're ripening, somebody always comes along and takes them. Personally I don't know if I would really want to eat a plum that was from the side of a New York City bus stop.

He laughs.

I planted it more for the aesthetic value than anything else.

I follow him north on Avenue C. As we walk he points to various features of his neighborhood.

This was a burnt-out building. Most of this neighborhood was a burnt-out derelict back in the late '70s, through the '80s.

There were lots of little-bitty gardens, the Lower East Side is famous for its gardens; they had chickens and the occasional rabbits, goats, pigs.

This was a weed store. This guy and his sons, they sold weed outta here. And they made sure that nobody went into the garden and did drugs. If you wanted to smoke a joint you can do that. But if you were caught down here selling dope, selling coke, his two sons would run you off the block with a baseball bat. Eventually they got rich, went back to Puerto Rico.

This was a coke store here, but it was one of your better quality coke stores in that it was actually a deli that also sold coke— as opposed to a lot of places that just sold coke and everything else in the store was fifty cents.

He laughs and cuts left into the Pedro Albizu Campos Plaza, a public housing development.

The projects we're cutting through, they were built during the late '70s, during the time when there was still money available for public housing. After the riots in the '60s in Detroit, Newark, Watts, places like that, the government couldn't figure out what was going on. So they put together a commission—they're so good at that—Governor Kerner was in charge, so they called it the Kerner Commission, and they sat down and studied the problem and they decided that the black flight during the '30s, '40s, and '50s from the South, up to the northern cities and the West Coast, had concentrated all these poor people, mostly black people, into these inner cities. And they were blaming the people—not the conditions—for their lifestyle. And they decided the best way to deal with this is to deconcentrate these spaces. Now how do you do that? How do you get thousands of people to move out of their homes and neighborhoods? Well, you cut off services. You cut back on the police, cut back on fire departments, you close schools, stop funding housing, and you let the drugs and the alcohol, you let all of that go on all during the '70s and deep into the '80s. Most of the kids that grew up in the projects, they had no choice: it was either deal drugs or nothing—or starve. So that meant that a couple of generations of mostly black and Latino youth either died in the gutter or went to prison and their lives were destroyed. These projects now, they're half empty still. There's no life. You see a few kids but not a lot. It's sad compared to what it was thirty years ago.

The New York City Housing Authority cares for 178,557 apartments. At any given point over three thousand are vacant. Turnovers and processing account for some of these but others sit empty for months or years awaiting required repairs and renovations. By the authority's own count, over three hundred homes have been empty for an average of seven years, some of them in aging buildings from the 1930s and 1940s, and the vast majority constructed before Jerry's arrival.

I got to New York in '75 from Texas, grew up in San Angelo, and I first moved to the Lower East Side in '77. I lived on the corner of Twelfth and A, directly overlooking the intersection from the third floor. I was sitting here one night—*he points up at the building in front of us*—I'd only been in the apartment a couple of months, and all of a sudden I hear this big boom right outside of my window. Now I'm enough of a country boy to know what a shotgun sounds like, enough of an ex-GI to know to drop and roll. So that's exactly what I did: rolled out of my chair and across the floor. I gave it a minute then I'm up against the wall and I'm looking out the window, and right in the middle of the intersection there's this cat standing with a shotgun, just like this—*Jerry holds an imaginary shotgun tight against his hip*—pointing straight up Twelfth Street. Then it's like something out of *High Noon*, he takes his shotgun and just walks right up the middle of the street. No cops, no nothing. I sat there for a good half an hour just watching. No cops ever showed up, cops only came down here either to dispose of bodies or to rob drug dealers. There was no other reason for cops to be here.

Tompkins Square Park was not a park you wanted to go bare-foot in, okay. Drugs like you wouldn't believe. I once walked around in one area of the park with a bucket and some thick welders gloves and picked up two hundred sets of works[7] just lay-ing around on the ground and what have you.

I didn't think of it until all the drug epidemics were over, but I've often wanted to mount all the drug paraphernalia that I found on the street in the shape of the New York City skyline. Another little art project I've always wanted to do—they would never give me the permits for this: I've always wanted to go up to the top of the Empire State Building with time-lapse cameras pointing down at Thirty-Fourth and Fifth and then just an hour or so before rush hour, I want to take like twenty gallons of different colored paint and splash 'em in the intersection and then let the cameras film the cars painting pretty pictures.

He laughs.

They would never give me a permit for that, I know better than to even try. But I still think that would be a great Andy Warhol, single shot—every different color of paint you can think of and then just let the cars come along.

Jerry stops at the corner of Thirteenth Street and pulls a half-smoked cigarette from his pocket. He holds it in his hand as he speaks.

This is the original squat—the one that everyone says was the first. This is where Rosario Dawson grew up—544 East 13th Street. She was hanging out on the front stoop one day and a Hol-lywood movie director came by and saw her and said, "She's gor-geous. I'm gonna make her a star."

He laughs.

And that's kind of what happened. Squatter child makes good—makes very good.

---

[7]   Everything one might need for an injection: a needle; a band of rubber to tie around the arm; a vessel of some kind, emptied of the drug it once contained.

This is Thirteenth Street, this is the famous block right here, this is the one where they brought the tank in on us. See the tall building here? It was taken over by junkies and the cops couldn't get 'em out, people couldn't get 'em out, they just kept trying and nothing seemed to work. The cops would come once every couple of months and raid the place and take everybody out and two hours later they would start drifting back in.

One day they took everybody out and people from one of the buildings here took a piece of orange fluorescent paper—like the notices cops post, you've seen 'em a million times—and they put a little NYPD police symbol on there at the top and they were like: "This building is closed due to drug trafficking. For further information contact the 9th Precinct." They put a chain and a padlock on the door; the junkies came by, saw it, turned around and left. After a couple days, people went in there and turned that from a shooting gallery into a squat.

In the spring of '95 there was a group that wanted this building. They're people that I call property pimps, they get tons and tons of money from the government and they'll fix up a building and put half that money in their pocket and they're just sitting there exploiting people and making themselves rich. They wanted this building. We took 'em to court and we were in court over a year, claiming adverse possession, claiming people had been in there for over ten years, that they had a right to it—they had run out all the druggies, they had done all the repairs, and they had saved these buildings when nobody wanted them. The judge was sympathetic, we won in his court; unfortunately we lost in the appeals.

That was in May of '95, and there was a lot of standing off and what have you in June. They were going to evict everyone and we came in and built a barricade of cars, and that's when they brought the tank out. It wasn't a real tank, it was an APC, an armored personnel carrier. When I was in the army in Germany I actually drove a few of those things. It doesn't have a turret and a cannon; it's just a big track vehicle, used to carry troops into a heavy combat zone. And they were gonna just drive it straight through the wall.

He laughs.

This was back during the Giuliani administration, and Bratton was police commissioner. They were both showboats but then at the last minute they realized what a media circus they had created, so they backed off with the tank.

They eventually evicted this building and put up scaffolding, put a little command center right here, put a cop there twenty-four seven.

Then on the Fourth of July, there's a fireworks show in the East River and the whole neighborhood is going this way, and all the cops are going down there. By this time I've got a garden over on Ninth Street and I've been sitting there drinking beer all day. Now I can hold my beer, at least I could back then—I don't drink a lot now. Unfortunately, when the beer ran out they were drinking wine, and you know beer and wine don't mix. Then we came stumbling over here and they should never have let me on that roof, drunk as I was—I acknowledge my part of it, I was drunk out of my mind. We went up on the roof and, being from Texas, I started screaming: "Victory or death." That was how Travis signed his famous letter at the Alamo. "Victory or death! William Barret Travis, Lieutenant Colonel."

He laughs.

These silly Yankees had no idea what I was saying, they thought I was paraphrasing Patrick Henry or something.

He laughs.

We had taken over the whole building, took 'em completely by surprise, there were people all up in that fire escape, we had a big banner across the front that said "Home Sweet Home." At one point they were dropping bricks off the roof to keep the cops from the front of the building. I was standing up there, I was really drunk, and this squad car came down the street. He got about right here and I'm like: "Damn, I can hit that." Well, guess who woke up the next morning in the tombs with attempted murder on a police officer?

He laughs.

Only felony I picked up, all these years.

We move closer to the East River, to the area the Dutch originally referred to as Burnt Mill Point because of an eighteenth century windmill fire. The neighborhood was largely uninhabited in the early nineteenth century when one of its first developers, the Dry Dock Company, started buying most of the land in 1825. The state legislature gave the company unlimited charter, including banking rights, to last "as long as the grass grows and the water runs." So after constructing dry docks to hoist boats out of the water for repairs, the company set out to build a complete neighborhood with a railway, a four-story Federal-style bank, shops, and tree-lined streets with three-story houses. Originally built for single families, most of these homes were converted into small apartment buildings in the twentieth century. Jerry points to the one with an added fourth floor and rooftop garden:

Ever hear of a McMansion? This is a McMansion. This is now a one-family home. See, they evicted twelve apartments, just slowly and quietly, and they didn't really evict them, they just bought 'em out. Then they came back and added like a floor and a half, put all this wrought iron stuff up top. It's been in several of the *Better Homes and Gardens*–type magazines and what have you.

This process—buying a building that was originally inhabited by one owner then broken up into several apartments and converting it back to a single-family home—is on the rise. "It's like a return to the Gilded Age," one real estate agent told The New York Times *in an article about the reinstatement of single-dwelling mansions with leaded-glass windows and marble fireplaces. In Brooklyn there is one listed at $13 million and in Manhattan the price tags range from $20 million to $44 million. The $44 million option has 14,000 square feet. A second real estate agent describes the surge of all-cash, largely in-*

ternational buyers purchasing these homes like this: "A townhouse or mansion is almost like a piece of art and there are buyers who appreciate that history and want to be part of it."

Jerry turns away from the McMansion with the trellised rooftop garden and walks closer to the East River. At the corner of Avenue D he points up at a five-story brick building with the unlit cigarette still wedged between his fingers.

The building on the corner, that's a former squat and one of the oldest buildings in the neighborhood, built in 1827. The original Dry Dock Savings Bank was in this building. Then it sat empty for a number of years. The Glass Factory came along, had it for about twenty years, then it sat empty for a few more years. Then in the early '90s the punks went in and took it over, and this became Glass House. This was one of the more famous—one of the more notorious of the punk squats down here. I guess because I live in a punk building and have for a long time now, I've witnessed a lot of what's happened, and I don't think the punks get enough credit.

These buildings don't always have electricity, so sometimes you have to tap into these guys—*Jerry bends down to knock on the base of a streetlamp*—and that's what they did here.

They went back inside and the lights were on. Then all of a sudden the lights started blinking. Then they went off. Then they came back on, and just started the process all over again. What they had done, they tapped into the "Don't Walk" lights. Being the type of people they were, they left the lights like that for a few days until finally it drove even them nuts.

He laughs.

So if you're going to squat, and you're going to tap into a pole, get somebody who knows what they're doing.

He laughs.

There was a woman named Linda Twigg, petite little woman just as sweet as she could be—if you messed with her, though, you would find out there really is a hippie Mafia. You did not want to mess with this woman. The building she lived in got evicted, and she ended up in Glass House for a while, and Herbert used to hang out with her in here. Ever hear of Herbert Huncke? He came from the Midwest to New York City, specifically to sell heroin. He's the guy that introduced Ginsberg, Kerouac, Burroughs, that whole crew. Linda was good friends with Herbie and he was sitting here one day, and he's like, "We called 'em *flops* and the beats called 'em *pads* and the hippies called 'em *communes* and you guys call 'em *squats*, but you know what? They're still flops."

He laughs and stands silently for a moment, taking in the building formerly known as Glass House. A smile breaks out across his face.

Two weeks after this building was evicted, Linda Twigg sent guys in to rescue several five-gallon buckets full of nothing but prime marijuana seed that had ended up in this building. Cops all up and down on the sidewalk.

He laughs and moves on.

Allen Ginsberg lived on the next block in the '60s but those cats lived all over this neighborhood; I can show you twenty different places where Allen Ginsberg, Kerouac lived. They hung out and worked in the West Village but they lived over here because the rents were lower.

I don't call this the East Village, by the way. The term *East Village* started with the Beats as a joke. They worked in the West Village: "Ha, ha, you live in the East Village," that type of thing, joking. Then the real estate speculators picked up on it. I, personally, consider it the Lower East Side.

Right around the corner here, on Eleventh Street, there were three guys that date back to the '50s, they're all Puerto Ricans: Armando Perez, Bimbo Rivas, and Chino Garcia.

Back in the '70s, they squatted a building in the middle of the block. It was unheard of to announce that you were squatting. Squatting goes back many, many decades, but to get right in their face just didn't happen. These guys not only got in their face about it, they put a wind turbine and solar panels on the roof—back in the '70s. Bimbo became known as like a neighborhood Latino poet; he's the one that came up with *Loisaida*, making fun of all the white boys who were starting to come down here: "Ah, you can't even pronounce it correctly, you're running around calling it Loisaida, it's Lower East Side!" Again, a joke.

Rivas, along with Perez and Garcia, founded CHARAS, a community center in an abandoned school across from their squat.

This is CHARAS. This school was empty for many years and they took it over. Nowadays it's empty again and it has sat empty for twelve, thirteen years. Giuliani stole it out from under them and this guy bought it for $3 million. He's not supposed to make a profit on it.

Gregg Singer bought the school from the city at auction for $3.15 million in 1998 and evicted CHARAS shortly thereafter. He has yet to get the approval for any of the varied plans he has submitted to the city. The building has been the subject of two decades of lawsuits, including one for $100 million in damages, brought by Singer himself, who claimed the city was blocking his development plans. Jerry points up at the windows on the top floors, overtaken by pigeons.

I don't know if you've ever heard the term *scalping a building*? In order to prevent a building from getting landmark status, which would place restrictions on its development, a landlord or a building owner—see above the windows over here? That building's been scalped. They took all the masonry off just so the building could not get historical landmark status. That's scalping.

Ornate stonework once framed the window Jerry is pointing at, but all that remains is a clump of broken brick—a jagged surface that reveals the violent lashes it survived. As we continue down the block and turn the corner, Jerry is still fidgeting with his half-smoked cigarette in his hand, still unlit.

We're now on Ninth Street, the next two blocks have so much history I forget half of it.

This is Serenity House. I opened up four buildings back in the

'80s, this is the only one still standing. We took it away from this guy, he was going to turn it into a halfway house and call it Serenity House. He would have got major grants, he'd have done a shitty rehab job and walked away with a pocketful of money. So we took the building away from him. That was almost thirty years ago and, as it is, this building has housed people almost every day since then.

Jerry turns and crosses the street.

This is Serenity Garden. I took the back third of this garden in '95 and announced that I was gonna build a place where I was gonna sit down, smoke blunts, drink forties, and play spades for the next few years, which is precisely what I did.

He laughs and we turn another corner:

This is Dos Blockos. A group called Everybody's Kitchen— they were just a school bus going around the country feeding people—they parked over here and a couple of people got off the bus and opened up this building and it became known as Dos Blockos. Dos Blockos, meaning, people who never go more that two blocks from their home.

This was a pretty wild building. It was the first squat on our scene—the hippies. Most of the squats over here were hippies and punks, they were counterculture squats, the other squats were what I call "working-class bohemian." They get up, they go to their jobs every day, they give as much liberal support to as many liberal causes as they can, and occasionally they do something. I'm not putting them down, just to say over here we were always hippies and punks, we were more likely not to have a job, more likely to get drunk and go out and do something.

We turn another corner and come upon La Plaza, which is filled with twenty-somethings sipping beers and parents shadowing children who are trying to run freely in the open space of the park.

This old rainbow hippie who had run rainbow soup kitchens, he showed up at La Plaza one day and took charge over here, stood right on the corner, started spare changing to get a bag of rice and a bag of beans. He started cooking and I'd say for the next year and a half we were feeding two hundred to four hundred people a day, seven days a week, on an open campfire, on the Lower East Side.

By the mid '90s I was living across the street and I had a key to La Plaza and I let the punks come in. The police tolerated the hippies and the activists, they tolerated the homeless and the hungry. They did not tolerate the punks. That's when they wanted to bulldoze La Plaza but we fought them on that, too.

Jerry takes me under the canopy of trees in the park to show me where there used to be a kitchen, then we head back to the street.

This building right here is what we call Mother Squat. One day this couple, Steve and Cathy, they showed up after squatting in Europe. Steve organized what we call the Eviction Watch List, this was a list of all the squatters and their supporters, and any time we had of any kind of trouble, whether it was from police, or landlords, we got on the phone and we started calling the Eviction Watch List. That's when we started getting more organized as squatters, that was December of '84. We took our cue from the gay community: closets kill. We now had four, five buildings, maybe a hundred people, and that's when we started getting in their face. Letting the city know, letting the neighborhood know, letting everybody know: we're taking these buildings—these are our homes and we're going to fight for 'em. And we did. We took the idea that these were our homes very seriously: you fight for your home.

We stand in front of Christodora House, across from Tompkins Square Park. Constructed in 1928, it originally housed European immigrants. By the 1960s, the building had been abandoned, and it later became the home for several organizations, including the Black Panther Party. Jerry points out an air-conditioning unit near the top of the building where a hawk nests. Then he crosses the street to enter the park.

I follow a half step behind him as he walks the park's designated path; he takes several pauses to clear his throat or clear his thoughts while he fiddles with his cigarette.

There were people living in this park, twenty-four seven, every day of the week, every day of the year.

This area right here, this is where we organized a tent city. There were a couple of people—I always use the expression, "burnouts from the '60s that hadn't quite burned out yet." A couple of them were sleeping in here and they started organizing. The homeless were just people, okay, they didn't want to be exploited by people like us, political activists with an agenda, but at the same time they knew we were pretty much talking the truth; they didn't want to fight the cops but they really had no choice.

In the late spring, early summer of '88, some landlords, a couple of cops, and a couple of people from the community board got together and started talking about putting a curfew on Tompkins Square Park. And one day in July, late June, early July of '88, they went around to every entrance of the park and they wrote in big letters: "The park closes at midnight." They left that up there for a month.

Now this was '88. Remember Morton Downey, Jr.? Well a bunch of us were doing Morton Downey, Jr. shows at the time, myself included. We were defending squatting, what have you. One time I had to debate Curtis Sliwa, founder of the Guardian Angels, and Morton Downey, Jr. in a nightclub uptown. Out of the eleven shows that I did on television, this one nightclub show was the only time that I actually got paid; they gave me $200 plus we got all the food and wine and what have you that we could drink. That was the same night they were going to set the curfew, so we called for a demonstration right here at St. Mark's Place and Avenue A.

Now again you have to picture this: the whole area is overflowing with homeless, as far as the eye can see: tents and shanties and people sleeping on benches everywhere. We went up, a whole group of us, the standard yippies. We got here 'bout 11:30 that night, about thirty people. I went and I got a case of beer, and I came back and thirty people went crazy for twenty-four beers. So I went and got another case of beer. Now I'm coming back over and I got these four cops about five feet behind me and got all these people in front of me, and I take my beer and I start going— *Jerry holds an imaginary beer over his head, shaking it in sync with his chant*—"Pigs out of the park! Pigs out of the park!"

Once everybody started to chant, I take my beer, I opened it up, and I sprayed down the cops. Needless to say the crowd went crazy.

He laughs.

Next thing you know, squad cars coming in—they were waiting for us. They busted four of us. That was the night of July 31st.

We cross to the south side of the park.

This is where the band shell was. Now, after the incident with the beer we called for another demonstration, the night of August 6th—one week later. I had spent some of the Morton Downey, Jr. money, paid for a couple of the leaflets, bought a hundred police whistles. We called for a demonstration right here at the band shell. Had they let us do that then we would have chanted our chants, waved our fists, and flashed our banners and gone home and that would have been it. But McNamara requisitioned all this heavy equipment, special trucks and what have you, and he parked them all right here.

This was a precinct commander, his name was Gerald McNamara. The man might have been a good cop, as far as cops go—I don't know—but he was a totally incompetent precinct commander.

They turned out all the lights, totally dark, and we were marching though the park, riling the people right and left. Someone brought these M-80s and they would light one and toss it and all the sudden you'd hear a big flash followed by boom!

Things started to get a little hairy.

Our plan was that at midnight we were going to leave the cops, we were going to go liberate Washington Square. Just leave the cops going—*in a dopy voice*—"Which way did they go?"

He laughs.

By eleven thirty we had a couple hundred people, we had had our drums and we had all the M-80s and lots of noise makers and we were attracting people and we're building up some tension, and one guy started taking a group of people up St. Mark's Place toward Washington Square too early. So I ran up and stopped them. "Whoa go back, you're going to blow it." So we all start turning around to go back into the park. These four cops stood across the entrance and they wouldn't let us into the park, never mind the fact that there were already a couple hundred people directly inside. So everybody started climbing over the fence and going around these cops. And these four cops started shoving people with their nightsticks.

McNamara is sitting back over here by the band shell, and he gets on his radio and calls a "10:85 forthwith, Tompkins Square." This is part of the old police ten code, "10-4" and all of that—okay?—"10:85 forthwith" means anybody who hears this, get here now. So cops in the surrounding area, they're showing up on the avenue, but there's nobody in charge because McNamara has completely cut himself off from everyone at the entrance to the park—us, the cops, everything. He doesn't realize cops are responding to his call. They're coming in, they're seeing the excitement, and they're just wading in like thugs, swinging. And McNamara is still over here by the band shell, "Ten eighty-five forthwith!" Cops had stopped coming in from the surrounding area because they're all here now. Cops are coming across the bridge from Brooklyn. They're coming from downtown because it's late and nothing's happening on Wall Street—they're coming from all over. And there is nobody in charge. "Ten eighty-five forthwith! Ten eighty-five forthwith!" Car 54, where are you?

He laughs.

Most of the activists didn't get hurt that night. We were all experienced. Most of the people who got hurt were coming out of bars to see what was going on. It was a hot summer night.

There was a helicopter fifty feet from the buildings. People coming out of the apartments to see what the commotion was, people coming home from Broadway, restaurants, movies—those are the people that got hurt that night. People went to the hospital. The least I've heard was 55 people; the most I've heard was 111. We fought the cops all up and down Avenue A, all night long. Six o'-clock in the morning they finally let us back in the park. We marched straight through to the door of the Christodora, went into the lobby, totally trashed the lobby, took a police barricade and rammed it through the glass doors. And then, well, went home and went to sleep.

Jerry laughs and raises the unlit cigarette to his mouth. It hangs for a moment, rising then falling against his lips with one slow, deep breath. He jerks the cigarette away without lighting it and says he's tired.

The reporting from The New York Times *shortly after the first riot on July 31, 1988, described the scene like this:*

> *Frustration with a daily life of poverty and oppression help explain why someone—who, [neighborhood residents] say, they do not know—began tossing beer bottles at the police during each of the two protests, starting violent street battles. [They] believe in this oppression with a passion altogether foreign to the vast, comfortable enclaves beyond the Avenue B border of Loisada. It transcends their political philosophies, which vary from eco-anarchism to communism to milder forms of socialism. And it is reinforced by the conviction, equally foreign to outsiders, that the plight of the homeless and the poor and the tragedy of AIDS are part of a Federal conspiracy to depopulate the cities for repopulation by the wealthy.*

The "vast, comfortable enclaves" mentioned in the article are now fully embedded in Jerry's neighborhood and have been for years. By the mid '90s, in fact, one building along the northern edge of the park,

not far from where Jerry and I stand, jumped in value from $5,706 to
$202,600 in a five-year span.

I generally put post-squat at '95, but technically it's '01.
That's when we made the deal with the city. Just as Giuliani was
leaving and Bloomberg was coming in, we made a deal where we
walked out with eleven buildings. One group was responsible for
getting the bank loans and then we brought them up to code.
Originally we had a total of about thirty buildings, over the course
of twenty years. Thirty buildings, two different bookstores, our
own newspaper, and at one point we even had a radio station that
broadcast from a different building every night. Could be heard
from river to river, from Twenty-Third Street to Canal Street.

Twenty-five years later, it's hard to make sense of it. If nothing
else, we helped a lot of homeless people, we fed a lot of people,
we helped a lot of people stay in their homes. I like to think the
Lower East Side squatters were the ones who put the word *gentri-*
fication on America's lips. Nobody knew about that word before
we started talking about it. Those riots and those confrontations
with the cops are what brought that to the foreground. We took
a problem that they had turned a blind eye to and we shoved a
light in their face.

And with that, he sparks a match to light the half-smoked cigarette
wedged in the corner of his mouth. Jerry lets his eyes close for a mo-
ment. He takes a deep breath and the ember at the end of the cigarette
glows brighter.

28.

ylan Gauthier is sitting at a booth in a shuttered luncheonette in Greenpoint, Brooklyn. It is night and the place is dark; the only light that hits his face is the ambient glow from the streetlamps, finding its way through the windows.

Personally I'm a little bit leery of creating enclaves. If you create what happened in the Lower East Side with the squats that are still remaining, you create this enclave where there's the right politics, the right relationships within the walls, but meanwhile the neighborhood's changing and you're still powerless. Those spaces were really inspiring and part of New York even when I came to the city. But I do wonder about that question: If the neighborhood changes will the space still mean the same thing?

I also wonder about what Bea would want to do.

Bea is in her apartment behind the luncheonette, presumably, but Dylan can't get her on the phone. Bea is seventy-nine, so there's a good chance she doesn't hear the ring. Eventually there is some rustling near the bathrooms at the back of the restaurant. Bea emerges, short and stout, mostly obscured by the lack of light in the space where she stands. We see enough to know she's waving us on so we follow after her. She is talking from the start, first something about how she left the door to the luncheonette open for us so that we wouldn't be cold outside but then most of what she says is hard to track as she speeds along in her thick Greek accent, her unsteady voice, swerving from one topic to another. I catch pieces:

Bea (to Dylan): On the corner, why do they put the tree?

Dylan: A million trees. Bloomberg. Purify the neighborhood.

Bea: It's a bathroom for the dogs.

Dylan: You're probably the only person that doesn't like the tree.

Bea: And the leaves—I have enough from the park.

As we near the door to her apartment, Dylan manages to interrupt Bea long enough to introduce me. She sort of turns around to look at me, nods, and smiles—a limited investment from someone who has already memorized enough names in a lifetime. I pick back up with what she is saying when we arrive in her living room, where she offers seats and beers. Dylan and I take the seats. She presses on the beers, and we promise that we'll get to them soon.

A single table lamp illuminates a room that has not seen fresh paint in years, or new furniture for decades. The plush, brown chairs are lumpy from innumerable naps and books and conversations. Oil paintings hung from the picture rail, and a selection of family photos—or, more precisely, a shrine to her grandchildren—is crowded onto a few shelves. Bea's last name is Koutros but:

Bea: You know if you're married your name is gone. You have to have your husband's name. You know the story. My name is actually Katrualis. I'm from Sparta. I was born 1934. February 14, Valentine's Day. Years ago, if you were my age, you'd be famous. Now people live longer. You know, the Greek people, they don't celebrate birthdays like you do over here. They are smart, after they are forty years old they don't want to know.

Bea and her husband, Louie, ran the luncheonette from 1963 to 2008. Even until the end the hamburgers were $1.25 and the cheeseburgers were $1.50—and the dusty menu posted behind the counter still proves it. Much of the place seems unchanged from its earliest days—the antique silver coffee samovars, the wooden icebox, the red linoleum countertops.

Dylan, thirty-five, is originally from Los Angeles and teaches at Hunter College, where he received an MFA in integrated media arts. He maintains an office in the former home of Franklin and Eleanor Roosevelt, which the city university system, CUNY, bought in the 1940s and reopened in 2010 as the Public Policy Institute at Hunter College.

He likes to be on the water, exploring the rivers and beaches and bays of New York. Dylan belongs to Mare Liberum, or The Free Seas, a collective that describes itself as an organization that has been "hacking the free seas since 2007" with roots in "centuries-old stories of urban water squatters and haphazard water craft builders." The group engages in a range of activism and work including building small seaworthy vessels; some are made of craft paper and wood glue, which ends up looking like a varnished papier-mâché canoe. One of the paper boats is stashed in the hall outside of Bea's apartment. Though Dylan has a place of his own down the street, which he shares with his wife, he is at home in this building with Bea. He became a regular at the luncheonette shortly after arriving in the neighborhood:

Dylan: I moved here in 2002, and Louie didn't come out that much but he was really the engine of this place. Thinking about the way they ran this for fifty years was, to me, an eye-opener when I first moved to the city. It was more than just a restaurant, it was a community space. And it wasn't that they weren't in it for the money, but they did enjoy communing with people and supporting the neighborhood. And so there was that: meeting them through that sort of initial exchange. Bea was like anyone's grandmother. She'd make a peanut butter sandwich if something was taking too long. Really sweet.

The room where we sit is cold and drafty. Bea wears a hooded sweatshirt, black sweat pants, and tennis shoes. She leans forward in her chair, like a boss giving orders.

Bea: I got married in 1955. My husband used to have an uncle who sent for him to come over. We couldn't come together. I can come after a few years, 1958, by a boat. Ten days, I think. A beautiful time. I was young. I'm an American citizen but not my husband because he was in the Greek army and he don't want to be American citizen. For me, I think if you're here long you're supposed to be an American citizen, no? My husband he say, "Naw."

Louie worked at a beer factory in Williamsburg, the neighborhood directly to the south of Greenpoint. After five years of saving up they bought this three-story building across from Monsignor McGolrick Park. They opened the luncheonette on the ground floor, taking the apartment behind it while renting out the remaining four apartments on the two floors above.

We opened in 1963. June 19, I think it was. We never closed a day. Only close early on the holidays. No vacations. It was nice all the time, people was nice, friends come all the time. It was fun. I had some Greek friends, they used to drink a little bit. For years, I was busy in the restaurant and everything was beautiful. I was young, easy at the grill.

The young people used to come, a lot of young people because I used to have good stuff and cheap prices. And they used to give me more tips than the prices for the food to help me pay the rent.

The health inspectors used to come all the time. And most time, no problem, good, perfect. They found everything alright. Maybe they write something down but no money or anything. If they say fix the floor, we do it—all those years. And now you see what's going on? If they find something—anything small: $200, $300.

Dylan: Sort of right around 2008, there was this market crash and Bloomberg was bringing in letter grades for restaurants, and it was making it even harder to be a small business in the city. So if you were running a scrappy diner, as they were here, the fridge wasn't the right temperature or you didn't have the right kind of lights, you were shut down.

Bea: I tell you everything is money now. Nothing else. Forty-four years and after they find something wrong—no gloves, no hat—they make it a violation. I say those plastic gloves they give you more trouble! Go to the sink next to you every time—you wash hands!

But everything's money. You don't believe? You know how many people they close because it costs too much? The health department closed us. Seven years ago. Even now, everybody think it was wrong. Everybody come into the restaurant and they say, "See the place is beautiful."

The day we closed, I tell you I was so upset with it. Very upset. My son say, "Ma, forget it. Don't bother."

But I stayed very, very depressed. All I dream is cheeseburgers and coffee.

Dylan: Louie was getting pretty sick at the time, too, pretty frail.

Bea: After the restaurant closed he laid down and he get stroke. The store closed in '07 and my husband died in '09. I say if they didn't do this maybe my husband still alive. Not because he loved to work.

She laughs.

But he never sit down. He always had something to do. He woke up at five o'clock in the morning, six o'clock downstairs. People come talk. He's not a hundred percent but at least he used to do something.

Old people, I tell you, they lay down all day, but I don't know if it's good. For me—I can't.

Dylan: When they closed down the space sat empty and dark and I think also at that time it became something it hadn't been before: there were makeshift memorials erected outside and people didn't know what had happened. Online there were all kinds of posts, hoping the place would reopen. So kind of this absence when it closed.

I also thought, living in the neighborhood, that it was this sort of generative absence. It was this dark space that people could project their dreams and plans and ideas onto. You could walk and wonder what's going on in there.

Then one day I saw her coming out and I hadn't seen her in years. It seemed like she was making more appearances out during the daytime and going around the neighborhood. And once I'd seen her that one time I started seeing her everywhere. So I was continuously talking about things going on in her life.

I came into the luncheonette one day, and she read all the letters she was given and had me give her advice, going over these offers.

Bea gets up and retrieves a stack of business cards from her mirrored coffee table.

Bea: Every day, they call me to sell the house. People, they want it.

They bother me all the time.

She points at one of the cards:

She's Greek, I think—or she's married to a Greek guy.

She hands the cards to me, one at a time.

I got a lot. I throw away.

As evidenced by the cards in my hand, she doesn't throw them all away.

Dylan: She was also getting offers from young entrepreneurial couples from the neighborhood who wanted to start a dream business in the space.

Bea: A Polish guy, he owns in Greenpoint—I don't know how many houses—he stops by every week. I say, "I don't want to move."

He say, "You can stay upstairs."

I have an old lady like me upstairs; she lived here since twenty years. I never raised the rent. I have four families in the apartments upstairs, above the restaurant. They pay $700, $800. No rent control, no lease. If I wanted to, I could raise the rent and make them to go. But you feel sorry for the people. How are you going to pay?

If somebody buys this place, what they do? They take everything down and they build.

I don't want to move from here. But the building needs a lot of work. I have damage from the hurricane. We try with the insurance, and they don't pay. If I showed you the bills from the house—forget about it. I'm scared to look at them.

She glares with distain at the pile of bills on the coffee table.

Six, seven thousand dollars a year—maybe more. The water bills, almost $800, $900.

The only new thing in the house is the boiler and the roof.

Dylan: The two most important things. Eleven thousand for the new roof two years ago. The boiler is six or seven years ago.

Bea: But you don't believe it for an old house, all the money they want to give you. A lot of people moved into the area. Now they say people move from Manhattan to Brooklyn. Young people now, like you are, I don't know how you can afford it. I think years ago it was easier. Now it's hard to find jobs. Too many people. New York has almost nine million, I think they say. It's what's in the papers.

Dylan: I don't want to live in Greenpoint in ten years if it changes to a certain extent. I am in a rent-stabilized apartment, so my rent won't go up too much, which means I might even be able to stay. But talking to people around the neighborhood who have rent-stabilized apartments, it's this feeling of golden handcuffs because you know that if you move, you'll be moving to Yonkers or East New York. And you'll be trapped there. Gentrification means all these different things in all these different cities but you can't really disconnect it from place.

Bea: Greenpoint was always nice. I never had problems. Only once I remember there was a man in the store. He was at the table and then he went in all the registers, took the money and run. Another time, another guy from inside the store went upstairs into the apartment. I used to have this beautiful stuff from Greece, always I used to hide them, and he run in and take and run away.

Twenty-five years ago, some Greek friends from Astoria, they try to take taxi to come over here. The driver said, "Greenpoint?" They don't even know where is Greenpoint. Maybe he don't want to come, I don't know. But now they say it's third best neighborhood. Park Slope is the first. Everything here is old. Every house is one hundred years old and up.

Always Polish people here. But now it's a mix. You can see every people here now. Everybody loves to come to New York, right? Everybody dream to come to New York, from all over—this is true. I don't know why. They think you could find easier job over here. But it's so hard. A month ago in Long Island City in Queens, they have some kind of job. They say $17.50 per hour and they sleep for two nights in the streets to see who is going to go first for the application. It's hard now to get good jobs.

The only good thing I tell you now is that the young people coming to the area. That's nice. But some old people like me they don't like it. They say, "Oh, it was better before." They don't like the noise. They complain. But it don't bother me. I say, "What's better? It's not better to see young people?" They make you feel better! If you go with the old people always we complain. They don't feel good, all these problems. The young people they feel better. It's nice to be young! I wish to be young like you!

She points at Dylan and me.

Enjoy your age!

Most young people, their parents pay. One girl she comes from Manhattan and I say, "How you pay the rent?"

And she say, "My mom and daddy help."

Bea shrugs.

If you have money, you do for your kids. I mean, what are you going to do, take the money with you? But how many have that kind of money? Now they say New York has the most rich people of the whole country. Everything is money now.

Dylan: I think since even before they were closed—Bea, you started getting notes under your door from speculators and developers and it hasn't stopped. If anything the offers have become more and more lucrative.

She has several notes from people who find her on the street and offer her $2 million cash to buy the building so they could ostensibly kick the tenants out and turn it into condos. We are right on the park here and it's really desirable real estate. Meanwhile parts of Greenpoint have been rezoned along the waterfront, the Newtown Creek, and there's the feeling that that's the new Greenpoint, and it's going to slide back this way and developers and real estate types are preparing for that flow of people. The Bloomberg model has been a very particular beast and it's driven by ideas of capital accumulation as this sort of panacea for fixing the ills of the city.

I've only lived here since Bloomberg's administration but reading about so many other administrations—you know, certainly Bloomberg and Giuliani instituted these paternalistic—I think it's beyond paternalistic: they didn't want to listen to the people in the community. They demonstrated this time and again. Their efforts to defund the community boards, or dismantle the community boards. At a certain point Bloomberg just said I don't think we can afford them, so we should just get rid of them. Excuse me? Who are you building the city for?

At a certain point you start to hear them speak what you've been imagining behind closed doors, only they're saying it in public and you say, "Wait, you're not supposed to be saying that in public." It's no accident, it's planned. Motivations? I don't know. There's capital. Their friends are involved. They're involved. It's this vision of taking back New York City. Bloomberg says my daughters now live in Bushwick or Bed-Stuy and fifteen years ago you couldn't live there. Really? You couldn't live there? Who the hell is "you"?

Bea: I'm here all those years. I never move from here.

My son says "Why? Just sell this and buy a condo something, a little house." But I don't want to move. If something happens to me, what are my sons going to do? They're going to have to sell.

My son, he lives in New Jersey, in a beautiful house. He says come over here. But sometimes it's not good to live with your kids. You get in an argument or something and you worry. And if you go to New Jersey you don't see nobody. Here you see people and talk. You get a few drinks and you see everything beautiful.

I like the noise. I don't like it quiet. Everybody knows me. And they give cans and bottles and I bring bottles to Key Foods. My son, he got mad at me. He don't want me to do that. But I don't want to throw them away. Bring it to Key Foods and make a few dollars.

My social security check is not even $300. And now I get my husband's check and it's still not high, $850 something.

Dylan: She recently said she would take $10 million.

He laughs.

I thought that was good. Why not? It's good to have your price.

What is gentrification? It is Bea in this moment, wrestling with herself, shaking her head. She does not deny what Dylan says about the $10 million but she does not like it either. Capitalism, by its own design, does not care who participates in free-market competition— only that there is competition; democracy, by its own design, cares deeply that everyone participates. So it would stand to reason that democracy might exert power over capitalism and enforce the inclusion of all neighbors when it comes to the development of their neighborhood. But enforcement is limited at best, so Bea must maintain this principle on her own. She does it by keeping her tenants, who are in good standing, in their homes at rents well below market rates. She does it by opening the luncheonette for neighbors to share meals. She gives Dylan a report on last night's dinner.

Bea: That was good but the night before was delicious—all the kind of vegetables.

Dylan: We were having informal dinners here and other people in the neighborhood were using it, too. It sort of became this community resource where you could say I want to have a dinner party, I want to have a birthday party—can we rent the space? She would always be happy to have people. And we had this one dinner and she seemed really happy, really glad to have people. We cooked this pasta she loved and talked about for weeks and she started saying, "Do you guys want to come back and do some more things like that?"

She proposed that if we want to keep doing stuff we could give her a little bit of money and figure it out. To me it seemed like without necessarily having the vocabulary for it, she was talking about having a form of mutual aid or assistance. She does own the building but her tenants pay just enough to cover the property taxes, water, electric—all this stuff that's been continually going up every year. Like she said, she hasn't raised their rent in over twenty years, so the top apartment is paying $700 a month for a two bedroom and two blocks away, new two bedrooms are going for $3,000, $3,400, which is insane.

So she needs some kind of money and it was kind of like, "Okay, we have this space. What should we do with it?"

I sent an email out to five or six people I knew who I'd been involved with in different projects throughout the city and invited them to think of what we could do with the luncheonette. And we formed into this collective that runs the space, tries to keep the walls and roof from caving in, putting time and energy into it, upgrading the electric and plumbing and all these things that we need to actually use the space and get it through the winter. Always with Bea there.

The model we've kind of hit upon is—it's in the federal tax code, the 501(c)(7)—is a member-based social club. We haven't formalized and there's talk about whether we will formalize but it seems like a good model to have a member-based club where members pay dues and that's what pays our rent and keeps the lights on.

Having been involved in some event spaces—the scramble to get the public to come in, not treat you like shit, not destroy anything—was something that I'd tried for too many years in New York and was sick of it. And I didn't think this was really the right place for it anyway. It's small. You get thirty people in here and it's pretty crowded. So rather than base it around programming, we're involving more members who shape the space, add to the space, plan events, invite friends over.

There are about thirty members. Certainly a lot of the people who would describe themselves as artists. There's a fair mix of educators, art history professors, urban planners, activists, a couple designers. I guess there are carpenters, who don't necessarily see themselves as artists, but builders. Couple of poets. Couple of musicians.

I think there was a pretty strong sense that we didn't want to get bogged down too much in talking before things started happening. I think that maybe there's a resistance to having too many meetings or formal kinds of concoctions, and that means you have to leave a lot of leeway for people to do what they want to do. We don't have any formal rule structure, or leadership structure. We try to have a meeting every month so that we can all be together and see each other's faces. And then we try to get the neighborhood involved in some way.

For me, a lot of the work I do as an artist, activist, or educator is all about different forms of collaboration. And here it's collaboration with the members of this collective and then there's this other collaboration with Bea and it's hard to describe. We never sat down and had the art theory talk about collaboration but she expresses what direction she wants things to take in the space and what's inside her comfort zone and what isn't, and it really is a full collaboration.

One of the things she told me was you can have things in here but it's got to be on the DL. She doesn't want inspectors. She doesn't want paperwork. She doesn't want the city involved at all. Which makes for a good collaborator in this scenario.

They both smile.

Bea: Dylan, you know, he's good all the time. I don't know if he wants to show only that. But it's no good to be perfect. If somebody's perfect there's something wrong. This is the truth, you know.

Dylan laughs.

Dylan: She's happy with us being under the radar and her preference would be to keep the space as it is for as long as she can. Hard to say what that means in the long run.

In terms of the long-term plan, it's dependent on Bea. Initially there are a few ways that you might be able to create something sustainable, and the 501(c)(7) might be one of them. It won't keep her from selling the building if, by some misfortune, she becomes sick, or decides to sell the building and move in with her kids. I think it's probably in the back of a lot of people's minds that we could try to fundraise and buy the building, but realistically it's a ton of money. It's nice to imagine that would have been possible at some point in New York City's history.

Our relationship with the neighborhood has been very multi-textured and multilayered and the old-time residents can't wait for us to reopen it as an ice cream parlor or a luncheonette. A lot of the kids want ice cream. A lot of the young, urban—not to put them in a group—but the younger small-business owners that move in here think, oh, there's no cafe here—bam—open a cafe. Or there's no bakery for pies, open that. There's no Korean restaurant, open that. I've had funny encounters with them and heard funny mumblings from them of, "Oh, you won't be there long, it won't last." Also criticism that we are somehow depriving Bea of the market value of the space. This is something we hear a lot: You're not giving her the market value of the space. You're not paying her market value rent. You're cheating her etc., etc. Not that people say this directly to us but you hear things. I think that's when you get into, "Why wouldn't she get the two million dollars?" Or, "Why wouldn't she take the six thousand dollars a month that an ice cream parlor was offering?"

You know what? Money: in the end, people better fucking realize it isn't everything.

The one thing I'll say as a caveat to the whole sort of experiment is I don't come at it with the feeling that just because you will it to be different, it's going to be different. You know, the rents go up or the neighborhood changes so much it's unrecognizable. So just by coming here and saying that we'd like to freeze development in this neighborhood: A) Is that even feasible? And: B) So you'll have this rarified patch?

For me this is an opportunity to make this model for using space that isn't necessarily quite destructive and doesn't quite lead to displacement. That's kind of a privilege that comes with this very copacetic relationship with the owner, which is something that you don't usually have or usually takes years and years to work out. Usually the building owners are the enemies. It's a weird thing.

Recently we've added a few new members who are urban planners who are involved in community groups. There's this whole other language of policy. I don't always know if it's the most generative or the most fruitful; it's definitely not something I had any contact with.

Urban planners and certainly the mayor's office try to "increase density" in these neighborhoods. There's all kinds of reasons like increasing the tax base and planning to compete with these megacities that are cropping up in China or wherever. But I don't know why you'd be trying to turn New York into Hong Kong or something. You're really going to add twenty million people to New York intentionally?

People who argue for density point to Paris, where development is extremely limited within the city so the world's elites are the only people that can afford to live there. They say if you freeze development in one zone then you get these historic quarters like

Fort Greene or Brooklyn Heights, and they're brownstone districts. They've become these little jewelry box places.

So on one hand we need to build more buildings so that there's more affordable housing, so that it doesn't just become this little jewel for whoever the worlds' rich are at the time—Koreans, Emiratis, whatever. Which is a compelling argument. But you also have people saying we need to bring in as many millionaires as possible, they'll help float the bottom. So it is complicated and confusing thinking, well, what's the alternative to this? You get to thinking, well, maybe we're talking in extremes. It's not Paris vs. Shanghai. It's not Paris vs. Rio. That's a lack of imagination. Why not think of how you can keep the people that are already in this place and they're happy and doing what they're doing. I don't know, consult with them? Invite them to live in new spaces that you're building. I think these things could be really easy and wouldn't create the same level of displacement.

We've also thought about not overburdening this space with meaning. You could come in here and turn it into a nonprofit and have things going on every night. But the opposition to that idea is that if you have some nights where nothing is happening some people walking by will peek in and it's just this kind of mystery. Why is there this dark storefront in this neighborhood?

If you leave the space dark then you create this sort of dream space, which I think encourages people to be productive actors in the city and not just accept the city as a built environment we move through.

Bea: "Maybe what will happen in life will happen," my grandma used to say that. My grandma say, "The time we are born, it's lying next to us, what's going to happen to us." As little kids she used to tell us that. But it's no good to believe that because then you wait to see. It's not good to believe that because then you're not going to do nothing.

Dylan: If you project yourself into the city and think of how you're able to change it then you're better capable of answering questions about what belongs there and what doesn't. The worst thing I think are these developments that they're putting up on the waterfront where literally every inch is completely planned and paved and everything is so orchestrated that you can't imagine anything other than what's there when you're standing there.

Bea tells me I should come over for dinner soon. She looks at her watch—it is late, and much colder than when we first sat down. Winter is coming, and her windows need repairs to keep out the wind.

The three of us walk back out to the luncheonette. The space remains unlit so it feels boundless. Bea is still pushing the beers. Dylan and I decline again—I don't know why, really. It's mainly me, I think, rushing to get back to my six-month-old daughter and wife. As I edge my way to the door, Bea reaches into a refrigerator under the counter. She pulls out two Budweisers and a couple of club sodas and insists we take the drinks for the road. I thank her and she apologizes because she's out of straws. I thank her again—for her time, not just for the beers—and she waves it off as though it was nothing:

I like the blah, blah.

She says blah, blah *with the coolness of someone who's been meeting new people for nearly eight decades—and the generosity of someone who's always open to the idea of one more new face. She tells me to bring my wife and baby when I come back for dinner.*

29.

*T*he earliest use of the word gentrification *comes from the British sociologist Ruth Glass who wrote about several London neighborhoods in 1964:*

One by one, many of the working class neighbourhoods of London have been invaded by the middle-classes—upper and lower. Shabby, modest mews cottages—two rooms up and two down—have been taken over, when their leases have expired, and have become elegant, expensive residences . . . Once this process of 'gentrification' starts in a district it goes on rapidly, until all or most of the original working-class occupiers are displaced and the whole social character of the district is changed.

It's a strong word, invaded, *but one that never leaves the mind when chasing gentrification in real time. Invasions can be grand—an entire neighborhood—or nearly imperceptible—a single building, one apartment at a time.*
"1059 Union."
"1159 President Street."
Money is always involved—it can't not be. And so is land. Land that is endlessly transforming under the subjugation of capitalization.

As Rob Robinson put it, "Make no mistake about it, that's what's at the crux of the problem in this country: land. The fight for land and property rights." Land as property: it's the idea we used to seize much of this continent and establish a nation, and it's the same idea that defines our aspirations as a culture: the American Dream of homeownership. There is something to the fact that in the five decades since Ruth Glass used the word gentrification to describe what she saw in London, all the other zeitgeist terms—urban Thoreaus, brownstoneurbia, et al.— have faded, and only gentrification remains. The idea of the gentry— and more specifically, the landed gentry—controls the space where we think and talk about land. Those who see land as a product, property valued at whatever maximum can be extracted and wired to Dubai or London or Los Angeles, strong-arm the conversation. But those individuals exist on a massive spectrum that also includes but is not limited to: those who believe the vitality of land depends on the diversity of classes and cultures that share it; those agnostic to land, who are happy to flutter through the various neighborhoods they inhabit in a state of transience; the homeless, who depend on the land for any food and shelter it can provide; fifth-generation residents who do not want the land to brook any changes from the day they were born; and those who refuse the idea of land ownership all together. On the last page of a pamphlet entitled "Squatting in New York City," given to me by Jerry the Peddler, I found the lyrics for "A Digger Song." This is part of the third verse:

> The sin of property we do disdain
> No one has any right to buy and sell
> The earth for private gain.

The sin of property.

Each of us defines gentrification in accordance with our own relationship to a piece of land, a neighborhood. And as is the case in all meaningful relationships, our feelings are conflicted; our actions, contradictory. We have hopes for what the land may bring us—profits, security, community—and we have fears about what it can do, what it *might become. As Niko, the real estate lawyer, pointed out to me, even an investor who has never been to New York has fears over its future: "The fear is that a terrorist attack will get people to leave and gentrification is reversed." Whether it is the possibility of global jihad disrupting a portfolio's steady growth or the challenge of finding a warm place to sleep, our relationship to land can't help but set the terms for how we talk about gentrification.*

Curtis Archer, executive director at Harlem Community Development Corporation and a colleague of Tom Lunke, recently said, "You know, I get kind of sad when I hear people talking about a 'New Harlem Renaissance' happening. Because let's remember: the Harlem Renaissance was built on what? Arts and culture. It was the voices that came out of this neighborhood that mattered. And this? This is economics, pure and simple."

Gentrification *is our word of choice because we have settled into the choice to let money frame our relationship to land. This abstract thing called money is, itself, in the process of abstracting land: a patch of earth where a building was constructed and used for work and shelter by one group of people has become an investment for another group of people in another neighborhood or state or country. The second group rarely enters the doors of the homes and businesses they acquire—they don't need to. Landowners, individuals and institutions alike, operate in a global economic system that cultivates absentee landownership, obscuring them from the people who populate their buildings. As Ephraim put it, "That's why we don't usually buy buildings with tenants because if you do, you have to go talk to them."*

It is not unreasonable to argue that the people who spend the most time participating in a neighborhood should also be the people who bring most of the money to that neighborhood. But in this era of steroidal global capitalism, international investment plays the leading role, and the people who spend the most time in a neighborhood and the people who spend the most money there are increasingly discrete groups. And as Cea Weaver pointed out, "The larger the gap between people who know about New York City housing and the people who own the buildings, the worse it's going to be for the communities."

As I write, Bill de Blasio is approaching the one-year anniversary since his election, and The New York Times *is reporting that the income gap is worse in Manhattan than anywhere else in the country. The top 5 percent of Manhattan households earned 88 times as much as the poorest 20 percent. More New Yorkers are living in poverty than last year and this trajectory shows no signs of abating with millions surviving on less than $11,170 per year.*

A development company called Extell recently won approval of its plans for a thirty-three-story condominium high-rise at 40 Riverside Boulevard in Manhattan, and they did so the way all big developers win approval for their plans: with the promise to designate a small portion of the available housing units, generally 20 percent, for "low-income" earners—a term defined by the city using different measures, depending on the type of project, but it is generally either side of $30,000 annually for an individual and $50,000 annually for a family of four. In the case of 40 Riverside Boulevard, Extell has made 55 of 219 units available for low-income earners. But in the construction plans, Extell was granted permission for one very important design feature of the building: two separate entrances, one for those who live in the low-income units (at the back of the building with no views of Riverside Park or the Hudson River) and another for those who have paid market value for their apartment (with park and river views). New Yorkers and the media at large now commonly refer to the entrance at the back of the building as "the poor door."

The de Blasio administration emphasizes that the Extell project had already won preliminary support from the Bloomberg administration, implying that the situation is beyond its control—the mayor's appointees are simply pushing the paper along.

If the interests of those who spend massive amounts of time in the city are never weighed against the interests of those who spend massive amounts of money in that same city then New York will not only become hollowed out and demoralized, but also economically unsustainable. The city of Detroit lost 35 percent of its population over six decades, and while the reasons were complex—and wholly different from the afflictions faced by New York—it's not inconceivable that in the era of global gentrification, New York, too, could shrink away at such a rate. The Motor City did not project vulnerability in the 1950s, and New York does not project vulnerability now. But with a fading middle class and a swelling population living below the poverty line, if New York does shrink, it will be because the pursuit of capital steamrolled all else. It will be because the idea of property completely seized how we think about land. If the needs and desires of the people who fill the streets and workspaces and apartments do not remain a priority, then this giant tent of ideas and perspectives that is New York City will lose its central post and collapse.

New York has always been defined by human interaction—and by new iterations of it. Even though modern technologies can weaken these interactions—"Look up!" says Shatia Strother to her neighbors— we still ride the subway, we still walk the street, we still gather at the bar, we still sit or stand or kneel in the house of worship. All of these people and all of these activities continue to provide a certain propulsion. At the risk of quoting a politician, Daniel Squadron might have put it best: "The greatest thing about this city is that we have the strongest collection of energy and expertise anywhere in the world." And the idea that New York might not be as diverse as it was when the senator's grandfather arrived at Ellis Island is, in Daniel's words, "Absolutely unacceptable. And it will mean we lose the city."

Endless variations on humanity maintain the city's notorious energy level—it's always spiking in one direction or another: if it is not sucking out your last current of breath and hope with hurdles and malevolence, it is, instead, charging you with an electric moment, revivifying you in an instant, and you feel yourself upright again, ready to march forward. If the diversity of income and skills and perspectives that allows for those moments of revivification—of exposure and opportunity—is trampled underfoot by the hegemony of capital and its insistence on class homogeny, then the transformation of the city will end. The devaluation of land will follow the devaluation of the people who used to call it home.

and who will go down in history as a person of great skill and integrity. You are a man of your word.

Chris Parris-Lamb, a man of tenacity and intellect who inspires me to become better at everything I do.

Tasha, dear Tasha, it ends where it begins—with you and your counsel and your proofreading and your ideas and your research and, most of all, the inspiration you radiate which has carried this project. Thank you for being the wildly creative and beautiful partner that you are.

"Money," said Dylan Gauthier, "people better fucking realize it isn't everything."

This conversation about gentrification must end with Bea. And that's precisely because it is impossible to write policy that does what she accomplishes. This type of reform, which prioritizes the health and accessibility of a neighborhood over any individual's—or corporation's—opportunity to maximize the value of property, can only be enacted from within. To imagine what might become of a neighborhood's dark spaces, those dream spaces—to really reckon with those possibilities—is to take the city seriously. It is what it means to be a citizen.

Look up.